ONCE UPON A HILL

Also By Carmine Vittoria

All You Need To Know About Soccer

Microwave Properties Of Magnetic Materials

Elements of Microwave Networks

Magnetics, Dielectrics, And Wave
Propagation With MATLAB Codes

Bitter Chicory To Sweet Espresso

Dal Caffe di Cicoria al Caffe Espresso

ONCE UPON A HILL

Courtesy of Mastro Fernando Masi

CARMINE VITTORIA

Purpo, Inc.
Key Biscayne, Florida

Purpo, Inc.
P.O. Box 490217
Key Biscayne, FLA 33149-9998

Copyright @ 2021 by Carmine Vittoria
All rights reserved,
including the right of reproduction
in whole or in part in any form.

Purpo is a registered trademark of Purpo, Inc.

Photos Courtesy of Anmarie Vittoria
Paintings Courtesy of Fernando Masi

For discounts, please contact Purpo, Inc. at 305-989-8522 or at the mail address.

Library of Congress Cataloging-in-Publication data is available

ISBN 978-0-578-320001-4
Printed in USA

Once again *reginella mia*, my wife Rie, came to my rescue.
She encouraged me and edited the book.
Thank you, I needed that.

Sources, Notes and Declarations

A mafioso, mafia member, pledges to an oath of secrecy (omerta) as to divulging his identity to the public. Violation of omerta can have serious consequences. No one in public or otherwise volunteers to talk about Mafia matters, but the author was able to decipher a story from normal everyday conversations with the two main characters in the book as well as with many of their friends. This is a heart-wrenching story of a mafioso who turned his life around. Trials and tribulations of a mafioso are being narrated from childhood. Historical facts, dates and names are cited in the book in order to establish a background for the characters introduced in the story.

As such, the story is mostly true but a few names are fictional for obvious reasons. Names of government officials and some of the mafia members are actual. A realistic picture of the life of a mafioso is revealed for the first time which is nothing like what is depicted in the movies.

Contents

Prologue

"*Once Upon a Hill*" is a sentimental story about the life journeys of two childhood friends, who emigrated in the late nineteen forties and early nineteen fifties to the United States in pursuit of the American dream. The journeys of the two friends, Guido and Vito, are described since their childhoods, when they were shepherds, grazing sheep in the Apennine Mountains near Avella, Italy. In America, one settled in the mid-west and the other on the east coast. Although these two regions represent very different lifestyles and customs, both readily adapted to the American diverse and ever changing lifestyles over the years.

In Italy, both boys were well aware of the Camorra (Neapolitan Mafia). As such, they were exposed to Camorra characters, although both were naive about Mafia families or syndicates in the USA. Even the FBI did not acknowledge the existence of the Mafia or Cosa Nostra in the 1950s. Hence, they never imagined that it could ever take roots in the USA. It all changed when Guido pursued work in a pizza house and later got into the lure of greed and money by working in trafficking contrabands. Vito pursued the hard knocks of academics. As quirks of nature would have it, they met forty years later and a glimpse of their separate life's journeys in America are revealed.

Both re-settled by chance in the same community of Italian immigrants whose culture was very familiar to them. Their common interest over the years as adults was their love for the game of bocce which they had played as children. Through their many encounters on the bocce courts, there emerged a life portrait of a mafioso (Mafia member) which is much different from the one usually depicted in books and in movies. Their friendship resumed under somewhat awkward circumstances. The academician suspected that his friend was a mafioso, but he chose to ignore it for convenience sake.

The renewed friendship was more important to him than the special circumstance of his friend. Alternatively, omerta (secrecy) forbids a mafioso to divulge his or her identity or line of work, and, besides, it is the type of private information that one needed not to know about. They carried on their friendship as if they were back up in the mountains playing the game of bocce that both loved. The bocce courts replaced the mountains in their minds. On the bocce courts, there was a smorgasbord of characters playing the game without revealing who they were: mafiosi, pimps, drug dealers, tourists, politicians, mayors, governors, actors, singers, police officers, medical doctors, scam artists, academicians, etc. It was indeed a fascinating and interesting mixture of characters, and they all got along.

The setting for this story is the North End district of Boston, but it could easily have taken place anywhere on the east coast where large communities of Italian immigrants settled. The story is necessarily fictional in order to protect names and places and also out of respect for privacy, but remained true to the special characters of people in the story.

As in most ethnic communities, Italian immigrants did not assimilate very well with surrounding communities and, in fact, they were completely oblivious to the American culture outside their neighborhood. In all those years, they never made peace with current American lifestyles or adapted well to the ever changing ways and customs. Their churches, local schools, social clubs and religious societies provided the social services needed to guide new immigrants into the new world. Alas, their support system shortchanged them from participating and engaging in new American trends in lifestyles. Their ways of being were stuck in the times of the forties and fifties when they emigrated, even though the world around them changed. They were frozen in time. If, in the year 1990, an Italian scholar wanted to study how people lived in Italy in the fifties, all he or she had to do was to take a walk in that community of Italian immigrants. They were relics of the past. In some sense, it was like watching a painting come alive in front of one's eyes. Thus, besides historical monuments in their neighborhood, there were relics of the past.

Not only did the Mafia thrive in isolated Italian communities but, also, Irish gangs festered in large communities of Irish immigrants in Boston as well. However, since the Irish immigrants were established long before new Italian arrivals in Boston, they were part of the fabric that governed the city.

Competitions and warfare among Irish gangs themselves and between Mafia and Irish gangs were unavoidable. After many years of turmoil among local gangs, there emerged one Irish gang leader who totally dominated the landscape of crime in the city. His name was James (Whitey) Bulger. Anything illicit was possible by Whitey and the establishment put on horse-blinders to cover up the crimes. The emergence of Whitey not only affected the type of illicit crimes to be condoned, but it also affected peoples' lives in all communities of Boston and nearby towns. In effect, he was the "emperor" of crime enterprise in Boston.

One place that was immune to all the gangs turmoil in Boston was the bocce courts. It was a place where people from all backgrounds, from the high and mighty to scumbags, came to unwind and relax from the hustle and bustle of the city. In short, it was an "oasis" in the middle of a busy city where tourists came to visit historical sites and restaurants. This was the setting where the two friends were most comfortable and relaxed in the company of fellow bocce players. It fostered a strong bond among them that transcended the differences of the social and professional standings. One was preaching the wonderments of science on campus, and the other attending to the everyday perils of the underworld. Although the two friends led very different lives, they didn't lose a beat from the days of shepherding when they engaged in a game on the bocce courts.

Today in the North End, the bonds that tied the old and new generations together for years have loosened, as well as in other Italian communities. It is the beginning of a new era, whereby the younger generation has assimilated with the new modern world of computers, I-Phones and social media. They moved to suburbia to share into the American dream of owning a house with a white picket fence. Someplace in the mountains of Cervinara, Avella, and many other towns there are two other shepherds planning their life journeys to the USA chasing their dreams, much like Guido and Vito did.

ONE

Once Upon a Hill

M onte Avella overlooks the order of things in nature from above it all and her strong icy blasts of wind reveal her mood and seasons. Fields of red poppies, chicory flowers, lavender violets, white and pink daisies, and wild dandelions adorn the farms and foothills of Avella and Cervinara in the spring, much like Monet's landscape paintings. The flowers in the spring reminded farmers and shepherds of time to prepare for the next crop and remove the thick wool coats on sheep. Since ancient Roman times, hazelnuts and olives from there have been exported to every corner of the world. The mountains have been a source of food in good and bad times.

The Apennine mountain range, from regions of Campania to Calabria, were settled by the Samnite and Volscian tribes [1-1], who were mostly shepherds and farmers. There was no demarcation or border separating these two tribes, as they herded their sheep in more or less the same territory, like nomads. The Samnites and Roman Legions were involved in a bitter war in 100 BC over the granting of Roman citizenship to Italians [1-2]. Avella was the only town in the Naples area that allied with the Roman Legions in defeating the Samnites. The Roman Senate rewarded Roman citizenship to all the allies who were loyal to Rome. As a result, Avella gained influence and size at the expense of neighboring towns, including Cervinara. Eventually, Rome granted citizenship to the rest of the Italians, since they contributed most of the soldiers to the Roman Centurions (the Roman armies).

The town of Avella is located at the foothills of Monte Avella, part of the Apennine mountain range near Naples. After World War II, Italy was in turmoil, especially in Naples, where people were starving and Communists dominated the political landscape. The Communist party in Italy had the largest membership in Western Europe and the intent of the party was to push Italy into the Soviet bloc countries of Eastern Europe. Basically, there was a civil war, but no one in the media dared to call it as such for fear of inciting one. Communists hunted down and killed Fascists at an alarming rate without court trials [1-3]. The Allied Military Government (AMG) [1-4] in Southern Italy replaced Fascist Mayors with members of the Camorra (Neapolitan Mafia) or the Mafia in Sicily. As a result, organized crime in Italy re-emerged stronger than ever before and people did not trust their government. In short, whoever survived the horrors of the War were thrust into the throes of anarchy. One could feel the tension of the times in the streets. To make matters worse, there was little food to be had until the implementation of the Marshall Plan in the late ninety forties [1-5]. Desperation prevailed throughout Italy and people were looking for ways to leave the chaos and emigrate to the USA, South America and Northern Europe [1-6]. The only place in Italy that was peaceful, quiet and with a plentiful source of food was up on the mountains, where shepherds had survived invasions and civil unrest for millennia.

Avella faces South and, on the other side of Monte Avella, Cervinara faces North. Thus, Avella is located on the sunny side of the mountain range and Cervinara the shady side. Whereas Avella has a splendid view of the Bay of Naples and Mount Vesuvius, Cervinara has a mountain view of the city of Benevento. The word translates to "good wind". It is always windy there, even in the summer time. In the winter, the wind can be strong and cold and it feels like shooting daggers. People run indoors to avoid that nasty wind in the winter. Both towns were home to clans of shepherds who took their sheep to graze on the mountains.

Vito lived in the town of Avella and he liked to believe, as a child, that good people lived on the sunny side of the mountain. Guido Alvaro lived on the shadowy side of the mountain, Cervinara. At Christmas time, it never snowed in Avella, but it did in Cervinara. Vito and Alvaro were good friends, as they were called upon to help in shepherding the sheep on the high mountains as they grazed the grassy fields. Shepherds usually lived in poor sections of town among other shepherd neighbors. There was little mingling between shepherd families and the rest of town. In effect, the town

5

Panoramic view of Vesuvius and the bay of Naples from the top of Monte Avella. The town of Avella is at the bottom of the mountain in the valley. The Clanio creek can be seen below heading toward Avella.

Panoramic view of Monte Avella as seen from downtown Cervinara. Avella is on other side of the mountain.

was split into two societies, the have and have not. In Carlo Levi's book, *Christ Stopped at Eboli*, [1-7], he refers to them as "gentries and peasants". Gentries represented the establishment: Mayor, police, business people, nobility, tax collector, i.e. town's people. The peasants represented mostly the farmers, shepherds, maids, waiters, service people, etc. As long as the gentries sought more power the more life was miserable for the peasants. The song, Anema e Core (Heart and Soul), was so popular after the War that it was adopted by the peasants as their National Anthem. Life as a shepherd was arduous and sometimes dangerous. Typically, two shepherds would herd their own sheep, as well as sheep owned by other shepherds. The shepherds of Avella and Cervinara shared the same grass fields on the mountains, as a truce was worked out between them to use the grass fields simultaneously. They met on Monte Avella with their sheep where they set out on their journeys from there to search for grassland.

The trek from Avella to their meeting point was straight uphill to the top of the mountain. The terrain was thick with under-brush, ravines, deep gorges and just nasty terrain. A creek, Clanio, ran from the side of the mountain down to the town. In the spring, rain water gushed down to the creek forming a river flooding the town. At some places, it looked more like a canyon than a deep ravine. It took about four hours to get to the top. This meant that one had to get up at three or four in the morning to get there on time to meet other shepherds from Cervinara. The most dangerous part of the trek was chance encounters with wolves, wild boars and poisonous snakes, such as vipers. Bears were extinguished long before Alvaro and Vito appeared on the scene. However, the reward for the arduous work was the return trip. The view of the Bay of Naples and Mount Vesuvius was stunning on the way back and wild berries were plentiful. Strawberries were the size of a fingernail, but so sweet. In addition, wild porcini mushrooms, asparagus, and other vegetables, as well as snails, were there for the taking. Mother always asked for the strawberries and Vito would reply: "Not ripe yet." He ate them and mother sensed as much.

The trip from Cervinara to the meeting place was a lot shorter, since Cervinara was located higher up on the mountain, just below the peak. However, the climb was a lot steeper and the gorges a lot deeper. On Monte Avella there was a small shack with a haystack roof and a cleared resting area for sheep and people. The shack was built from a mixture of mud and small and big rocks, enclosing the sleeping quarters. The roof was a compilation of thick hay or straw strung together with twine. This type of shack probably dated as far back as the era of the Samnite tribes. Shepherds referred to it as simply the "haystack". The front door was covered by a thick bundle of hay at night to keep warm. Cooking was done outside the haystack. Usually, after one week or longer on the fields of grass, the journey ended with festivities and a picnic on Sunday. Grazing took place along the mountain chain of the Apennine mountains running north-south of Italy, as far south as Calabria and as far North as Frosinone, near Rome.

While one group of shepherds roamed the mountains for grassy fields, other shepherds waited their turn in town, resting and/or making dairy products like cheese. On the mountain trail, their protection from the many wolves and wild boars was secured by large shepherd dogs (a mixture of German shepherd and Collie) who guarded the compound of sheep and shepherds at night. Wild boars can be quite ferocious and dangerous when cornered or while protecting their little ones. They have no fear and will strike at anyone or anything in their way. Alvaro and Vito were instructed to climb the nearest tree, when charged by one of them. Although boars are much heavier than shepherd dogs, they easily outran the dogs. These big dogs were principally guard dogs, and, therefore, were tied down near the haystack for most of the time. For the purpose of rounding the sheep into a controlled herd, smaller and quicker dogs were utilized. The bigger dogs were treated as common "property" to be shared by all shepherds, as they remained on the mountains most of the time, unless injured. Smaller dogs or puppies were trained by a shepherd in town and eventually returned to the mountains.

Along the grazing trail there were camping grounds similar to the meeting point on Monte Avella. The grazing season started in spring soon after the sheep were sheared of their wool coats. It ended in late fall, depending on the snow accumulation on the mountains. During the snow season temperatures and the chill factor were quite unbearable. At that time, sheep were returned to town to wait out the winter season. The camping grounds along the grazing journey were spaced at sufficient distances so that shepherds could rest for the night after grazing the grass fields. However, sometimes the small quarters had to be shared by multiple groups of shepherds. In those days there were no I-phone or wireless communications to contact other shepherds in the area to make arrangements for resting grounds. Pork and beans was the usual meal of the day. After a while, anything else tasted better.

These grazing trips lasted seven to ten days and were unbelievably hard work. Sheep forever darted out of line or easily wandered off on a cliff that, most of the time, overlooked a canyon or a deep crevasse. The more serious problem was steering the sheep away from clover leaves and/or grass laden with fungi or bacteria, which are poisonous to them. Danger was always around the corner and the name of the game was to anticipate problems before the sheep did. It was Alvaro's and Vito's responsibility to bring the stray sheep back to the fold. It was no fun for either of them. Whatever free time that they had, they loved being outdoors, seeing views of the sea from the top of the mountains and running after dogs chasing wild boars. They lived in a world transfixed in time, contrary to the one in the valley. Shepherds were far removed mentally and physically from the political turmoil below in the valley.

Sunday was a special day; young and old participated in the game of bocce. The setting was more like a picnic of various shepherd clans. In a fire pit containing charcoal, just like nomads in the middle east, they grilled a baby lamb. The taste of the roasted lamb was delectable. After a steady diet of pork and beans, it was heavenly to taste the roasted lamb. In addition, ricotta cheese, roasted boar meat, asparagus, and pies were spread out on a large table. Shepherds helped themselves to the food. The sheep were secured inside a clearing area, and guarded by dogs all around the perimeter. The competition in bocce games between shepherds from Cervinara and Avella was fierce. No prisoners were taken. The ribbing and foul language among shepherds was extreme. It was almost life and death competition. Afterward, everything about the games was forgotten and each went his separate way. However, Alvaro and Vito kept playing until dark and were at each other's throat to win. They bet whatever little money they had.

Guido and Vito started shepherding on the mountains at the age of eight after the War. That was the age when shepherd children finished their education at the third grade level, enough to read and write. However, Vito continued his schooling past third grade. The first one to break away from the cycle of shepherding was Alessandro, Vito's brother. He was the first child in the family's history to go past fifth grade in elementary school and attended the lyceum. The environment on the mountains was hazardous and dangerous, but it taught the children to be mentally and physically self-reliant. In some sense, they exhibited a streak of independence early in life. Alessandro was ready to pursue schooling soon after the War. Vito's household consisted of grandmother, mother, and brother. Alessandro helped with shepherding during spring holiday and summer. Vito answered to his uncle Don Camillo. Don Camillo was the younger brother of Vito's father, Mario, who died at the beginning of World War II in the desert of Libya. At that time, Don Camillo was too young to be drafted into the Italian Army. Shepherding was the family's main means of carving out a living, since Samnite nomads appeared on the scene circa 200 BC.

Guido was supervised by his much older brother, Davide. They were orphans. Their father, Raffaele, married as a teenager a beautiful older woman named Tamarina, who died in childbirth, when Davide was born. Tamarina's family owned a knitted sweater and seamstress shop in downtown Cervinara and depended on the shepherd community's goodwill for the sheep's wool. Raffaele married again, years later, to Carmela in an arranged marriage, just before WW II, uniting two shepherd families from Cervinara and a small town nearby, Paolisi. Like Mario, Raffaele also died in Libya. Tragedy struck this family once again, when Carmela, Guido's mother, died relatively young from influenza after the War. More people died from influenza and complications from it than any other sickness. This was due to a lack of medicine In Southern Italy at that time.

The two uncles became guardians and caretakers of the orphans. One uncle represented the paternal side (Alfredo) and the other, the maternal side (Simone), Carmela's brother. The uncles were associated with the Camorra and involved in the sale of contraband American cigarettes stolen from the American Naval base in Naples [1-8,9]. Both were appointed Mayors of their respective towns, Paolisi and Cervinara, by the AMG with the recommendation of Vito Genovese [1-10], who was employed by the US Army as a translator and liaison to the populace. He had the rank of a Sergeant in the US Army. Genovese was a former Mafia underboss, sottocapo, in New York City.

Genovese was deported to Italy in 1937 by the US Immigration Office, because he was indicted for murder in a gangland slaying. He was cleared of the murder charge, as the key witness never appeared in court. He returned to New York City in 1947 to assume the leadership role, capo, of a Mafia faction once headed by "Lucky" Luciano (Salvatore Lucania) [1-11]. Luciano was also deported to Italy in 1946 as an undesirable alien, but never made it back to the USA. He died in Naples, Italy, in 1962. Apparently, he was not welcomed by a dominant Mafia faction in Sicily, where he was born. During WW II, Genovese was responsible for recommending to the AMG former mafiosi as mayors in the Naples area, including Cervinara and Paolisi, as well as in Calabria and Sicily, to replace Fascist mayors. What a nightmare! It was like having foxes guard chicken coops. It was no surprise that Genovese was acquainted with Alfredo and Simone, since all three were involved in the sale of stolen cigarettes from the American base in Naples. Also, they were neighbors, since Genovese was born in Tufino, a stone's throw from Cervinara and Paolisi.

The first thing that Vito and Guido had to learn in order to help out was to be able to control the smaller dogs and keep them away from the big guard dogs. The smaller dogs were trained to respond to a loud shrieking whistle from a shepherd. It was imperative that the whistling be very loud so that the dogs could hear the command from a distance. The whistling was generated by placing both the thumb and forefinger on the tip of the tongue and blowing hard on the fingers. It was not trivial, but after much practice the boys graduated to be shepherds. However, the next obstacle to overcome was the fear of the elements: cold, wind, rain, wild animals, hunger and being alone on the mountains. Being left alone, it allowed them time to adjust/adapt/live in harmony with nature surrounding them. They learned to accept nature on its terms, in good or bad times, much like the ups and downs of life itself. Shepherding was hard work with little reward, but there was no other choice after the War, better than starving. Tending sheep was the lifeblood of the family for generations. One accepted the role from childhood.

Rainstorms on the mountains were nothing like the ones in the valley. At least in town, one could hide from a storm. On the mountains, there was no place to hide. The violent storms evoked the worst fears in the young shepherds. Rain came down in sheets of water, as the wind threatened to lift them up in the air. They held on to trees and boulders as their life depended on it. With clouds hovering over the mountains, visibility was considerably diminished. Lightning and thundering from all sides just made the situation frightening and perilous. For the young shepherds, it was so scary as they imagined how hell must be. The older ones had seen this before. Dogs and sheep "declared" a truce by bunching together. Remarkably, the weather down the valley was sometimes sunny! After the storms, the splendor of mother nature revealed her best behavior, rewarding the shepherds for her indiscretions. The scene up on the mountains was one of serenity and thankful to be alive. Birds appeared suddenly out of nowhere to greet the shepherds. The sheep started to move about demanding attention. Dogs chased the sheep back into the fold. The view from the mountains was nothing short of spectacular. Visibility was so clear that one could see the mountains of Sorrento. The young shepherds were confused by it all. How could nature be so cruel on one hand and be so gentle and beautiful on the other?

The team of Don Camillo, Vito, Davide and Guido gathered about every six weeks at the top of Monte Avella. Vito can still hear Don Camillo shouting at Vito's bedroom window at four in the morning, "Get up, you lazy bum." Vito jumped out of bed and ran out in a jiffy. His grandmother, Nonna, who was Don Camillo's mother, was the Matriarch of the shepherd clan in town. She was basically judge and jury of whatever disputes occurred among shepherds. She was a master cheese maker and produced wool which she sold at the farmers' market in town. She woke up before Vito and prepared breakfast for the whole family.

Still Don Camillo complained to Vito, "What took you so long." They straddled the Clanio creek with one hundred sheep or more and about six dogs that were always full of energy and very well trained. Don Camillo led the way, with Vito closing up the rear and the dogs keeping an eye on straying sheep sweeping from side to side, preventing the sheep from entering extraneous hideouts in town. In the spring and fall, the wet seasons, the creek swelled with water and the sheep were forced to move on a very narrow path alongside the creek all the way up to the top of the mountain. However, in the fall season the two boys were not available to help Don Camillo or Davide, since they were attending elementary school.

Schooling was intended only to learn enough to sign one's name on a document, which was about third grade level. Vito could hear Don Camillo gasping for air, as he was carrying food supplies, while encouraging Vito, "Just a couple of more minutes of this, and we will be there." It really was a no-man's-land as they neared the top. The foliage was thick and the passage was getting more narrow and steeper to climb. However, at the top, it was

The Clanio "river" dries up in the summer. However, in the rainy season, it fills up to both banks of the river. Rain water flows from the top of Monte Avella (foreground) to the town of Avella.

a serene scene, as if one were on top of the world with no one else around. It was such an eerie feeling, almost spiritual and surreal. The sight of the large guard dogs wagging their tails non-stop made Vito forget about the arduous trip.

One had the feeling that, at that height, prayers had a better chance to be heard by God, since it was so close to the sky. Mount Vesuvius appeared to be so close, but yet so far. There was a vast windswept plateau of a field of grass, and a huge picnic table next to the haystack. Don Camillo immediately set up housing by starting a large fire near the shack and cooking some Porcini mushrooms which were growing in abundance nearby. Vito rounded up the sheep in a cordoned off area. By that time, everybody was exhausted, including the smaller dogs. Other food supplies were brought over by the Cervinara's team of Davide and Alvaro, who often waited for the Avella group. They did not have to struggle with the foliage and the water flow in the creek. Fortunately, the creek dried up in the summer at the bottom of the mountain, but not at the top. The dryer weather made it easier to climb to the top, but still that water flow in the creek was unpredictable. A little shower would induce a torrent flow in the creek. It was a love and hate relationship between the creek and the shepherds. Water from the creek was desperately needed, but too much of it was a nuisance to say the least, and sometimes catastrophic.

Finally, the big dogs were released and allowed to roam together with the other smaller dogs for a short while. Guido and Vito had time to play around with the bigger dogs whose ugly appearances belied their friendly nature. The younger shepherds were really excited to see such a warm welcome from all. Alvaro and Vito immediately ran to the area where it was hard and flat and engaged in a game of bocce. There was a lot at stake at those games. The loser had to milk the sheep. Both shouted insults at each other, "Tu si nu scugnizzo" ("You are an orphan scum bag.") That was the beginning of the game to unnerving each other. In truth they liked each other and loved to tease. For a change, they did not have the adults on their backs commanding them but indulged in playing a child's game "on top of the world". What a feeling!

Both Vito and Guido were taught to keep the sheep bunched up with the help of the smaller dogs while the adults guided the sheep toward grassy fields. The big dogs stayed close to Davide and Don Camillo. Vito and Guido, together with the smaller dogs, would flank the sheep from side to side and drive them toward the middle of the herd. It was fun for both of them. They enjoyed working with dogs. They learned to whistle like Don Camillo to command the dogs as they pursued the sheep. Occasionally, a wolf attacked a sheep in the middle of the night. A ferocious fight ensued between them. Usually, it took the intervention of Davide or Don Camillo to chase the wolf away with a special heavy-duty stick. One end of the stick was shaped into a large circular wooden head, about 4–5 inches in diameter. One blow from the heavy end of the stick was enough to drive the wolf away. The shepherds were more upset than afraid of the wolf, since they had to get up early in the morning to continue their search for grassland.

The shorter excursions into the grassland extended from Monte Avella to the East and West mountain range toward Avellino and Caserta, respectively. On longer treks, they headed in the North-South directions. The Apennine mountain range extended along the latter direction. Don Camillo knew all the "sweet spots" where grass was not yet grazed. Usually, lunch was prepared near the "sweet spot". The object was to return to camp and have enough time to enjoy a feast. Along the way, Don Camillo and Davide would have time to hunt for wild boars and search for mushrooms, asparagus, etc. Besides pork and beans, sometimes bread and cheese complemented the dining with porcini mushrooms. Metal traps were set at night to capture a wild boar. The two boys worked their butts off and, by the end of the day, they were exhausted. They concluded that this was no way to make a living. They often talked about what they were going to do when they grew up. "I am going to own a restaurant in America," Guido would say. "I am going to be a philosopher," Vito would answer. Guido became visibly upset and countered, "That's bullshit. You cannot make a living doing that." That stumped Vito. These conversations went on the whole time, when they had a break from work. Each day the boys' goals or dreams for the future changed.

The boys looked forward to returning home from the long journeys. The sheep were left behind so that a new "crew" of shepherds took over. However, the smaller dogs returned to town with the boys. It was all downhill and a lot drier. By the time they returned home, their basket was full of vegetables, porcini mushrooms, berries and snails. Don Camillo taught Vito which mushrooms were poisonous, which were most of the colorful ones. Sometimes Don Camillo carried a small wild boar home to share with the family. Usually, this called for a celebration that made use of food secured from the mountains. In particular, a favorite recipe called for porcini mushrooms, fried in virgin oil, spread over a bed of cooked macaroni. Hard cheese, prepared by mother and grandmother, was grated over the dish. The taste was truly out of this world and yet so simple. Snails cooked in special broth was a starter dish and wild berries in yogurt the final dish. Sometimes, a meat dish of wild boar followed the macaroni and the salad. Home-made wine was served during dinner. The boys were allowed to drink wine diluted with water. The dinner made the hard work on the mountains worth-while. The mountains truly took care of the shepherds' needs at a time when food was in short supply throughout Italy during the War.

With the coming of summer, people were looking forward to religious festivals in Avella. It was the only time of the year, when the have (townies) and the have not (shepherds) socialized together. There were four major festivals scheduled, starting in June and ending in September. Saint Francis Festival in September was the biggest one. It started early in the morning on a Friday.

Saint Anthony church, left of the picture, and monastery that sponsored Saint Francis festival in Avella.

A tambourine player and trumpeter walked around the streets drumming a tambourine early in the morning to announce the festival. It was intended to wake up the children to follow them in their merrymaking; the more noise the better. Vendors from nearby towns showed up in the afternoon to sell their wares. The favorite food item was a slice of pork cut from the head of a pig which had been cooked in boiling water and herbs. The sliced piece was doused with lemon juice and other condiments. In addition to food and toys, tricksters showed up with card tricks and hand tricks. They were basically thieves stealing from youngsters. Most often, the Carabinieri (local police) chased these thieves out of town. On Saturday, more vendors came to town as well as merry-go-rounds, carousels and exotic rides. People prepared for Sunday events when, usually, an out of town orchestra was invited to play classical music or opera. Anticipation by the town residents was overwhelming, especially by the children.

Cervinara then was not a big enough town then to sponsor festivals. They just had a procession of the Statue of San Rocco on Sunday. Davide and Guido had time to visit with fellow shepherds when they visited Avella for the festivals. Alvaro and Vito resumed their grudge match in bocce as if nothing else mattered. The adults loved to watch these two go at each other playing bocce in the street so fiercely, just outside Vito's grandfather's wine shop. There was no letting up by either one of them. It was not hate that drove them; it was passion for the game.

Finally, the adults put a stop to this spectacle, when invited for a big lunch at Nonno's (Vito's grandfather) home. Afterward, a siesta and a bocce game with only adults participating. The adults would not allow the two boys into their game. They didn't want to be embarrassed by either Alvaro or Vituccio (little Vito). Like a lizard, Nonno basked in the sun and took it all in stride sitting on the sidelines sipping wine flavored with peaches. Side streets were the only places where dirt roads were flat enough to play bocce. The ribbing or the chattering took on a life of its own, bordering on absurdity, but it was welcomed by all. This was a prelude to the afternoon dance of the "Tarantella" (The dance of the spider) by local artists dressed in costumes dating back to the middle ages.

Dancers dancing to the Tarantella. In the early days of the dance, the male held onto a colorful string, as the couple gyrated around a centered pole.

Dancers held onto a colorful string hanging from the top of a tall wooden pole, like a maypole, avoiding each other as they circled around the pole, dancing in the rhythm of the music. The music was very lively, upbeat and reminiscent of Neapolitan music of yesteryears. After the dance, there was a competition among the young men of town to climb to the top of the wooden pole greased with soap and lard. The winner was rewarded financially and with assorted food items.

The staging for the orchestra was in the main Piazza, and people rushed there to place themselves in front of the stage for the evening performance.

During the performance no kid dared making a fuss as they were on a short "leash". It was an opportunity for adults to see a major production in a small town setting and they demanded quiet, period. Poor performances were rewarded with rotten tomatoes or eggs. Sometimes a dead cat was tossed onto the stage to register unhappiness with the performance. Opera singers were recruited from the San Carlo opera house in Naples. By late evening, the streets were full of people taking their passeggiata (social walk), and kids and thieves waited for the fireworks. It was ideal for thieves, since the streets were extremely overcrowded for them to slither among people like snakes. Festivals in the North End of Boston today are, more or less, a replica of those festivals in Avella during the late forties. Whereas festivals in Avella are no longer practiced; in the North End, it has maintained that tradition.

In 1948, Italians in Southern Italy finally exercised their free will and aspirations after many years of being harassed by Fascist thugs and by the Camorra. Unfortunately, crooks and thieves felt the same way, but more so. Not only did they enjoy the same liberty and freedom as everyone else, but they had the freedom to pick and choose whatever illegal activities, and victims, to their hearts' content, without consequences. There was no law and no public order. In the Naples area, the Camorra intimidated or bribed people to vote for their candidates.

Davide and Don Camillo were staunch Communists. During the War, they were members of the Partigiani (partisans) group that helped sabotage German transportation vehicles in the Avellino area. The political affiliation of partisans was mostly with the Communist Party. Don Camillo was the leader of the Communist Party in Avella after the War. He helped Davide in organizing the Communist party in Cervinara. Before the 1948 election, Alfredo and Simone were mayors of Cervinara and Paolisi, respectively. The two towns were in close proximity to each other. Both uncles let it be known to all in town that they were receptive to bribes for "favors".

Alfredo and Simone were not Communists; they were opportunists working for the Camorra. Before their appointments as mayors by the AMG, they were involved with the contraband of cigarettes in the Naples and Avellino areas. About one-third of supplies earmarked for the Navy base in Naples found their way into the streets to be sold on the black market. Italian cigarettes were atrocious and extremely expensive. For the same price, people preferred the American brands. Tobacco stores in small towns did not carry American cigarettes unless they dealt with the Camorra. Most people rolled their own. Alfredo and Simone thrived in the black market from not only cigarettes, but American products: clothes, shoes, food, etc. stolen from the base.

As incumbent mayors, Alfredo and Simone were not encouraging competition from the Communist Party in the election of 1948. They had too many things "to fry in the pot". The Carabinieri were accountable to both mayors and it was an easy thing to bribe them with American cigarettes or money. Thus, the contraband of American cigarettes enjoyed the protection of the Carabinieri. Life was beautiful for both mayors. Politically, they were Fascists at heart, but could not run for the Mayor's office as Fascists, as that party was abolished after WW II. So, they ran under the banner of the Christian Democratic Party. Even their nephew, Davide, recoiled when he heard of his uncles' affiliations, but blood was thicker than water. He resigned from the chairmanship of the Communist Party to help his uncles, Alfredo and Simone. Communists detested Christian Democrats, because that was the only party preventing them from taking over the rest of Italy. The Democratic party barely eked out a small margin of victory in the 1948 Election in Italy.

In view of the fact that their uncle, Alfredo, was holding the town of Cervinara hostage, Davide and Guido did not envision themselves as shepherds in the future. They saw themselves helping out and abetting their uncles in their good fortunes. They wanted some of the action. Shepherding for them was a temporary job to survive the hard times immediately after the War, principally starvation. The two brothers saw that an opportunity to get away from shepherding and working for their uncle was a lot easier and more profitable. For a change, they were going to partake in the easy life, la dolce vita, like their uncles.

The modus operandi were no different between Cervinara and Paolisi, where the two uncles ran City Halls. Cervinara was a small town of about five thousand people then. Paolisi was smaller. Most of its people lived off the mountains and their main trade was selling dairy products, wild boars, knitted sweaters, and all other things related to the sheep or dairy industry. Ninety per cent of the population tended sheep. The mayoral election of 1948 in Cervinara was a classic example of buying an election in those days. Davide and Guido knew the lay of the land in Cervinara. They "taught" every shepherd how to vote. Elections at that time required the voter to sign his or her name on the ballot. Most of the shepherds never attended school and couldn't sign their names. They signed an X on documents. However, Davide taught them how to sign their names and gave them a monetary reward for voting.

As in any election in Italy, there were something like 25–30 parties and each candidate was allowed to plaster posters on city walls. However, in both Cervinara and Paolisi, an ordinance was passed by City Hall whereby only certain walls might be covered by posters. As it turned out, only posters of Alfredo and Simone were posted before any other party. Thus, posters from other parties were excluded, since there was no room left to place any others. The Carabinieri strictly enforced the ordinances, as they were paid off by the uncles. Needless to say, Alfredo and Simone received 70% of the vote. The Communist party gathered 18%. The rest of the parties received the remaining votes.

People of Avella also voted overwhelming for the Democratic party in their election. The Communist party never won a mayoral election in Cervinara, although they easily won in other towns nearby. Davide and Guido's hard work was duly rewarded. Alfredo acquired a café/bar in which Davide was appointed manager and Alvaro the waiter. The populace was ready for diversion like a café after the War, and Alfredo made sure that he owned the only one in town. Davide and Guido didn't have to leave town to sell American contraband cigarettes. They sold them on the premises. Indeed, the brothers had a cozy arrangement, but totally illegal. Who cared? People loved American cigarettes and were willing to pay for them, especially Camel cigarettes.

The Carabinieri were accomplices to the shenanigans taking place in the cafe, since they loved American cigarettes as well. That period of time marked the end of shepherding for Alvaro and Davide, and the beginning of the indoctrination into the Camorra. Life in a café/bar was easy, especially when their backs were covered by the mayor and the Carabinieri. The chief of police, Maresciallo of the Carabinieri, was bribed by the Mayor and walked around town like a General or a peacock in heat. All the women in town ran for cover when seeing him. However, the brothers' ultimate dream was to emigrate to USA and own a cafe of their own.

Contacts between Guido and Vito were somewhat sporadic soon after Guido worked at the Café. When Vito heard about Alvaro's good fortune, he sought a waiters job at cafes in Avella, but no luck. As in Cervinara these jobs stayed in the family. Nevertheless, he too abandoned shepherding as the work was much too harsh for his liking. He saw no future in it. His older brother, Alessandro, led the way out of shepherding by turning to soccer and academics. Vito followed in Alessandro's footsteps.

Because of the economic turnaround in Italy at that time, young people were leaving farming and shepherding in droves. They became aware of and attracted to alternative lifestyles in Italy as well as in the USA and Northern Europe. USA was becoming a window of opportunity and a glimpse into the future. It gave Guido and Vito hope and a dream to chase.

TWO

The American Dream

In the late 1940s and early 1950s, there was an exodus of young people from Southern Italy to the USA, South America and Northern Europe. The U.S. immigration laws of the 1920s resulted in long waiting lists for the small number of visas available to those born in Italy. Exactly 249,583 people were waiting for admission into the United States after the War. The annual quota allowed for immigrants from Italy was 5,666. When WW II came to an end in 1945, an estimated 7 to 11 million people were displaced from their homes in Germany, Italy, Austria and the rest of Europe. However, the US position toward Italian immigration to America was dramatically affected by the new wave of refugees especially from Southern Italy. The Truman administration supported admitting a number of European refugees over and above the existing immigration quotas for the USA, [1-6]. The law passed in 1948 authorized the entry of 200,000 displaced persons over the next two years. In 1950 the entry to America increased to 415,000 displaced people. The law stipulated that preferential treatment be given to people who were in resettlement camps, or refugees. It also gave preference to relatives of American citizens who had housing available for refugees.

A number of Vito's friends, including Guido, left Italy for the USA. Guido visited Vito at one of the many festivals in Avella to inform him that he and Davide qualified as refugees whereby they did not have to wait long to emigrate. However, they never interned in a refugee camp. They left town in less than a year, after informing Vito, and settled in the State of New Jersey. Their uncle, Simone, "cooked" the application papers to qualify himself and his two nephews for the refugee visa requirements. The only refugee camp that Simone camped in was at City Hall in Paolisi and Guido and Davide in the cafe in Cervinara. Clearly, the Camorra had connections all the way up to the American base in Naples and the Consulate Office, where the application paperwork was processed.

In general, it took much less time to emigrate to the USA under the Refugee Act than sponsorship visa laws. Hence, the Camorra specialized in expediting scam refugee visas for money via the Consulate Office in Naples. For the Camorra, it was a lucrative business in view of the many immigrants desperately wanting to emigrate. Vito and his brother, Alessandro, were not aware of any special visa laws that they could take advantage of. Besides, they didn't have the money or contacts with the Camorra to accelerate their departure to the USA. They did it the hard way. Fortunately, they were sponsored by their grandfather who was living in Aliquippa, Pennsylvania. In contrast, refugees do not need sponsors.

Guido and Davide emigrated to Sturmville, NJ, in 1950 under the Refugee Act of 1948. Their clever scheme to qualify for the Refugee Act was nothing short of brilliant. They claimed that their uncle Simone, in New Jersey, would provide housing and jobs for both of them. Uncle Simone had emigrated to USA six months earlier, soon after the passage of the Refugee Act, 1948. How he was able to qualify as a refugee, when he was living comfortably as the Mayor of Paolisi, is still a mystery. In their application as refugees, they claimed that they were orphans interned in a refugee camp in Benevento. All documents were forged and signed off by the Mayor of Cervinara who happened to be also their uncle Alfredo. With all of their paperwork in order and signed off by custom officials and American Consulate in Naples, their application put them at the head of the line waiting to emigrate.

A large Italian immigrant community lived in Sturmille, NJ. The only advantage to living there was that the town was located within a stone's throw from the George Washington bridge, the gateway to New York City. Half of the population of the town worked in NYC and the other half worked in local restaurants, bakeries and in pasta manufacturing. A super highway split the town in two with oil refineries on both sides of the highway. Simone bought a three family house. The plan was for Davide and Guido to convert the ground apartment into a pizzeria, when they showed up.

It was an excruciating five year wait for Vito's family to secure clearance from the US Immigration Office. The amount of paperwork in the application process was so enormous that lawyers were employed to expedite it. The legal aspect of it overwhelmed everyone in the family, including Alessandro who, at least, could read the documents from the Immigration Office. The first two lawyers, employed by Vito's family, were opportunists who pounced on desperate people. At that time, half of the town applied to emigrate. The first lawyer didn't know the difference between the Refugee Act and Truman's sponsorship visa program. He relied on connections that he had with the Camorra who were then involved in human trafficking as it pertained to the Refugee Act. The lawyer took the money and disappeared without bothering to contact anyone in the Consulate Office in Naples.

The second lawyer also had connections with the Camorra, but at least knew that the family was not eligible for the Refugee Act. Application papers were compiled for the sponsorship program. However, like the first lawyer, he disappeared as soon as he was paid, never to be seen again. The worst part of it all was that two years were wasted languishing in not knowing the status of the application. Finally, a third lawyer was hired. He quickly informed the family that due to the enormous number of people applying for the sponsorship program, it might take longer than usual to emigrate. He asked to be paid only after the approval of the Consulate Office was in hand. Basically, it put the family at the end of the line. The process was painful, arduous and tested the patience of the whole family. Preference was given to immigrants with special skills who could easily be placed in the work force. Members of Vito's family had no skills that would enable them to take jobs upon arrival. Nevertheless, they were not deterred from applying.

The application process involved a number of steps. Each step of the application needed to be signed off by officials like the Mayor, Chief of Police and even the postmaster. It was pure agony to follow each step carefully. Most of the time these officials were not around, and when they were around they stuck their hands out for a bribe. After the written part of the application was completed, an interview with the American Counsel General was scheduled in Naples. What a pompous man! But what choice did the family have. For all intent and purpose, he yielded as much power as the King of Naples in medieval times. He was dealing with desperate people, and, the worst part of it, was, he enjoyed the situation. Apparently, the family did not grease the palms of people working at the Consulate Office, mostly hired local Neapolitans. However, waiting those five years and being able to dream about emigrating to America was worth every minute and Lira (Italian money) spent.

Vito's family settled on First St. in Aliquippa, PA. That city block was mostly settled by Greek immigrants and few from Southern Italy. There was an apartment complex inhabited only by African American residents. The apartment complex was located next to the house where Vito's family lived. It was a form of segregation in housing, although it was not called as such in northern states like Pennsylvania. In southern states, it was common to have segregation across the board in housing, restaurants, hotels, clubs, bars, etc. Also on First Street, there was a café (owned by Tony Massimo), drug Store, Mosque, Greek Cafe and a Turkish gambling house, three bars and an empty lot where kids played stick ball. On Sunday afternoon, African-American residents came out of worship in white robes extending from head to toe singing Gospel music, as they strolled across the empty lot. It was all strange to Vito: the music, the robe and the timing of religious festivities in the middle of a lot. The empty lot served many purposes, besides stick ball among neighborhood kids.

There were many other customs that Vito had to make peace with. For instance, teenagers formed youth clubs and roamed around town looking for other clubs, in other districts of town, to pick fights after school. These confrontations were prevalent throughout the east coast, especially in New York City in the fifties. From today's perspective, it was simply crazy behavior. An immigrant caught in this whirlwind of madness was rather confused. It was probably a takeoff from the movie, popular at that time, West Side Story or On the Waterfront. In short, Vito was not tuned into the latest craze of American teenagers. The only things that he could relate to were playing basketball, football and stick ball with teenagers in the empty lot.

It took Vito about nine months to transition into the regular school system. A week after arrival, he and Alessandro attended a remedial school in Ambridge, PA. Most of the attendees were immigrants from Southern Europe: Greeks, Italians, Spanish, Albanians, etc. Their ages ranged from six to sixty. The teacher was an elderly Italian-American woman who was well versed in English, Greek and Italian, but she demanded that only English be spoken in class. Initially, students were introduced to verbal skill exercises, writing and progressing into American history, geography and math skills. This allowed the teacher to separate students into sub-groups according to their skill levels. Individual lessons were imparted to the sub-groups to upgrade their academic skills. At the end of the school year, the teacher made academic recommendations as to what grade level a particular student should be assigned in the regular school system.

Remarkably, Greek and Turkish immigrants got along very nicely on First Street. On the island of Cyprus, Greeks and Turks have been at each other's throat for centuries, trying to annihilate each other and taking possession of the island. Today, the island is split in two. One half governed by Greek and the other half by Turkish governors. On First St., a Turk and a Greek immigrant co-managed the "Turkish Coffee House" which featured Turkish coffee and gambling. However, the relationship between the two partners was too cozy, especially between the Turk and his partner's wife. The neighborhood became suspicious of the dalliance of the two, when all of the offspring looked like the Turk. They were carrying on an affair for many years.

It was discovered years later, when the Greek partner was examined by a medical doctor for a serious disease and deemed to be infertile. The Greek patient could not have conceived any children, although his wife gave birth to six. Upon learning of his medical condition, the Greek partner was seen marching toward the Coffee House with a machete in his hand. His partner was nowhere to be found. The Greek family was distraught and the children were in total shock. The ages of the children ranged from ten to the mid-twenties. The family split up with the older children, ashamed, leaving town and the wife moving to another part of town with the younger children. It was the talk of the neighborhood. Tony mediated peace between the two partners, and they patched things up so that they could work together again. Tony was the Mafia boss whose territory included the Pittsburgh and Youngstown areas and, basically, he told them that he would replace them unless they were able to work together. They didn't kiss and make up, but found a way to work together. After a couple of months, all was forgotten, and both lived in harmony. The family reunited with the mother, husband and small children moving back to the old house. The older children never forgave their parents. As for the Turk, he was invited to their house from time to time on special holidays.

Vito met his friend, Enrico (Rigo for short), on the empty lot during a game of stick ball. Rigo was a football player for the High School team. Together, they were the odd couple of the neighborhood. Rigo was over six feet tall and 230 pounds and Vito was a skinny runt, just over five feet. He introduced Vito to the games of football and basketball. He also introduced Vito to shady games like rolling dice in secluded buildings. Vito was hired as a "lookout" man while they rolled dice. Vito came to learn the American slang, and expressions like seven come eleven, Nina from Pasadena, snake eyes, etc. At these games, Rigo warned Vito not to ask too many questions about where Pasadena was. Many years later Vito learned Tony was a Mafia boss, as reported in the NY Times, but never was aware of it then. Just thinking about those days gives Vito the shudders. Yes, it was a wild neighborhood, but Vito liked the excitement in contrast to the dormant world atop Monte Avella.

Every day, Vito was exposed to something new and strange that caught his attention. For example, the first time he saw African-Americans in white robes singing out loud coming out of church, it blew his mind for he never saw such a spectacle before. In truth, the singing was rather captivating and melodious. He didn't know what to make of it, but it was spectacular and very theatrical. On summer days block parties were common on the empty lot. One day, a man was walking around wearing only a raincoat, although it was not raining and the temperature was in the 80s. Protruding on the side of his coat was a sharp object which was discovered to be a butcher knife. Everybody scooted out of the man's path thinking, "A raincoat in this heat and a knife?" He was looking for his wife's lover.

Out of nowhere, Tony appeared on the scene and simply said, "Put that away." The man was so scared that that he got on his knees pleading for mercy. Vito could not grasp what just transpired. It appeared that the word of God came down from the heavens to strike fear in this man's heart. Vito never connected Tony to any powerful influence for he was nice to Vito. "Strange", Vito murmured and said to no one in particular: "What a country, so much to learn." What a difference it was living on the mountains versus surrounded by all these "nut cases" on First Street. Everything was a blur that never registered in his brain. After a while, he just gave up thinking about it and went with the flow. He simply assimilated with what was going on.

Tony's café was located in the middle of First Street. To the left of the café there were three bars, an air condition store, a pharmacy and a tire store. To the right was a butcher shop, gambling place and an all-purpose convenience store. Diagonally across the street was the empty lot where children played stick ball. In one memorable game, the rubber ball was hit high over the shoulder of Vito. He turned around, a-la-Willie Mays, to catch the ball over his shoulder onto the street, in front of an incoming car. Unbeknownst to Vito, the game had spectators, all the wiseguys of the café. They were gambling on the outcome of the game. There was a long dispute among the kids whether or not Vito caught the ball. The dispute went on for a long time until Tony and some of his cohorts shot out of the café with rolls of C-notes, hundred-dollar bills, in their hands to settle the dispute. "He caught the ball," Tony blurted out, just like an umpire. That was the end of the dispute. Probably, Tony won some money on the outcome of the game. Thereafter, Vito had free and open access to Tony's café.

As one entered the café, there were small tables and chairs placed against the wall. Single spinning stools aligned along the counter faced the coffee machine. The small kitchen faced all potential customers. Interestingly, Vito never saw anyone pay for anything. About ten to fifteen adults usually had breakfast or lunch there. Sometimes, they would gather into a private room with Tony and run out of the café, like firemen chasing a fire. Jesse and the Sanchez brothers were regulars at the café but disappeared right after lunch. Two burly young men followed Tony everywhere he went, except to the bathroom. The strange thing about the customers was that the neighborhood residents did not frequent the café. Vito never put much importance to this omission. Obviously, the neighbors were boycotting the café for some reason not obvious to Vito. Perhaps, the neighbors may have been aware of Tony being a Mafia capo.

In the room next to the kitchen, there was a billiard table, where Gino, Tony's son, and Vito often played billiards. The most interesting room to Vito, located in the basement, was the gym where amateur boxers trained for the "Golden Gloves Matches", to be held in Pittsburgh, PA. Vito loved to train with the boxers. Every evening there would be sparring matches. In a sparring match, the sparring partner engages the boxer entering the competition, whereby the sparring partner only defends punches thrown at him, but does not counter punch. Basically, the sparring partner is the equivalent of a moving punching bag. Vito did not understand the role of a sparring partner. He decked the boxer in the first round. The older brother to the boxer in training came out of nowhere to challenge Vito, although he was much older and bigger, 180 versus 135 pounds. Once again, Tony came to the rescue. He asked the boxer-in-training and his brother leave the gym. There must have been some heavy gambling going on for Tony to step in. However, that was the last time Tony allowed Vito in the gym. Vito's family informed Tony that Vito did not have permission to train as a boxer. Tony honored the request. Furthermore, Rigo's mother did not allow Rigo to go near the café and advised Vito to do the same. Vito didn't understand why, but he knew something was amiss. Gambling, and only gambling, pervaded with the same people coming in and out of the cafe the whole day.

Rigo's family was large, four boys and two girls. The mother's name was Beatrice, as in Botticelli's painting in Florence. The father, Ferdinando, was an interesting character. Punctually, every Saturday at one pm he would sit down in a comfortable chair, with a bottle of wine, cheese and bread, and listen to the Firestone radio program airing operas from the Metropolitan Opera house in New York City. Sometimes, he would sing along. The rest of the family ignored him, but Vito loved to talk to him about operas as he had encyclopedic knowledge of them. He would explain to Vito the difference between the singing voices of Enrico Caruso and that of Beniamino Gigli and would compare them both with American singers of the time, baritone Robert Merrill and tenor Richard Tucker. Also, he would explain the highlights of the opera that he was listening to. Truly fascinating. He heard the greatest singers of all time at various opera houses in Brazil, Argentina, France and NYC. Ferdinando was born in Abruzzo, Italy, and traveled or worked in various countries. Being an anarchist at heart, he was thrown out of a lot of countries for his political activities. In Aliquippa, he worked at a steel factory. Whenever Vito came into his house with Rigo, he would warn Vito not to step into that café, but never explained why.

A typical scene in the cafe for gambling went as follows: In the fifties, the best boxers in the world were in the USA, but Mafia pretty much manipulated the game of boxing. In this particular boxing event, it matched two fighters who were ex-world champions: Archie Moore and Ezzard Charles. The newspapers reported the bickering between the boxers as to who should wear the white trunks. Traditionally, the champion wore the white trunks. In this case, neither boxer was the champ. Betting in the café was heavy and strong, one hundred to thousands of dollars was exchanged. Tony declared, in front of everyone, that he would bet ten thousand dollars on the boxer wearing the black trunks, implying that he was offering 50–50 odds on the fight, even odds. It appeared to be an honest and fair bet. To put things in perspective, the salary of Joe Di Maggio of the Yankees was about one hundred thousand dollars. The starting salary of an engineer was eight thousand dollars. Yes, Tony won the bet, all of it. Both boxers wore black trunks. Only after many years did Vito reflect back and conclude that there was something "fishy" then. Tony must have known, a priori, that both boxers would wear black trunks. There were many signs to indicate that there was something amiss about this café, but Vito was totally oblivious to all of these obvious signs.

Looking across the street from Vito's window sill in his home he could see Jesse walking down the sidewalk toward the café, only half a block away from the café. Jesse was an African American who spent a lot of time in the café and was a good friend of Tony. A uniformed policeman was approaching Jesse from the opposite direction. They were about fifty feet apart, when Jesse stuffed a bunch of small white papers in his mouth and started chewing the papers. By the time the policeman reached him, he had devoured the papers. Yuk! Vito hurried down the steps and zoomed across the street to ask Jesse what happened. "I was hungry", he retorted. Many people gathered around to ask as well. Jesse just continued walking, as if nothing happened. Further inquiry with the neighbors revealed that Jesse must have eaten the numbers written on papers by him. These were the numbers that people gambled on for the night lottery controlled by organized crime. Vito never connected the dots to make the logical conclusion that Tony was a Mafia boss.

Another incident that should have alerted Vito was relayed to him by none other than Tony himself. Tony claimed that he was vacationing with his family up in the Pocono Mountains in Pennsylvania. He was talking to an audience of friends seated on a bench in front of the cafe. He went to the Poconos, PA, every summer, according to him. There was a lot of entertainment at night, from famous artists and nightclub artists to others performing on Broadway. However, one evening the whole bunch of them were surprised by Federal agents at a town nearby, Apalachin, NY [2-1]. He claimed that he was lucky to avoid capture by them. He never explained why he was there and why he had to escape from the FBI. The story in itself sounded innocent enough to warrant some sympathy. However, years later Vito compared the timing of the famous "Apalachin meeting of the Mafia" with the time Tony visited the Pocono Mountains. No surprise that it occurred at the same time. Unbelievable! At the Apalachin meeting in 1957, Mafia bosses from New York, Los Angeles, Chicago, Detroit and other big cities met near the Poconos for the purpose of establishing a national Mafia syndicate with five capos (bosses) coordinating or managing the syndicate. Tony must have represented the Pittsburgh area. The meeting was necessitated because of the extradition of "Lucky" Luciano to Naples, Italy, in 1946 where he died in 1962, [1-11]. The meeting was organized by Luciano's underboss Vito Genovese, who became boss of all bosses and headed the syndicate, [1-10].

Vito himself was a gambler at heart. He loved to gamble on football games. His friend in high school, Wrona, taught him how the odds were calculated in Las Vegas for college and professional sporting events. The name Wrona was short for his Polish name, Wronjakowski. There was a large community of Polish immigrants that emigrated to Aliquippa after the War. They settled at the other end of town, Tenth Street, near the High School. After many back and forth conversations with Wrona, Vito decided to gamble one hundred dollars on a professional football game. Wrona preceded Vito in placing his bet for one hundred dollars. Vito followed Wrona into the gambling place. The place was no bigger that a small hallway, fifteen feet long, and the proprietor was sitting behind a counter. In addition, there was a small private room, behind the counter, no bigger than a closet space. It could have been, perhaps, a toilet. He was so sure that he would win that he was willing to plop a bundle of money even though he was only a teenager. *Besides, Wrona exuded confidence and Vito trusted him, since* Wrona gambled there on a daily basis. Wrona was ahead of the game and won more than lost. The owner asked Vito for his name. As Vito placed the bet with the bookie, the bookie excused himself to place a call in his small "toilet" office. When he came out, he barked at Vito: "Get out of here." Vito, distraught, retorted, "You just took Wrona's money, what's wrong with mine." In a threatening tone he reiterated, "Get the fuck out here." Wrona and Vito were stunned. Fear showed in Wrona's eyes and he just walked out. Vito was enraged, but the man threw the money to the ground. What to do—nothing. The man showed total contempt and was threatening.

The next day, Tony calmly addressed the episode of the previous day. "I don't want you near that place." Vito thought that he was being a hypocrite, as there was so much gambling in the café. Also, how in the fuck did he know Vito went to that gambling place. These episodes proved one thing. It should have forewarned Vito that Tony was tied up with that gambling place, but it never occurred to him that Tony was a big, big time racketeer. On the other hand, although Tony was connected with the Mafia, he had a good heart. He simply did not want Vito involved with gambling. It could only have led to misery and who knew what else. Tony knew the road ahead and did not want Vito or his son Gino to go that way.

About that time, Vito was saving money for college and was desperate for a summer job. The country was in an economic down turn, and there were no summer jobs. He knocked on doors of every business in Aliquippa, begging for a job. He asked Tony if he could be his golf caddy. Clearly, Tony did not need a caddy. He had a small golf cart stored away at the private club. He paid Vito double salary for caddying once a week. Every Friday afternoon, Tony, Willis, Consigliere to Tony, and Vito rode to a golf club in Tony's car. A Consigliere is basically an adviser to a capo (boss) Mafioso in all matters. Vito was not aware of any special connection between Willis and Tony. Mr. Willis was the owner of the air condition/appliance store, but no legitimate business was ever conducted in that store. Every time Vito walked past the store, it was either closed, or Mr. Willis had his feet up on a desk with no customers. There was no cash register in the store. He looked like an old distinguished Irish gentleman who knew his way around. He wore a straw hat even in the winter time and had a carefully trimmed moustache. He was about six feet tall, slender, with whitish-blond hair. He was the splitting image of actor David Niven, except for the light complexion. He looked like a man of leisure who had disdain for money and who tipped Vito a C-note ($100) after playing golf.

Years later, Vito discovered that Mr. Willis was no Irishman, but a Sicilian-American born in New York City. His father emigrated from Sicily and his mother from Ireland. His real name was Cuglielmo. Since few Americans could pronounce that name, he changed it to Willis (short for Williams which is the literal translation of Cuglielmo). It is quite common in the Mafia for its members to assume nicknames or any names that fit their images. Every time Tony and Mr. Willis wanted to have a private conversation, one of them would drive the golf ball into the woods and asked Vito to fetch the golf ball there. Sometimes, they asked Vito to go fetch the ball, although no one hit the ball into the woods.

Yes, there were signs for anyone not so brilliant to recognize that Tony was associated with organized crime. Psychologically, Vito was not ready to accept that conclusion. He was not naive and was well aware of the Camorra in Avella selling contraband American cigarettes in the Naples area. Even teenagers smoked American cigarettes. He liked to believe that he had arrived into the world of "Alice in Wonderland", when he emigrated to America. Furthermore, he liked to believe that the US government could never allow the scourge of the Mafia or Camorra to exist in the USA, but it did. Joseph Valachi's testimony to Congress in 1962 removed that picture of "Alice in Wonderland" from Vito's mind once and forever. Valachi [2-2] revealed that, indeed, Mafia syndicates or factions prevailed in all major American cities. Even then, Vito refused to believe that Tony had anything to do with the Mafia. He rationalized that Tony was too accessible and too nice a person to be involved with the Mafia. Vito was wrong. The New York Times in 1994 reported that Tony was forced to retire from the Mafia, as a pipe bomb exploded in his cafe. By the end of summer of 1958, Vito saved enough money to pay only for tuition. He borrowed the rest of the money to pay for room and board for one year and left Aliquippa for good to attend college.

Nowadays, Vito reminisces about those strange and awkward times. There is one scene in the movie, "Goodfellas", that depicted, more or less, Vito's time spent at Tony's cafe. In one scene mafiosi in a café were praising a teenager for refusing to give evidence against one Mafia mobster. In watching that movie, Vito was reminded of what could have been in store for him. Today, he gets cold sweats just thinking about it. As a teenager, the first thing that Vito had to give up, which was dear to him, was his love of the game of soccer. He played the game, since he took the first step in life. It was considered a "foreign" sport in the 1950s by most Americans and Vito did not want to appear as a foreigner. No one at that time played soccer, except at a small University in Saint Louis, Missouri. The University imported all of its players from Europe and South America. He yearned to be an American and to be accepted by other teenagers. He learned to play baseball, basketball and football in order to assimilate completely into the American dream of becoming a professional athlete someday or at least get a scholarship to a college. He soon realized that being small in stature was not going to impress anyone at college level athletics. Universities did not grant scholarships to runts.

Vito stumbled onto the study of physics by accident. At the urging of Wrona, Vito enrolled in the physics class as a freshman in high school. In the first day of class, the teacher handed out books for students to read in class. On the first page and line, in bold letters, it read: **What is Matter**. It threw Vito for a loop, since he just learned the expression "what is the matter" as a way to greet people. To say that he was confused is an understatement. Looking around, he saw other students reading past the first page. He wondered, if he was in the wrong class. He was too embarrassed to ask anyone, even the teacher, about it. That evening, his mother was shocked to hear that Vito went to the public library. Usually, he hung around basketball courts. It didn't take long before he came across the name of Fermi in almost all of the physics books that he perused. He tried to make sense of what Fermi did, but it was useless. He vowed that someday he would get the hang of it.

Fermi was an Italian nuclear physicist admired by all Italians and the world at large. He split the atom to discover new elements in the Periodic Table of Elements, although his initial studies were in the field of general relativity. Element number 100 in the Periodic Table is named after him, Fermium. Splitting the atom experiments at the University of Rome (La Sapienza campus) in the mid 1930s cost him about $160. Today, high energy physics experiments cost more than tens of billions of dollars. Ironically, Fermi had a similar problem of being accepted by the physics community of Europe in the 1930s. According to Fermi's wife's diary [2-3], Fermi met much resistance to his approach to physics from colleagues in Germany, when he went there for his sabbatical leave from the University of Rome. After all, in those days, Germany was the center of the universe in the studies of physics. However, Fermi was re-assured by a Dutch physicist, Ehrenfest, who was an early pioneer in quantum physics, to keep doing what he was doing.

Most of Vito's friends knew very little about Fermi. They were into baseball cards. Wrona was the only one who knew about Fermi. He went on to become a great physicist himself. He was truly a genius in numbers and figures. He was able to determine the methodology by which odds were calculated in Las Vegas on professional and collegiate sports betting and Vito was impressed. Vito had a dream that one day he and Wrona would go to Las Vegas and win a bundle of money. Mafia bookies relied on Las Vegas odds only. Wrona placed his bets locally based on his calculations and was very successful at it until a Mafia bookie put a stop to his gambling. The bookie refused to take his bets. He was ahead of the game and that is a "no, no" in the Mafia. They are not in the business of giving grants to students or foundations. Wrona rarely studied but scored all A's in his exams. He and his sister survived the Holocaust but not his parents, grandparents and some relatives. He emigrated from Poland under the Refugee Act and settled with his uncle in a Polish community. Often he and Vito played baseball together after school until the Pittsburgh baseball team invited him for a tryout. However, he bypassed the tryout in order to pursue academic studies at the University of Chicago.

THREE

Hello Dolly

Leaving Aliquippa for College was the best thing that could have happened to Vito. For one thing, it removed him from Tony's café. Although Vito often socialized with people in the cafe, he had a queasy feeling about it. The people there were tough characters who kept to themselves. Vito had the feeling that it was no place to hang around and there was no future in gambling for him. He was admitted to Toledo University, Ohio, which was a small private school with an enrollment of about 7,000 students. Most of the students were from Ohio and vicinity. There was a small contingent of students from as far away as India, Sweden and South America. At Penn State, his first choice, as a foreigner, he was considered an out-of-state student, although he had been a resident of Pennsylvania for five years. That did not sit too well with Vito, especially when he was required to pay five times more tuition than residents of Pennsylvania. Also, he didn't particularly like to be labeled a foreigner. Luckily, Toledo University did not require SAT scores at that time for entrance requirements. Tuition was the same for all students.

During recess from the University of Toledo, Vito would return to the café and visited with Tony. Conversation was not about anything in particular, but more like old acquaintances getting together shooting the breeze. Tony would ask Vito about school and what Vito was majoring in. More importantly, Tony wanted to find out what school his son should apply and how the process of admission worked. Of course, Tony was concerned for his son, like any father would be except, perhaps, he was thinking in terms of whom to bribe at the University. To Tony, the University world was a strange one, of which he understood little. Eventually, Gino was the first one in his family to attend a university and Tony was proud of that. By the time Gino graduated from Penn State University, Vito attended graduate school in Connecticut. Gino went on to become a lawyer employed in the Federal Office of the Attorney General in Pittsburgh, PA. Thus, in contrast to Michael in the movie, "The Godfather", Gino took a detour, away from the Mafia.

This time around, Tony appeared to be more jovial than usual. For a change, he could smile. He was proud to announce the birth of his grandson to anyone who came by the cafe. Apparently, Rosalie, Tony's daughter, eloped with Carlos Sanchez about the time Vito left for Toledo. Rosalie was a wild one in high school and very rebellious, especially with her mother. They argued about Rosalie's relationship with Carlos. The dalliance between the two was no secret to anyone on First Street. Tony was the last to know. It must have been very hard for Rosalie to leave home and put Carlos in mortal danger in the name of love. Carlos was an "employee" of Tony and drove Rosalie and Gino to the high school. When Rosalie worked in the cafe, it was obvious to anyone there, except to Tony, that something special was taking place between the two. Rosalie and Carlos moved as far away as possible to avoid the wrath of Tony after they eloped. However, reconciliation was thrust on Tony's lap, when Rosalie contacted her papa about the birth of his grandson, Anthony. Tony broke down and cried, wanting to see his first grandchild and to convey to Carlos that all was forgotten and forgiven. Thus, history repeated itself, as Tony's father had also eloped on the birth of Tony himself.

Vito found college much more intense and challenging than high school, but it just meant that he had to buckle down more. However, he was not ready for the avalanche of students coming from all over the world and the USA with different cultures. Once again, he had to adapt to a new school environment with diverse lifestyles. He was comfortable with the cozy setting of First Street in Aliquippa, but that didn't prepare him with what was coming. Fortunately, he discovered that he could easily relate to new friends, whose backgrounds were in farming. He appreciated and understood the mind set of these farmers. Toledo was located South of Lake Erie. Only a couple of miles south of Toledo was "corn country" and farmers there represented values of mid-America. It was impressive to view acres upon acres of farmland, as far as the eye could see, so near a big city. Vito spent a lot of time working on the farms as well as going on those long treks on the mountains of Avella. When his friend and roommate, Laird, invited him to his family's farms, it reminded him of those painful days on Monte Avella which he didn't want to think about anymore. He didn't want to be a prisoner of those memories.

However, not everything was rosy with other roommates. Some were just not ready for university, either academically or psychologically. For instance, one roommate, Patsy, who aspired to be a pharmacist, had almost a complete inventory of pills stolen from the pharmacy where he worked in Cleveland, Ohio. Anytime a student in the dormitory asked Patsy for a pill to cure an ailment, he would provide it. No one questioned the wisdom of his quackery. Anyway, Vito had a headache one evening and asked Patsy for an aspirin. The next morning, as he was urinating in the common bathroom, about ten or more students were peeking at the color of the urine. It was blue! Yes, Vito's face turned different shades of blue and red. Bare chest, Vito ran to Patsy's room to ask him about the pill. Patsy reassured Vito that his bladder was fine and Vito should consider himself lucky that he didn't give him a pill that induced urination in red. Vito retorted that he was going to wring his neck and see what f…g color it was going to be after he choked him. He then planted his hands around Patsy's neck. Fortunately, two burly football players separated them. Patsy flunked out after one semester. The flunking rate of the freshman class was near 50%. In the Ivy League, it is less than 1%. Obviously, elite universities do a better job of recruiting students, since they can draw from a better pool of students in high school.

Laird was a former Air Force sergeant attending the University on the GI Bill. His family owned a farm that grew only corn. He was proud of himself, self-assured, good hearted, very religious and respectful of the land. As a former shepherd, Vito understood those values. Not only did he relate to them, but he embraced them wholeheartedly. Often Vito and Laird would visit that farm. Vito sympathized with the hard work farmers went through, much like the farmers of Avella. His friend loved to say: "Cut the bull and get to the chase" which Vito could relate to as that was how he felt about many things.

Vito's approach to science, even in the early developments, was simple and direct. He took special pride in getting to the essence of complex ideas. Academically, Laird was an above average student and very good at performing experiments. In the Air Force, he operated a radio and had a license as a HAM-operator. When Laird introduced himself as a HAM operator, Vito became totally confused. He wondered why ham had anything to do with radios. Laird explained that the word HAM stood for the initials of the names Hyman, Almy and Murray, who operated an amateur radio station at the Harvard Radio Club in 1908. Vito was clumsy in putting together electrical engineering experiments. His friend would call him Lefty. However, Vito's analytical skills were unmatched; that saved his ass in school and was the main reason that he was able to graduate from Toledo University.

The city of Toledo was a multi-cultured town. There were communities of Hungarians, Polish, English, and French-Canadians. Italian immigrants were few and spread all over the city. In all his years there, he never found an Italian restaurant that suited his taste. In addition, it was nearly impossible to get a decent pasta dish there. The only Italian pizza restaurant, Mario's pizza, managed to undercook a pizza. Vito discovered that the owner was a Polish immigrant who shortened his name from Markowski to Mario. It is impossible to screw up the cooking of a pizza, but he did it. Mario claimed that pizza al dente tasted better. Vito felt like stuffing him in the oven and overcooking him just to show how it was done. It didn't matter what Mario did; people were flocking to his pizzeria.

About once a month, Vito and his school friends would dine out in the city on Hungarian goulash and apple strudel. The Hungarian community was established in the late 1950s after the Hungarian revolution against the Soviet Regime. Hungarian refugees escaped the yoke of Communism in Hungary to settle in the mid-west, and in Toledo in particular. The cuisine at Toledo University's cafeteria was strictly American-style, meat and potatoes with gravy. This was difficult for Vito to adapt to in the beginning, but eventually, he made peace with that cuisine.

Vito survived his freshman year, at which point he had to decide what degree to enroll in. He decided to pursue electrical engineering only because he thought that he would learn about the physics of electron motions in a field. That was a mistake which he finally corrected in later years. Clearly, Vito had a lot to learn, besides books, about university life in general, but he went with the flow and assimilated as best as he could. His decisions about the curriculum showed how Vito's lack of language skills misinterpreted the implication of his choice of courses. Yes, electrical engineers are well aware of electron motion in electric fields, but inside an electron tube, not in general! Fortunately, his familiarity with electron tubes landed him a summer job with the Navy designing electrical circuits for the first generation of computers. The job went a long way in paying for school bills. However, Vito was on a mission to undo that mistake. He signed up for as many physics courses as possible under the guidelines and requirements of the Electrical Engineering (EE) department.

Furthermore, he embarked on learning about the field of magnetism on his own. At Toledo University there were no experts in this field, even in the physics department. Nevertheless, Professor R. A. Chipman, chairman of the Electrical Engineering department, encouraged him to pursue that field of study. He welcomed Vito to his office anytime he wanted to talk about magnetism. Professor Chipman always asked the right question to steer Vito in the right direction in the approach to the new field of study. This was the typical Cambridge (UK) style of teaching, one on one. However, magnetism had been around a long time. The Chinese invented the compass, using magnetite, in 200 BC (Han Dynasty) and the Greeks discovered lodestone (magnetite) in 2000 BC. Vito was caught in an uncomfortable world of no man's land. His language skills were nearly non-existent, either in English or Italian. His verbal skills in English, at best, were poor and he was no longer comfortable speaking in Italian or Neapolitan dialect. A man without a native language. Career wise, he was not here or there. He was a cross between an engineer and a physicist; what a mess to be in. It just made him work harder at improving his situation.

Upon graduation from Toledo University, his adviser, R. A. Chipman, prevailed upon Vito to enroll in the Applied Quantum Physics program at Yale University graduate school, since he himself received his Ph. D. in science from Cambridge University and undergraduate at Yale. Vito was also accepted by three other graduate schools offering Electrical Engineering Ph.D. degrees. Professor Chipman explained to Vito that Yale was not just an ordinary school, "You will get to meet interesting people and personalities that you normally don't get to see at other schools specializing in engineering". Vito had no clue as to what he was talking about. Professor Chipman added: "At least, at Yale, courses in the new program will be taught mostly in the Physics Department". That was welcome news. He wanted out of the Electrical Engineering field of study and be able to tell his mother that he is not an engineer anymore and couldn't fix her TV, radio and appliances.

It didn't take long for Yale to make a prophet out of professor Chipman. In one instance, as Vito was entering Woolsey Hall, the main auditorium at Yale University, he could hear, in the background, a singing voice very much similar to that unique Louie Armstrong's style. Vito said to himself, "Nah, it can't be." So, he ran up the steps to the second-floor balcony section of Woolsey Hall. Yes, it was Louie himself. What joy to hear him singing "Hello Dolly" with Carol Channing, who was the star of that show. Other entertainers were pianists Vladimir Horowitz and Arthur Rubenstein and many others, but Vito didn't have time to see them all. Yes, there were interesting students with impressive resumes who went around campus incognito, like G. W. Bush, 43rd president of the USA, but, frankly, they had nothing to do with where Vito was heading, to obtain the degree and get the f..k out of there! He couldn't stand the few of them from far-away lands with elitist attitudes, bad mouthing the USA about everything under the sun. By that time, he was a proud American naturalized citizen. In these lively conversations with law students, like J. I. Lieberman, U.S. Senator from Connecticut for 24 years, and foreign graduate students, they engaged in strong political exchanges during dinner at the Law school cafeteria. These talks were enlightening and left an impression on Vito. The main topic of conversation was the Vietnam war. Vito frequented the Law School cafeteria, since it served the best food on campus.

It was through these informal or accidental encounters that allowed Vito to meet or hear about individuals who eventually became famous celebrities or politicians. One instance stands out among many. Often at lunch, he would mosey to George's restaurant, a Greek diner, located nearby a research laboratory where Vito worked. He ordered George's specialty, lamb stew, from behind the counter, as undergraduate students were waiting to place their orders. Vito overheard one of them say, "Can you imagine the nerve of that walking idiot coming to the class near the end." It was unavoidable to hear that. "Who is the walking idiot?" Vito asked George. He took Vito aside and replied in a low voice, "He is the son of a famous Yalie, who was a Navy officer of a PT boat in the Pacific during WW II." George was friendly to Vito only because Vito would greet him with "how are you doing" in Greek. Vito learned that expression from First Street In Aliquippa, a Greek neighborhood. Vito surmised that the walking idiot could not be one of the Kennedys, since none of them attended Yale. But who? George was not willing to tell who he was. He was not that friendly after all. That walking idiot later became a powerful political figure.

Vito met his future wife in the "whale" building on Yale campus. The building housed indoor sports events, such as: hockey, basketball and youth events sponsored by the city of New Haven. It was named the "whale", because it was shaped like it by design. In the winter, the building also served as a skating rink for Yale students. Vito was trying to learn to skate but spent more time sliding on the ice than skating on it. However, one girl, who was very smooth at it, skated just past him on the ice and caught his attention. If only he could skate that well, he thought. But his true intentions were otherwise-how to meet her. He decided to skate backwards and "accidentally" bump into her. After many tries, the magical accidental bump occurred. Sitting on the ice, both laughed at the incident, although he was the cause of it. It was an understatement to say that Vito was a clumsy skater. It seemed that both wanted the accident to happen.

View from second floor balcony in Woolsey Hall, Yale University.

Her name was Annmarie. She was from Denmark, where her name was shortened to Anna. She was a visiting student scholar and part of a group involved with cancer research at the Yale pharmacology department. She had arrived a month before the skating episode and was on a J-1 non-immigrant Visa which meant that her stay in the USA was for only 18 months. They dated infrequently due to their busy schedules. Sometimes, each ate alone in the Graduate School cafeteria while the other was busy at work where they shared Vito's dining card, issued by the Graduate School. Their favorite hangout was at Morrissey Hall, where Kentucky Blue Grass music was played on weekends. After about a year's dalliance, they were married at the Yale Divinity School Church in a Catholic ceremony. After marriage, the J-Visa deadline loomed over their heads.

There were two contradicting applications of the Immigration Laws in regard to Anna. On one hand, the J-Visa required that she absolutely had to return to Denmark after the 18 month stay. On the other hand, spouses of American citizens automatically qualified as American citizens, [1-6]. The international office at Yale, dealing with immigration issues, declared that the J-Visa mandate superseded the marriage law. That ruling dampened the spirits of the newlyweds until a clarification by Congressman Robert Giaimo's office declared that the marriage law was more applicable than the J-Visa requirement. Hallelujah! Giaimo's office advised the two to inform the Immigration office in Hartford, Connecticut, immediately about their marital status. The problem was that their transportation to Hartford was problematic. The passenger door of their old car would not close. So, they closed the door with a rope while Anna sat in the back seat, as they drove to Hartford with much apprehension.

With the arrival of their first child, the newlyweds had a difficult time paying their monthly bills. Vito sought financial help from the school's department Dean. The Dean was an affable person with a sunny disposition, typical of a Greek immigrant that Vito was very familiar with on First Street. Vito explained his dilemma. Like the Greek logician of yesteryear, Aristotle, he said to Vito, calmly pulling his fountain pen from the shirt pocket, "Before your marriage, you and your fiance had two salaries and both of you got along well financially. After marriage, there are still two people and two salaries. Then, why do you need more money?" As he was talking he drew two circles to represent two people, Vito and Anna. Vito, asked permission to borrow his pen and drew a little circle beside the two larger ones. The Dean broke into a big smile, just like a proud grandfather, and said, "Yes, I see. We have to get some extra money for you."

Vito entered Yale with pre-conceived ideas about the physics of magnetism. He was self-taught at Toledo University about that field of study. His mentor at Yale was about to undo every home-made notion about magnetism that Vito brought along. The professor was both a mentor and a tormentor, but he loved the exchanges with the mentor. After all, the professor was the world expert in this field of study and recognized as the "Michelangelo" of magnetism. However, when they played a game of ping-pong, on their breaks, all the cordiality between the two went out the window. They tried to "annihilate" each other. In physics, there is such a thing as the "annihilation" mathematical operator, but not in real life. After all these years, the mentor and the student have kept in touch.

The mentor, Michelangelo, was a graduate of Oxford University and his thesis received well deserved acclaim internationally. He emigrated from Austria, when he was eight years old. His expertise was in low temperature magnetism. He was an unassuming person who did not like to boast about his abilities. Vito learned about those abilities soon enough. He liked to believe that he was a hotshot in mathematical calculations but, one day, his mentor showed him a neat mathematical trick that totally devastated Vito's confidence as a hotshot. Once disarmed of his special pride, both entered a new phase of professional understanding. Vito was the student and the mentor, the teacher. Michelangelo was a very gentle and soft hearted (a sentimentalist) person in his mentoring of Vito. At the same time, he demanded a lot. That was exactly what Vito needed, a kick in the ass.

The highlight of Vito's graduate school training was to attend three courses by Michelangelo and three courses in the physics department by Professor Willis Lamb who was a student of Fermi. Both Fermi and Lamb won the Nobel Prize for physics. Remarkably, seven of Fermi's students also received the Nobel Prize in physics. No other Nobel Laureate can claim that successful mentorship. Professor Lamb loved to talk about Fermi's ideas on physics. In one particular lecture, Professor Lamb introduced the problem of electron scatterings from nuclei. He presented the modern theory and then he would say, "Now, let's introduce Fermi's primitive and medieval ages approach to this problem." One could sense that there was much admiration and love between Professor Lamb and Fermi. The point was that although Fermi's approach appeared to be primitive and somewhat outdated, it still contained the essence of modern theory. However, what professor Lamb did not realize then that Fermi, according to the diary of Fermi's wife's, he read very old books on physics, written by monks in the sixteen century.

According to Fermi, these monks were good physicists and very original, [2-3]. However, their books never saw the light of day, and did not appear in open literature. Fermi bought those books at flea-markets in Rome when he was a student at the University of Rome.

In 1938 Fermi was awarded the Nobel prize in Physics for splitting the atom. Once in Stockholm, he and his Jewish wife, maiden name Laura Capon, never turned back. There was too much turmoil in Italy with the Fascist party and in the rest of Continental Europe, especially Germany with its views on racism. They boarded a ship in Stockholm and emigrated directly to New York City, although it was in the middle of winter, the peak season of storms in the Atlantic Ocean. He was employed by Columbia University on arrival. Fermi died, at the young age of 54, of stomach cancer due to radiation emitted from nuclear chain reaction experiments performed at the University of Chicago.

FOUR

University of Hard Knocks

Vito lost contact with Guido once he left Cervinara. Davide and Guido settled in Sturmville, NJ, moving into a house owned by Simone, their uncle. The two brothers occupied the apartment on the second floor and Simone, with his wife and niece, Lena, on the third floor. Their pizzeria was located on the ground floor. The timing of their settlement could not have been any worse, since there was great infighting in the New York City-New Jersey area among the five Mafia families in the 1950s. The turmoil resulted from "Lucky" Luciano's being deported to Italy as an undesirable in 1946, [1-11]. The five families [4-1] operated in five different Boroughs of New York City: Staten Island, Manhattan, Brooklyn, Bronx and Queens. Prior to his deportation, "Lucky" Luciano was head of the commission that regulated the interplay among factions or families. The commission consisted of five members representing the five factions plus the overall capo, Luciano. Only the commission sanctioned the killing of a mafioso. The killing of a mafioso, not sanctioned, was enough of a provocation to start a war among factions. Indeed, that was the case that resulted in the turmoil of the ninety-fifties into the early sixties.

The setting of the movie "The Godfather" took place about that period of time, illustrating the interplay among the five families, but also about episodes taking place in the 1920s involving the murder of mafia bosses Joe Masseria and Salvatore Maranzano [4-2]. So, the movie was a mix of events taking place in NYC between factions in the 1920s and 1950s. The movie depicted the infighting between the older and the younger generations of capos (bosses) in New Jersey and New York City, as reported by newspapers nationally. Since the deportation of Lucky Luciano, there was a vacuum in Mafia leadership. As a result, there were a number of would-be younger capos wanting to take over. In particular, Vito Genovese, [1-10], took over from Luciano by eliminating younger rivals within his faction in 1947. Whereas in the 1920s the young mafiosi replaced the old guards, in the 1950s the old guards retained their leadership, like Genovese and Bonanno. Leadership in the Mafia was not gained by the electoral process, but by intimidation, violence and by the gun, as depicted in the movies.

Simone and the two brothers were affected by that turmoil, since Simone and Genovese went back a long time. Anyone siding with a faction was dangerous, because it put a spotlight on that person. They were partners in the contraband sales of American cigarettes in the Naples area during WW II. It was only natural for the two to collaborate once again in the trafficking of heroin and cocaine in New Jersey. Genovese was the kingpin of heroin trafficking, since he organized the importation of opium in very large scales from Turkey to Sicily after the War. Simone's past association with Vito Genovese was an excellent recommendation for him to be indoctrinated in the Mafia and be part of Genovese's family in New York City. Genovese was the big boss then. Within the Mafia families, he was referred to as Don Vitone, big Vito. Pizza was becoming a popular fast food item rivaling the hamburger in the 1960s. Simone set up a pizzeria, and drug dealing in the pizzeria, not much different from his cafe operation in Paolisi. As in the past, his nephews, Davide and Guido, were running the everyday operation of the pizzeria.

For Simone, the only diversion from managing the pizzeria was gambling on dog races at the Meadowlands, East Ruthford. Besides, it took him out of town, away from the smell of oil refineries in Sturmville. He kept records of all the results of dog races, since he had lived in Sturmville. He had a crackpot idea that the winning numbers associated with the dogs were cyclic. It never occurred to him that the lifetime of a dog running everyday at the races was very short, compared with the cyclic period of him betting on dogs; hence, the likelihood that the same dog wearing the same number was remote. After a short duration on the racing circuits, these greyhound dogs disappeared from sight; most likely, re-appearing as dog food. At least, it got him out of town.

A four-lane highway, Hwy 95, running in the north-south direction separated the oil refineries from the town. The house, west of the highway, was located only 30 feet from the highway. Oil refinery tanks were built on the other side. Coming from Paolisi, Italy, breathing that pure mountain air, it must have been a shock for the whole family to breathe such foul smelling air. The stench and the orange-brown colored plume that hung over the area reminded locals to take whatever opportunity to get out of town. High power lines seemed to be everywhere. The high school that Guido attended was next to high power lines. In those days there were no publications reporting correlation between high power lines and cancer. In short, Sturmville was not a healthy place to live.

Oil refineries along a major highway in Sturmville

Guido could be seen playing basketball every day, come rain, come shine or snow. He was a social animal who loved to interact with all the kids in the neighborhood. The town was settled mostly by immigrants from Southern Italy. The local barber was from Cervinara. It had the highest density of Italian pastry stores on the entire East Coast. Also, Italian pasta was produced there and exported throughout New Jersey. The only benefits of living there were the low cost of food and its proximity to New York

City. The boys often went to Yankee Stadium, cafes, Broadway, movies and walked around the shops in New York City.

Guido joined the Pony League baseball team as soon as he arrived in New Jersey and he was a very good player. Playing the game was natural to him. They could have played sissy ball, and he would have been there just to be among the crowd of kids and a ready-made audience. It was so important for him to be accepted by his teammates and the crowd. He was in a hurry to learn English and assimilate into the American culture. In playing baseball, he had an advantage in that he was quite adapt at playing an Italian kid's game. The game was about hitting a tiny piece of wood with a heavy stick as far as possible, avoiding other children from catching it. The tiny piece of wood was cut from a small branch of a tree. It was catapulted up in the air from the ground, and swatted away. If caught, someone else swatted the piece of wood. Up on the Apennine mountains, Italy, the heavy duty shepherd stick was used to swat it away. Clearly, this exercise developed strong eye and hand coordination. On the very first time at bat, Guido hit a baseball so hard that it cleared the fence and the scoreboard behind the fence. He was the smallest player on the field, though the oldest. On one defensive play, he grabbed a line drive off third base diving at it and grabbing it with his bare hand. He received a standing ovation. When he returned to the bench, the coach asked him, why he didn't use the glove. He answered, "I didn't have time. I only had time to dive at the ball like a soccer goalie", all the while hiding his sore red hand.

Davide didn't have time for school or to participate in extra-curricular activities. His time was spent on opening up a new pizzeria. His school education was only to fifth grade, enough to read and write. For him that was sufficient for where he was heading, a career in the Mafia. He was helped in managing the pizzeria by Simone's niece, Lena, and Guido. However, during daytime, Guido was at school or playing baseball or other sports. Guido was required by state law to attend school to the age of sixteen. There was no doubt that the two brothers were headed in the same direction in their careers. The relationship between the two was more like that of a father-son, since Davide was much older. Yes, they had their spats in the past as any two brothers would but always resolved their differences. If anything, their bond was stronger than ever before.

Guido was an average student in High School, but earned varsity letters in baseball and football. In ninth grade he tried out for the baseball team as a center fielder. At that age, most kids were intimidated by the size and speed of pitches thrown by senior pitchers, but not Guido. He stood in that batter's box digging in his heels, challenging every pitch thrown at him, much like a bull waiting for the matador to charge. Older pitchers were exasperated by his tenacity at bat to the point that they would aim pitches at his head to move him away from the batter's box. Guido was challenged before by wild boars up in the Apennine mountains and came out alive. He was not about to be intimidated by them. The coach loved every minute of those classic confrontations. Of course, he had to have him on the team. Guido was a pugnacious and confident little bugger, and the spark plug of the team.

In football tryouts, again he was the smallest player, but he tried out as an offensive guard. He was built like a fire hydrant and weighed only 145 pounds, going up against players as big as 200 pounds or more at the line of scrimmage. In those days, players at the line of scrimmage played two-way football, offense and defense. Guido played middle linebacker on defense. He was a ferocious blocker on offense and a sure tackler on defense. Running-backs loved to run behind his blocking as they knew Guido was going to take his man out of the play, regardless. He was a starter for four years both in baseball and football. However, his career as a football player did not extend beyond high school, although he was recognized as the best guard in the state. No college or university would consider a lightweight at the line of scrimmage. However, the odds were in his favor to extend his career in baseball. He was good enough to be tabbed in the local newspapers as the next Phil Rizzuto of the Yankees, even though he played shortstop sparingly. The only difference was that Phil could not bat his "weight", whereas Alvaro could bat for average. Guido couldn't stand that label for he hated the Yankees. Frankly, Guido had other plans for his career with his brother who was the ultimate friend and mentor.

In high school, he would often invite his buddies from football to come to the pizzeria after a football game and have a party with cheerleaders and friends. Davide and Simone did not mind as long as there was no alcohol involved and the place was cleaned up afterward. In those days, rock and roll was the music of choice and played as loud as possible. Neighbors complained about the noise, but police cruisers just drove by the pizzeria and did nothing about it. They were rewarded with pizza. Besides, they were on the take from Simone. That was Guido's dream come true to partake in an American party in which he was the master of ceremony. When he was up on the mountains, all he talked about was America this and America that and the latest craze of the U.S. youth. Finally, he had arrived with the American new wave of music and youthful enthusiasm taking place in front of his eyes, he was on top of the world.

However, there was another craze among the youth which was not so healthy. It started on the East Coast and, in particular, in New York City. Gangs of young people would gather at Central Park and have an old fashion brawl. It didn't take long for this type of exuberance to get out of hand. These youth gangs were often referred to as "jitterbugging" gangs [4-3] whose purpose was to protect their turf and fight over girls. The introduction of drugs in later years brought an end to these gang fights. They were divided into ethnic groups: African-Americans, Italians, Puerto Ricans, Irish, etc. They were romanticized through mediums like the movie, "West Side Story". In all, about 6,000 members and 200 gangs roamed the streets of New York City. This craze soon spread like wildfire to the mid-west.

Fights were a common occurrence, and some teenagers were injured. In one instance, Guido was cornered by members of the Red Wings youth gang in high school in the boy's bathroom to urge him to join their gang operating in East Harlem. This gang consisted mostly of young Italian-American teenagers. One of them stuck a cigarette into Guido's elbow. In lightning speed, Alvaro grabbed the teenager by the balls in one hand and the other at his neck in a choke-hold, shouting, "Don't come near me or I will cut your balls off." That was the end of the harassment. Guido could not afford to put a spotlight on himself with the police by joining a gang, since he was operating a pizzeria with illicit business on the side. Davide and Simone would never have allowed him joining anything else. They had green fishes to catch, money.

Davide was not as sociable with strangers as Guido, but very sociable with friends from the past and family. He had too many things in his mind, managing a pizzeria in addition to trafficking, predominantly, in heroin. There were four people running the store: the niece of Simone's wife, Lena, Guido, Simone and himself. Lena was in charge of the cash register and waitressing. However, all sales were cash as to avoid paying sales taxes. Guido made pizza in a wooden fired oven, Davide was the host and Simone came into the store sporadically only to give Davide a list of people who came to pick up "special" orders of pizza. Special meant drug pickups. Simone took care of the business end of the illicit trades and Davide the pizzeria. As before, Genovese had his sticky fingers on the illicit business in New Jersey, since he was the kingpin of heroin trade. He was the one who initiated heroin trade soon after the War in Sicily in large scale and exported it to the USA. Before his appearance in Sicily, heroin trade was comparatively small. Thus, drugs were sold just as easily as pizza, as incoming drug supplies were intermixed with regular pizza supplies.

Lena and Davide behaved more like a married couple even before their formal marriage in New Jersey. They were raised in the same shepherd clan in the Cervinara-Paolisi area. The two attended the same public school to fifth grade. Beyond fifth grade, students attended the "Scuole Media" in either Benevento or Avellino about 15–20 miles away from Cervinara. Davide and Lena maintained their puppy love relationship in the USA and it was a foregone conclusion that they would get married soon after arriving in the USA. A private wedding ceremony was planned at City Hall. Lena was six months pregnant and she wanted to keep it private. The birth of a baby boy was important to Davide as it kept the family name alive. There was only one member of the family in the USA besides Guido and Davide who carried the same last name, and Simone had no children. Uncle Alfredo in Cervinara was the father of two boys and two girls.

Although Guido remembered the glory days of the Yankee's baseball team in the 1950s, his favorite team was the Boston Red Sox. Ted Williams was his idol and he often went to Yankee stadium to watch the rivalry between the two teams. He was lucky to escape alive from the stadium when cheering for the Sox. At Fenway Park, he was right at home watching and cheering for the Red Sox. It was only a three-hour train ride to Boston from New York City. For whatever reason, he liked Boston's historical settings and traditional values. However, he himself was a rebel-rouser who liked to stir things up. He excelled in baseball to the point that Rutgers University offered him a baseball scholarship. In those days, it was easier to enroll at a university, since SAT scores were not part of the application package for college admission. Certainly, his SAT score would have been a hindrance to being accepted. Nevertheless, he turned down the scholarship so that he could pursue his American dream of chasing the mighty dollar. Dealing in contraband was very profitable then. Money did not grow on trees, but the revenues from dealing heroin came close to that.

The two brothers were more interested in latching onto Simone, who was a "made man" in the Mafia, and begin careers of their own in the syndicate. Their plans for the American dream were right on schedule and everything looked rosy. Davide was becoming an "earner" and, in the eyes of the Mafia, that counted for a lot of respect. However, the boys did not plan for the turmoil created by the Mafia wars which were engulfing the New Jersey and New York City areas. A new order was taking place in the Mafia hierarchy with new faces replacing the older capos. Genovese, Gambino and Colombo replaced three of the "old" five capos in New York City in the 1940s. Now they were fighting for their lives to hang onto their power. There were too many killings throughout New Jersey. On a beautiful spring day, two undercover police detectives showed up at the pizzeria inquiring about the whereabouts of Simone. No sooner had they inquired, Simone walked into the pizzeria, was apprehended and driven away in a police car with a flashing blue light. Simone never returned to the pizzeria. He went missing for a long time. There was no record at the police station of him being charged for anything. Furthermore, his body was never found. Rumors circulated in town that Simone was looking for dog race tracks under sea. This incident proved only one thing: there was no loyalty among mafiosi. Genovese failed to protect Simone in a turf war where more than one syndicate was operating. Apparently, he felt that Simone, being in New Jersey, was expendable. Genovese's faction operated mostly in NYC.

In normal times, Davide would have been indoctrinated into one of the Mafia families in NYC or New Jersey. They decided it was time to move south as far away as possible from New Jersey to the Fort Lauderdale-Miami area and start all over again. However, this time they intended to develop their own contacts with the syndicate. For sure, staying in New Jersey would not have been healthy. Their future in the Mafia would have been problematic and possibly suicidal for them to carve out a living. Simply put, they would have been targets and, therefore, vulnerable to a takeover of their pizzeria. They were at the bottom of the totem pole in the eyes of the Mafia in New Jersey or NYC, since they were not indoctrinated by any faction. In addition, there was no way of telling when that madness of killings was going to end, because they were not in the circle of people in the "know". For once in their lives, they were on their own, plotting their own destiny. Yes, these were scary times, but they didn't lack confidence and had big dreams. Making pizza was, at least, one of many things that they planned to do in Miami.

They landed jobs at a small hamburger joint, owned by a long-distant cousin, in Hollywood, Florida, near the beach. Within one month, they bought out their cousin's place and made an offer that the cousin could not refuse. This was capo Trafficante's [4-4] territory in the Mafia organization operating out of Tampa Bay. No night club, Italian restaurant, café, bar, etc. could operate without the blessing of Trafficante. This meant that their cousin was not even on the radar screen of the Mafia in Florida, since his restaurant did not generate sufficient money to make it worthwhile for the Mafia to protect the business. But the Tampa faction heard about the success of the two brothers operating a pizzeria in New Jersey. Hence, permission was granted to Davide and Guido to buy the joint at their price and convert it into a pizza restaurant.

The brothers were an instant success with the beachgoers and their status was raised to associate members of the Mafia. An associate member has to prove to the Mafia that he is worthy enough to be a member. However, an associate member is not a "made" man of the Mafia, but performs service for the Mafia that benefits both parties. A "made" man is one who goes through a ritual similar to baptism where a small amount of blood is drained from a finger onto a burning figurine of a Saint in the presence of Mafia members, reciting words that exalt Mafia brotherhood, almost a cult ritual. In essence, a mafioso takes an oath that requires him to divorce from society and join a cult of mafiosi (supposedly an honored society among its members). An associate member is on a short leash to prove himself as in probation or purgatory. A mafioso may refer to another mafioso as "our friend" to others, but an associate member may not qualify as "our friend".

Guido finally realized his dream to be in America and soak up the sun on the beaches of Miami. He embraced everything that the Southern culture had to offer. Adoring the sun like a lizard, he was happy as a wild boar in mud. He loved women, worshipped the sun, made a bundle of money, and the future looked bright. He couldn't wait to become an American through and through, i.e., a citizen. Florida living enhanced his dream about America: beaches, parties, sun, nightclubs and easy living, especially when hordes of college students came to Florida for spring breaks. The first thing that he did, once in Florida, was to change his first name Guido to Sonny, which was a common adopted name of a lot mafiosi. The name Guido got in his way to become American through and through. His favorite entertainer was Sammy Davis, Jr., who visited Miami quite often. He loved the glitz exhibited by entertainers like Jackie Gleason in Miami. Obviously, he assimilated well with the new American lifestyle. By then, he was an equal partner to ownership of the pizzeria.

Besides being the co-manager of the pizza place, Davide was a taxi driver operating in the Miami-Fort Lauderdale area. No one knew his whereabouts. He often traveled to Texas and New Jersey. Sometimes he transported drugs; other times, he traveled with large amounts of money to designated casinos. He served as a courier between Miami and Las Vegas and often traveled to Havana, when the Mafia was operating a casino, where his contacts were with high level mafiosi. He was trusted by the hierarchy of the Mafia to reserve suites at the Miami Fontainebleau Hotel, when entertainers and capos came to town. It allowed him to rub shoulders with the capos and sottocapos of the organization. Certainly, the two brothers gained visibility in the Mafia organization and that is what they desired. In short, they were the movers and shakers, and earners in the parlance of the Mafia.

All this came to an end, when Castro took over Cuba in 1959–60. However, it was not until 1962, when he declared himself a Communist and chased the Mafia out of Havana. The movie "Godfather III" depicted the situation, more or less, at those times. Castro realized that he needed cash and, hence, confiscated luxury hotels and casinos from the Mafia to attract tourists from all over the world. As for the Mafia, they just moved on to greener pastures and built new casinos in Las Vegas and elsewhere.

FIVE

Highway 95 Corridor

The world was not prepared for the avalanche of cocaine throughout the world in early 1960s. In particular, cocaine powder and marijuana from South America was being smuggled by the tons into safe houses in the southern states of the USA. Money generated from it surpassed bootlegging in the 1920s. Once again, the Mafia was served with a bonanza of options to exploit: casinos, heroin and cocaine. It was a whole new ball game. The Mafia could not possibly exercise total control over cocaine smuggling, like heroin, since the main suppliers were the cartels in Medellin, Colombia. However, they were itching to get into cocaine smuggling on a large scale. They already had a network in place dealing with heroin smuggling. Cocaine was shipped to the USA by land and sea. The state of Florida was the main target of the cocaine export by sea which, in turn, was distributed to the east coast and beyond. The land route, via Mexico, found its way to the west coast, and mid-West. In a very short time, there was an epidemic of cocaine importations throughout the USA.

Davide's timing was exquisite in setting up a pizzeria in Miami, when cocaine appeared on the scene there. They owned the pizzeria and that alone was sufficient to support the family. Also, pizza was about to become America's favorite meal, competing with the hamburger fast food diners: MacDonald, Burger King, Hardy, Wendy, etc. By and large, Sonny and Davide were sitting pretty in Miami. Availability of cocaine was like icing on the cake. It was reminiscent of the times in Cervinara, when they were managing the cafe and selling American contraband cigarettes on the premises. Cocaine was at their doorstep. This was what Sonny had dreamed about. His American dream came true beyond expectations. Miami was sufficiently away from Trafficante in Tampa Bay so that they could operate autonomously. Also, it allowed the brothers some independence which they didn't have before.

The expression "cocaine cowboys" surfaced in the Miami newspapers to describe all the shooting among cocaine dealers who dealt directly with the Colombian cartels. Some flew private planes to Colombia to purchase cocaine directly from the cartels to distribute it in Florida. Cocaine powder was received as a finished product and did not have to be chemically processed as much as heroin. Thus, it was easy to store cocaine in Davide's pizzeria for the purpose of distributing it up north along the East Coast via Highway 95. Flour, pizza dough, and cocaine powder were perfectly color-matched, all in white.

Davide and Sonny soon established a network of people who received and dispersed cocaine. Cocaine dealing was all about a network of contacts, not necessarily with mafiosi. After all, cartel members and distributors were not mafiosi. It involved relatives, friends, indirect connections to the cartels, and mafiosi. Thus, some contacts were not expected to adhere to the omerta code. This is a code of silence about the existence of the Mafia and its members to be exercised among its members as well as with non-members. Violation of the code can result in mortal consequences. The brothers were walking a fine line between omerta and cohorts who had nothing to do with the Mafia. The purchase of cocaine was rather straightforward. It was a matter of contacting one of many "cocaine cowboys" in the Hollywood-Miami area. Negotiation with the "cowboys" was always handled by a trusted third party. Money for the purchase was made available by buyers in the Northeast, again through a third party.

Thus, money passed from the buyer to the two brothers via a third party and cocaine flowed in the reverse direction. In effect, the brothers were no different from pimps matching buyers with cocaine sources, whereby they provided temporary storage of money and cocaine in their pizzeria with the protection of the Mafia in Tampa Bay. However, that protection cost them money that they had to give to capo Trafficante in Tampa. At no time or place, were the brothers in direct contact with the buyers or cocaine sources, but it involved trusted third party partners, who may or may not have been mafiosi. Once in possession of cocaine powder, the brothers facilitated the flow up north by distributing through other pizzerias along interstate US Highway 95.

The book *"The Pizza Connection"* by Shana Alexander [5-1] gave a very good account of the distribution network along Highway 95 and elsewhere in the mid-west. Cocaine was loaded into cars and driven up and down the corridor, making stops at pizzerias. The drivers were not necessarily mafiosi. Usually, friends of the family volunteered to drive in order to make some extra money or take a vacation in Florida. Davide and Sonny soon earned the respect of the higher-ups in the Mafia as earners willing to share their wealth with their capo. If a drug deal went bust, the capo would enter the picture and there would be repercussions, but the brothers had no need to know what the consequences were. It was none of their business. They paid for that protection and that was the end of it.

In Sicily, this type of protection money was referred to as "pizzu". The literal translation of pizzu is roughly, "a little bite of something". The word was first introduced to the American lexicon in the movie, "The Godfather". In the movie, a mafioso extorted protection money from local businessmen for doing business in his neighborhood or turf. Originally, fruit, olive oil, and other food item exporters from Sicily paid the "Mano Nera" [5-2] (black hand or sometimes called Mafia) for the privilege of exporting goods, especially to the USA, since the Mafia was the conduit to America at the beginning of the 20th century. Most exports originated out of Palermo, and, hence, this practice was localized there. Eventually, it spread into the hinterland, where the produce were grown. Thus, the Mafia takes the first "cut" on profits or skims off the top without any risks. The underlings took all the risks perpetuating the system.

Although the brothers co-owned the pizzeria on Ocean Drive, Miami Beach, their homes were in Hollywood. This was a way of putting some distance from the drug scene. Life was good and the pizza business alone was thriving. Beachgoers seemed to love pizza and Sonny loved to mingle with the crowd at the beaches. At that time, nightclubs featuring disco music were popular among the young, who came to the Fort Lauderdale and Miami areas in droves for their spring breaks. There were parties every night and Sonny was in heaven. The brothers were on a cloud riding the wind, as they were not exposed to or threatened by drug dealers and drug addicts during their operation.

This time marked an interesting period. Music was influenced, for the first time, by the appearance of new drugs, LSD (Lysergic Acid Diethylamide), cocaine and heroin, as it was popular among the young. Rock and roll music of the 1950s began to give way to psychedelic and disco music. Usually, changes in musical compositions and styles are byproducts of class changes in society induced by great events like the Industrial Revolution, war, and the Depression in the USA. The hippie generation appeared on the horizon about that time influencing the music style. Sonny could not be any happier with the new sounds of music, especially disco music.

Out of the blue, Sonny's wings were clipped with the appearance, at the pizzeria, of a beautiful young woman looking for a job. Suddenly, all of that macho or guappo stuff usually emanating from Sonny went out the window. He was basically shy but he went gaga over this girl. Of course, Sonny employed her immediately without an interview and told her to come to work the next day, although there was no need for an extra employee. Both Lena and Davide were surprised and puzzled, to say the least. For one thing, the pizzeria was not just about making pizza! It was a family business as well as an illicit one. They reconciled among each other on how to handle the new employee, who became a cashier clerk. Not much happened between the two, only work-related conversations, until Davide stepped in. "Look Jesse, Sonny has hot pants for you, but he is too tongue-tied to tell you. Make sure to make it look like he is the initiator, if there is anything going on your part." Jesse was the name of the new employee, short for Joselmina. Yes, Davide was a man of few words; he didn't beat about the bush in declaring Sonny's interest in Jesse. The crudeness of his language was reflective of a shepherd, but the directness was reflective of his dealings with rough characters in the Mafia.

Davide was the head of the family. In an Italian family, the oldest child is usually looked upon as the head and protector of the family in the absence of parents. One thing about Davide was that he was a man of few words, and it was very difficult to dodge his words, just the opposite of Sonny. Davide was relegated to be the disciplinarian in the family which was needed to run the family and an additional burden to deal with the capos. To have two clowns running around partying would have been detrimental and, perhaps, suicidal for both. Of course, Davide enjoyed the good times as much as Sonny, but life chose another role for him.

The magic spark between Sonny and Jesse occurred by accident when they heard disco music coming from the beach area, overcrowded with college spring breakers. They looked at each other, as if asking themselves: what the f..k are we doing here at night? Within a millisecond, they closed shop and joined the party on the beach. Ever since, they discovered that they were of the same kindred spirit. They loved everything that the American youth was hooked on, including music. Sonny was no longer tongue-tied in the company of Jesse. He was in his element and enjoyed the moment to the fullest. Jesse introduced Sonny to the Miami community of "little Havana" consisting mostly of Cuban refugees. In little Havana, they often frequented a nightclub which featured only Cuban music. Their dancing to the Flamenco music was nothing short of an exquisite display of passion for each other.

Jesse's family escaped Cuba under duress, when Fidel Castro took over the Cuban government [5-3]. Her father, Ruiz, represented the wealthy and old establishment. Ruiz owned a tobacco farm and cigar factory before Castro's takeover. He exported Cuban cigars to a Tampa cigar outlet store controlled by Trafficante Jr., known in those days as the silent Don. Mr. Ruiz was a staunch supporter of President Batista, a corrupt President, who opposed Castro in the Cuban Revolution. The Mafia had been bribing Batista for years while operating a profitable casino in Havana since the late 1940s. As is well known, Fidel Castro overthrew President Fulgencio Batista's government in Dec. 1959. The world was enamored of the new revolutionary. Little did they know that Fidel was a true Communist of the Karl Marx mold. It was to Fidel's advantage not to tip his hand early to the world. Within two to three years, he consolidated his stranglehold on the government and declared himself a Communist. The world of Jesse's family went topsy-turvy in that span of time. They became destitute and poor when they eventually escaped to Miami. Mr. Ruiz worked as a clerk at a supermarket and the mother, Lourdes, as a waitress at a restaurant. Her two brothers moved to Detroit, Michigan, working in an auto factory. Jesse remained with the parents.

Initially, there was popular support for the revolution until Castro established a Communist State in the Caribbean for the first time. Lourdes and Jesse were die-hard supporters of Fidel during the Revolution, as he confiscated their farm and the tobacco factory and declared allegiance to the Soviet Union, a Communist Country. Farms, properties, luxury hotels, bank accounts, factories and casinos were confiscated by the Communist State. The campesinos, farm hands, who participated in the revolution on the side of Castro were short-changed in terms of land reforms, although health care services and schooling were free under the Communist regime.

Once Fidel Castro consolidated his power, he reneged on his promises to the campesinos. Whereas, before the Revolution, they worked for private landowners, after the Revolution, they worked for the state at much lower wages. In effect, the campesinos were short-changed twice in terms of land reforms and wages. There was no financial compensation for the properties taken over by the Communist regime. Ruiz's youngest son joined the Revolution initially, but the elder one detested the Che Guevara and Castro brothers crowd. It was not unusual for families to be split politically during the Revolution. Most people in Cuba were ambivalent about Castro until he declared allegiance to the Soviet Union and Communism. There was no middle ground after that. One either left Cuba by whatever means, or supported the regime and put up with the misery.

Soon after the Revolution, Ruiz's family was employed by the State as farm laborers. The family was allowed to work on their farm at measly wages, just enough to support themselves. For the first time in his life, Ruiz had to till his own land. They shared housing with campesinos, who once worked for Ruiz on the farm. The situation was becoming so intolerable that one by one the campesinos left the farms to escape to the USA, and Ruiz was stuck with more work. The campesinos built makeshift rafts that were vulnerable to sharks and storms, making the journey to the Florida coastlines very dangerous. Mr. Ruiz was too old to undertake such a trip on a raft.

The family bribed a local fisherman with whatever left over money they had from the past to take them to Florida, preferably to Miami, on a small boat. The planning of the trip was complicated, but rather ingenious. Cuban militias patrolled the beaches twenty-four hours a day. There was a window of opportunity between 1:00 and 3:00 am. Perhaps, the militia guards were asleep, when patrolling of the beaches stopped. The family waited until the low tide coincided with the timing of the escape. The boat was sufficiently small to be hidden just below a water protection wall. Four members of the family were lowered into the boat. The brothers stayed behind planning to make the trip on a raft later. The fisherman rowed the boat a short distance and then connected car batteries to a small make-shift engine fastened to the boat with metal wires. The advantage of a battery driven motor was that the engine made very little noise.

The engine consisted of two car batteries (24 volts), one motor, a metal rod attached to the motor internally, and blades from a fan welded to the rod. Engines for Tesla cars, today, are based more or less on a similar principle, except, today's batteries are more efficient. The trip itself was uneventful until they landed on the beaches of Key West, ninety miles away. Mr. Ruiz kissed land upon arrival. The fisherman decided to stay, leaving his family temporarily back in Cuba. He returned a month later to pick up his family, but this time with a more powerful engine, driven by gasoline firmly attached to the boat. Upon return, near the Cuban coastline, he used the make-shift battery-driven engine to quietly approach the coast. A lot of Cubans, who dared to escape Cuba on rafts, never made it to the Florida coastline. The US Congress passed a law that went a long way in helping Cuban stragglers come to the USA. The law is often referred to as the "wet-foot" policy. It meant that any Cuban refugee who was able to land on American soil or beaches were automatically granted asylum.

Cuban refugees who made it safely to Miami formed the largest community of South Americans. Their dream was to go back to Cuba and reclaim their properties, especially the elders. The younger generation assimilated readily to South Florida as well as to other parts of the country. They succeeded as business men, professionals, politicians and leaders of their communities. However, the elders still clung to their dream of one day resuming their former lives in Cuba. Every day, they gathered at the famous Versailles Restaurant, one of many Cuban restaurants in Miami and Florida, to commiserate about old times and talk about the day when they would free Cuba. Some of them were veterans of the "the Bay of Pigs" invasion on April 17, 1961 which turned out to be a fiasco [5-4]. The consensus among them was that President John F. Kennedy double-crossed them.

Cuban refugees, who were involved in the Bay of Pigs invasion, felt betrayed by the President. As it is well known, Kennedy promised air support during the invasion. Without air support, the invaders were sitting ducks. They were readily rounded up by Cuban soldiers on the beaches. To this day, remaining Cuban compatriots of that era have not forgotten or forgiven the Kennedys and never will. The CIA personnel who trained Cuban refugees for the invasion in South America were caught in a very bad predicament. The CIA interceded with the Kennedys to provide air support, to no avail. After all, it was Kennedys initiative to invade, although training of Cuban refugees by the CIA started during the Eisenhower administration.

The Bay of Pigs invasion was nothing more and nothing less than a ruse by the Kennedy brothers. They had no intention whatsoever of putting the Mafia back in operation at running casinos again in Havana. Hence, they just went through the motion of an invasion with no American firepower to back it up. No Americans took part in the invasion, although one American was captured on the beach. It is not clear to this day how that came about.

The Kennedys owed the Mafia big time for delivering the state of Illinois in the 1960 presidential election. For the first time in the history of American politics, dead people voted, thanks to the "miracles" of Sam Giancana [5-5], Mafia capo of the Chicago syndicate. Obviously, the Mafia wanted to get back to Havana by cashing in on the IOU owed by the Kennedy brothers and demanding them to "own" up to their debt. It was a Faustian deal between the two parties. The Mafia didn't "buy" the ruse [5-6]. Joe Kennedy, the President's father, knew better than to double cross the Mafia, as he had many dealings with mafiosi in Prohibition times. In a preemptive move, the Kennedy brothers requested Hoover, head of the FBI, to investigate Mafia syndicates, although Hoover was chasing would-be Communists in the USA, specifically in Hollywood, CA, at that time. As it is well known, President Kennedy was shot in Dallas on Nov. 22 1963. The Warren Report concluded that there was only a single perpetrator. The report has been debunked ever since it was published.

Prior to the death of President Kennedy, Carlos Marcello [5-7], boss of the New Orleans Mafia, convened meetings of all the people disgruntled by the Kennedys, except for CIA agents. However, the CIA was well represented by Cuban refugees who were involved in the Bay of Pigs invasion and hired thereafter by the CIA to do odd jobs here and there. For example, these were the same refugees caught in the Watergate affair years later. At one of the meetings, Davide drove Florida Mafia boss Santo Trafficante Jr. in a Lincoln Continental from Tampa to the Airport in New Orleans. From there, Santo took a taxi to the meeting and instructed Davide as follows: "Get rid of all receipts of road tolls and meals and don't mention to anyone that we were here. Drive the car straight back to my house." The mode of transportation from Tampa to New Orleans and return changed each time. No two trips used the same mode of transportation.

Davide had a suspicion, but he dared not say anything about it, even to his immediate family. Davide and Sonny were able to put two and two together, and arrived at the same conclusion: the attendees there were up to no damned good as regards to the Kennedys. Trafficante foresaw what was coming next and suggested to the brothers that they get as far away as possible, to the moon if possible. Quoting Trafficante: "It may not be so healthy to stay here in Miami. I cannot protect you in the long run." The meetings in New Orleans were not the usual Mafia meetings, because not all attendees were mafiosi. Quoting Hoffa [5-8] after Kennedy's assassination: "I told you that they could do it. I'll never forget what Carlos and Santo (Trafficante) did for me. This means Bobby is out as Attorney General." Quoting Marcello to a colleague: "You tell him (Hoffa) he owes me and he owes me big."

Hoffa disappeared from earth in 1975 and his body was never found. Sam Giancana was assassinated, also, in 1975, and John Roselli in 1976. Before being killed, Giancana was allowed to cook his favorite meal: fried red peppers and Italian sausages. Jimmy Hoffa was president of the International Brotherhood of Teamsters Union. It was alleged that he diverted membership union fees to the Mafia for many years. He was investigated for corruption by the Attorney General's office under Robert Kennedy. All the attendees of the meetings in New Orleans either disappeared or were assassinated except for Marcello and Trafficante! Both died of old age. It is amazing how many mafiosi wanting to put themselves on record as having participated in the conspiracy to kill Kennedy. Was it a form of braggadocio on their part? Nevertheless, much doubt has been raised on the Warren report since its publication.

Back in Miami, Lourdes never made peace with the new music of the young people like disco and Beatles' music, or the partying on the Florida beaches in the spring. To her, that was an example of Western decadence. She was a diehard Communist from the days of the Revolution who could not adapt to the changes taking place in Miami and the rest of the world. In Cuba, before the regime took her farm and factory, she held an important position and had many perks subsidized by the Castro government. In Miami, everybody in the family had to work at menial jobs to eke out a living while Ruiz was planning another counter-revolution at Versailles Restaurant with other former Cuban land owners. It was just talk about nothing. Even today, there is empty talk among the older Cuban refugees wanting to go back to Cuba and resume their lives of old times. The nice thing about wishes is that they don't cost money and make no commitments, if they don't come true.

The hatred for the Castro brothers was so deep that one could "cut it with a knife". A tourist at Versailles Restaurant once remarked to Ruiz: "If you want to kill Fidel so badly, why not hire someone to shoot the SOB?" Ruiz replied, "We Cubans are not like the Mafia." Yet, it was OK for someone else to do the shooting so that they could resume their past lives. If it were up to Ruiz, he would not mind invading Cuba every year until the Castro brothers were overthrown. Lourdes would tease Ruiz about when that day will come, and, then murmur to herself: "Never as long as the Castros are in power!"

Miami represented everything that Jesse ever expected from a Western country: Beatles music, disco, parties, nightclubs, young people all around on the beaches, and Sonny. It didn't take long for Jesse to be "cured" of Castro's propaganda. Sonny opened the door for Jesse to all things that she had heard and had seen from a distance in Cuba. She wanted to see and taste it all, physically and mentally! Sonny was happy to oblige. He loved Jesse for her wild spirit and sense of adventure in anything American. Both were starving for anything which had the American "label" on it. They often went to nightclubs together dancing to the new beat in music. They went to "Studio 54" nightclub in New York City. Wherever they went, Sonny drew attention from wannabes, non-earners in Mafia terminology. Sonny was a "made-man", mafioso, and, more importantly, an earner. However, Jesse had no clue as to why Sonny was so popular.

Ironically, Sonny and Jesse were anti-establishment, or anarchists at heart, but yet, they enjoyed all the things that the bourgeoisie class or the capitalist society had to offer. They had more in common than that. Sonny and Jesse married in Miami. The wedding was an elaborate one with more than 300 guests attending and who's who in the underworld in Florida were invited. By now, Sonny was a respected mafioso and was expected to behave as such. Jesse was six months pregnant and it showed. The Mafia hierarchy would have cut his balls off, if Sonny backed out of the wedding. The Catholic church usually does not condone such a late marriage, but, by greasing the palms and with a modified wedding dress to cover up the belly, the wedding went on schedule. For the honeymoon, they went to Boston.

Sonny had visited there often as one of his destinations on his drug journeys north along the highway 95 corridor. He had a lot of friends in Boston who also emigrated from Avellino area of Italy. It was his desire to someday settle in Boston. By then, he was comfortable assimilating anyplace in the USA for he felt like pure-bred American. He had a pretty good idea what the country was all about and he loved every bit of it.

In addition, Sonny saw an opportunity to finally settle down in one place. He was tired of running around looking over his shoulder for people like Marcello in Louisiana, Trafficante in Miami and Genovese in New Jersey. Yes, they were Mafia compatriots, but these individuals, as in the case of Simone, had no qualms about rubbing anyone out without hesitation, if it fit their purpose. That was one of the reasons the brothers left New Jersey and, eventually, to Florida. The other reason was that he felt at home in Boston, because of a large community from the Avellino area. For a change, he could pick and choose a place to his liking and manage his own pizzeria. This meant that their cocaine network, organized in Miami, would still be in place to assist its distribution in Boston. Thus, the move to Boston fulfilled his ultimate American dream. Most likely, Jesse had a lot to do with sharing the same dream, perhaps for different reasons. Most importantly, Sonny wanted to separate from his brother and chart his own course. Besides, his reputation as an earner would go a long way toward attaching him to a new Mafia faction in Boston. For a change, Davide followed in Sonny's footsteps, but managing a separate pizzeria. Thus, Sonny took the lead for the first time in the decision-making for the whole family.

After the birth of his first child, Sal (Salvini), Sonny traveled to the North End section of Boston with Davide while Jesse stayed behind in Hollywood, FL, with Sal. The brothers' plan was that once the local boss gave his approval for their permanent move into his territory, Jesse and her child and Lena with her two children, could join them. Sonny could not very well explain the real situation to Jesse. Sonny explained the trip to Jesse as an excursion to appraise real estate. Of course, that was a bullshit story, as he was well aware of house prices in the North End. He had been there often enough to know the price of everything in sight. He rented a beautiful apartment near Copp's Hill Burying Ground and Davide rented in Medford, MA.

It didn't take long for the brothers to attract the attention of the Mafia in the North End, as word spread like wildfire that "our friends are in town". However, the brothers could not engage in any other illegitimate business without the approval of the sotto-capo (underboss), Turiddu [5-9].

It was no secret to Sonny, who was a "made" man among fellow Avellinesi or Cervinara. Such information travels at the speed of light among mafiosi, especially among friends from the same area. It didn't take long for the brothers to be introduced to Turiddu "as our friends", "amici nostri". The Mafia in the North End was a loose organization of autonomous members, spread from Boston to New Hampshire. Their illicit businesses included number rackets, sports gambling, horse race fixing, shylocking, heroin smuggling, slot machines, and prostitution. Most money was generated from protection money from bookies and local businessmen. Turiddu was involved in shylocking, lending money to bookies. This was an ideal situation for Davide and Sonny for they had complete monopoly over the distribution of cocaine from Miami to New England.

At the meeting, between the brothers and Turiddu, they explained how they ran their cocaine drug trafficking along Hwy 95 and how omerta can be compromised, since some of the contacts might not be mafiosi. However, they reassured the underboss that their network of contacts had been in operation for a long time without incidental disclosures to police investigators. The two brothers steered the conversation toward operating cocaine drug distribution centered around pizzerias. They wanted some autonomy in their operation, much like what they had in Miami, but still affiliated with the Turiddu's faction. Of course, the pizzu payments would be made to Turiddu to provide protection against scrupulous dealers. That was music to Turiddu's ears. He could finally get into the new profitable deals of cocaine smuggling and collect protection money.

The brothers offered powerful contacts with the Florida network who had direct personal connections to the cartels in Colombia and, of course, capo Trafficante. It was a no brainer for Turiddu. There was no reason to doubt that the brothers could continue to be earners. The brothers' reputation preceded their arrival in the North End, since they were part of the network trafficking cocaine between Miami and Boston. There was no hesitation on the part of Turiddu, since there was no other competition for the cocaine smuggling, not on the scale being proposed. The brothers got what they wanted from the meeting; autonomy over their cocaine operation in suburbia plus pizzerias of their own. Eventually, Sonny set up a pizza restaurant on Lancaster Street, North End, where Sonny was the owner of the establishment. Davide opened up another one in Medford. The pizza making business alone was enough to financially support their respective families and pay for pizzu to Turiddu.

Turiddu already had a headache in his hands with two groups fighting over control of the heroin distribution in the North End as well as in the rest of Boston. One group consisted mostly of the new arrivals, zips, and the other the Irish gangs led by James "Whitey" Bulger [5-10]. The word "zips" referred to Sicilian mafiosi who spoke only in a dialect that no one else understood. Cocaine distribution would not interfere with the heroin mess, since different networks of smugglers were involved. The old nemesis, Whitey, was muscling into the North End, South Boston, Dorchester, Roxbury, etc. in the name of Martorano, who worked with the Irish gangs. At this point in time, there was much work to be done by the two brothers: family affairs, re-acquaintances and re-establishing contacts with the network of the cocaine trade in Florida.

With the arrival of the rest of the family to the North End, Sonny was busy opening up a pizzeria on Main Street. Jesse no longer worked in the pizzeria as she had her hands full with the newborn son and decided to buy the apartment that Sonny rented on Copps Hill. He was becoming a damn good pizza maker. His creative spirit came alive. His specialty was Neapollitan pizza Margherita using fresh ingredients of Buffala mozzarella and fresh tomatoes, no tomato sauce, on a very thin crust. The other specialty was his recipe for white sauce clam pizza. The recipe called for grated Parmegiano-Reggiano cheese, roasted garlic, virgin olive oil and fresh clams on the pizza. The transactions at the pizzeria were strictly cash so state and local taxes were not declared. This practice is associated with the Mafia since the 1850s, but it dates further back. In Roman days (circa 80 BC), Sicilian farmers sold their grain to the Romans without paying taxes to the Quaestor (tax collector). However, tax payments came in the form of commissions paid to the Quaestor (bribes), but, again, they were rarely paid. It was a habit inherited from the past.

Jesse's mother, Lourdes, came to Boston in order to baby sit Sal and help out around the house. She stayed until the family settled in their new house and Sal was old enough to take his first step. Thereafter, Lourdes was very happy to return to her own family in Miami. The main reason that she went back was that she hated the cold and clammy weather of New England. Being raised in Cuba and acclimated to Miami weather, she just could not cope with that Boston weather. Besides, mother and daughter had a fundamental difference of opinions about American culture as pertaining to the new generation of youth.

It didn't take long for Davide and Sonny to reach the so-called "earners" label by others and Turiddu. Both brothers had established in Hollywood-Miami a well-oiled network to run cocaine up and down the east coast along the 95 corridor long before they moved into the Boston area. This new operation was a piece of cake, since all of the contacts and network were intact, as before, in Miami. Being in Boston, they were in close proximity with buyers of cocaine. Together, they generated a lot of money, legal and illegal, for which they paid pizzu to Turiddu. The brothers did not complain, since life was good.

Jesse misinterpreted the attention that Sonny was getting from mafiosi and wannabes as being popular with people and friends, although he had an engaging personality. She never made the connection. Sonny was not about to educate her about the Mafia and never explained what he did for a living, other than making pizza. However, he was willing to pay a tutor to educate both Jesse and himself in American history so that both could pass the exam for American citizenship. Citizenship in the USA requires having basic knowledge of American history and to be able to converse in English. By this time, Sonny was as American as apple pie and ice cream.

The movie "The Godfather" was just coming out, Nixon declared war on drugs, major Mafia capos were dragged to Capitol Hill for investigation by Congress, etc. However, Davide and Sonny were sitting pretty. Their cocaine contacts in Florida and New England flourished to the point that the operation was running smoothly. Turiddu left the brothers alone to carry out their business. Jesse conceived a baby girl named Carmela. For the first time there was an influx of Vietnamese immigrants in the Boston area after the Viet Cong offensive in Saigon. A snapshot of the early 1970s showed that these were the best of times for the Mafia in the North End. Unbeknownst to Turiddu, the worst of times were lurking around the corner.

Irish gangs were at each-others' throats killing each other at an alarming rate over the heroin trade and it was spilling over into the North End. A volcano was about to erupt in the Irish gangs with the emergence of Whitey Bulger. Eventually, it would have repercussions for the Mafia and Irish gangs throughout Boston. Once again, Davide and Sonny were about to be in danger without realizing it and their lives threatened, much as in New Jersey and Miami, with the emergence of Whitey. The price mobsters pay for being in organized crime is they are forever looking over their shoulders and they live in fear of not knowing when to look over their shoulders.

SIX

Only in Boston

Equally motivated as the Alvaro brothers were the Bulger brothers [6-1], James (Whitey) and William (Billy). Whitey became a force to be reckoned with in the Irish gangs during the 1970s, and Billy in Boston politics. How strange that these two sets of brothers (Irish and Italian) should have crossed paths years later in Boston, although they were a world apart at birth and brought up in very different cultures. The impetus for Whitey's rise in organized crime germinated in prohibition times, long before he was born. During prohibition times the Mafia and Irish gangs blossomed from rag-tag crime groups to syndicates in organized crime.

In the 1920s, immigrants were full of hopes, aspirations and dreams when they arrived in America. So were the criminals. Prohibition of alcohol presented the perfect opportunity for crime. The 18th Amendment was ratified by Congress on January 17, 1920, leading the way for alcohol to be sold illegally at a profit. The law prohibited the production, transport and sale of alcohol, but it was legal to consume it. This should be compared with present day laws in some States where medical marijuana is produced, transported within the State and consumed and sold over the counter legally. However, it is illegal to transport medical marijuana across state lines. States and local communities derive taxes from the sale of legalized marijuana, but profits from the sale of alcohol during Prohibition went directly to crime gangs and no taxes. An ideal illicit business for all the mobsters.

That moment in time was the turning point in the make-up of the American Mafia. They were no longer a bunch of misfit immigrants hustling here and there in small groups. They soon realized that it was more profitable, if they organized in numbers. Syndicates were formed after the elimination of the old establishment of the Mafia in the 1920s, Joseph Masseria and Salvatore Maranzano. The young "turks" as represented by Meyer Lansky, Lucky Luciano, Benjamin (Bugsy) Siegel, Joseph Bonanno, Vito Genovese, Joseph Profaci and Arnold Rothstein were much quicker in realizing the opportunities presented by the Prohibition Laws. The older capos were just too slow in seizing the moment. Hence, the young "turks" had no choice but to eliminate the internal strife. Meyer Lansky, [4-2], modeled syndicates within the Mafia in the image of an American corporation. Rules were introduced to regulate relationships among syndicates. More than 300 members were associated with a syndicate in New York City, for example. The main purpose of a crime syndicate was to sell alcohol to quench the thirsty needs of America while eliminating competition by the gun, rule or no rule.

This is not to say that the Mafia was not organized earlier. It was organized long before the 1920s in Sicily as a loose band of farm managers who exploited landlords in controlling the export of farm products all over the world. Landlords lived in luxury all over the world leaving farm managers to run the large farms. The managers exercised complete control in the hiring of farm hands and exporting goods. As such, they amassed tremendous wealth, power and political influence over the governance of a town. In effect, they became the "real" padrone, boss, of the farm and the town. Most often, the landlords were at the mercy of their managers for meager financial handouts. However, whatever local organization set up by the padrone was never at the level of a large syndicate of the ones in the 1920s. Profits from bootlegging allowed mobsters to organize, hire lawyers and accountants, brew-masters, truck drivers, thugs, and to bribe police, judges, mayors, etc. It was not a question of whom they bribed, but who was not bribed. There was more than enough money to reverberate throughout city halls of big cities. The capo mafioso of organized crime in New York City during the prohibition times was Charles "Lucky" Luciano, [1-11]. He was lucky, because he was abandoned as dead by competing mobsters, but somehow survived. At age 23, he worked for gambling boss Arnold Rothstein, also involved in bootlegging. By the mid-1920s, Luciano was a multimillionaire and New York's top bootlegger.

Bootlegging was prevalent throughout the USA. There was an alleged connection between bootleggers in NYC and Boston. Patrick Kennedy, father of Joseph P. Kennedy [6-2], imported whiskey to Boston before prohibition and owned saloons there. At the end of prohibition, Joe Kennedy owned Somerset Limited (whiskey brand) and imported high quality whiskey. In 1972, Francesco Castiglia, also known as Frank Costello, claimed on his deathbed that he helped make Joe a rich man during Prohibition. Costello was a notorious Mafia boss in New York City in the 1960s. It has long been alleged that Joe Kennedy, father of US President John Fitzgerald Kennedy, made his money bootlegging during Prohibition.

Decades after Prohibition, known Mafia mobsters, Meyer Lansky and Frank Costello, claimed that they both worked with Joe Kennedy to bring in liquor from the high seas to the east coast, referred to as Rum Row. Bootlegger Owney Madden shipped liquor during Prohibition to night clubs owned by Joe Kennedy. Author of *"Paddy-Whacked" (Untold Story of the Irish Gangster)* [6-3] claimed that Joe Kennedy financed shipments to Rum Row on the high seas from Europe, but did not smuggle these shipments to the east coast. This was a way to circumvent the Prohibition Law, since Joe Kennedy was not involved with transporting liquor to the USA. Coast Guard records of boats during Prohibition, which were seized with liquor aboard, showed one delivery to Nantucket Sound. Aboard the boat, there was a nautical chart showing liquor drop-offs to Hyannis port where the Joe Kennedy family had a new summer home in 1926.

Medicinal liquor could be acquired with a doctor's prescription during Prohibition. This was a common way to obtain liquor, as the permits were readily available or faked. According to Joe Kennedy himself, he obtained permission to bring in large amounts of medicinal liquor. Records of the permit applications were destroyed in the early 1950s at the National Archives. The abolition of Prohibition of alcohol was ratified by Congress on December 5, 1933. Just prior to this date, Joe Kennedy used ships belonging to existing smugglers, like Costello, to carry medicinal liquor across the Atlantic Ocean to New York City. Such a trip would have been entirely legal. After Dec. 5, medicinal liquor could be sold freely at a very good price. All of the above evidences were circumstantial in proving that Joe Kennedy was a bootlegger, but he operated just outside the reach of the law.

In Boston, Mafia bootleggers operated out of the North End on a relatively small scale compared with the competing Irish and Jewish mobs led by Frank Wallace and Charles «King» Solomon, respectively. People of other ethnicities were also involved. However, the Gustin gang [6-4] was one of the earliest Irish-American gangs to emerge as bootleggers during Prohibition. The name Gustin gang came from a street in South Boston which was off Old Colony Avenue. The leaders of the gang were Frank Wallace and his brothers Steve and Jim. Their specialties, in the mid-1910s, were looting, hijacking trucks and armed robberies. In terms of high-power bootleggers, the Gustin brothers were small timers until they owned a few boats. They smuggled liquor in international waters to deliver it to various sites on the South Shore including to customers and nightclubs owned by their brother Billy. They could not get out of the habit of stealing. For example, they used fake badges of Prohibition agents to rob rival bootleggers.

A truce was declared between the Gustin gang and the Mafia and a meeting was arranged to discuss a "modus operandi". The meeting was called by Joe Lombardo, underboss of the Mafia in the North End, to patch up the differences between the two gangs, since the Gustin gang was running wild, stealing from everybody. On December 22, 1931 at the meeting in 317 Hanover St., North End, all were disarmed except for the mafiosi. Frank Wallace and Bernard Walsh, representing the Gustin gang, were killed. The ambush was led by Lombardo. Thereafter, infighting between the various factions of the Irish gangs only made the Mafia the dominant criminal organization in Boston. Many years later, when Whitey Bulger appeared on the mob scene, the killing of Frank Wallace served as motivation to even the score with the Mafia some day, and he did.

James (Whitey) Bulger [6-5] was born in 1929 and grew up in public-housing projects of South Boston. James was nicknamed Whitey because of his light complexion. He was the oldest of three brothers: James, Jack and William. Billy and Whitey were as different as night and day. Whereas James was of light complexion, Billy was dark. Whereas Billy was the studious type who eventually earned a law degree, Whitey dropped out of high school. Billy loved to read the classics. Whatever little reading Whitey did was about Sun Tzu, Hitler (Mein Kampf), and WW II. Billy [6-6] saw himself as another Cicero in modern times scheming, like Cicero, about how to get ahead politically. Like Billy, Whitey was equally ambitious, but heading into a life of crime. Billy thought of himself as bigger than life. Perhaps he tried to make up for his small stature, a Napoleonic complex.

Whitey had an uncanny ability to get into trouble, which included male prostitution, bank robberies and murders. With that type of resume, it didn't take long for him to join an organized Irish gang in South Boston. In 1943, 14-year-old Whitey was arrested and charged with larceny. By then, he had joined a street gang known as the «Shamrocks» and would eventually be arrested for assault, forgery and armed robbery. The gang specialized in hijacking commercial trucks and selling off stolen merchandises, and small-time drug dealing in South Boston. He was sentenced to a juvenile reformatory for these crimes. Shortly after his release in April, 1948, he joined the U.S. Air Force. He spent time in the military prison for several assaults and was later arrested by Air Force police in 1950 for going absent without leave. Nevertheless, he received an honorable discharge in 1952 and returned to Boston. The discharge was secured via a political «twisting of arms» of Air Force officials. In 1956, Whitey served his first term in federal prison, when sentenced, and jailed in the Atlanta Penitentiary for armed robbery and truck hijacking. He was eventually transferred to Alcatraz jail, CA. In November 1962, Whitey was transferred to Leavenworth Federal Penitentiary and in 1963 to Lewisburg Federal Penitentiary, PA. Whitey's third petition for parole, in 1965, was granted after he served nine years in prison. He would not be arrested again for 46 years. After his release from Lewisburg, Whitey worked as a janitor and construction worker before becoming a bookie (numbers racket) and loan shark under mobster Donald Killeen, whose gang, the Killeens, dominated South Boston for over twenty years.

In the mid-1960s there were five Irish gangs [6-7] and one Mafia crime syndicate. The five Irish gangs were concentrated in the following areas: Charlestown, Somerville, South Boston, Roxbury, and South End. The demarcation between turfs (territories), where crime gangs operated, was not as sharp as turfs controlled by Mafia syndicates in New York City or in Chicago. The lack of demarcation of turfs among gangs led to wars among Irish gangs. Areas like Dorchester, Mattapan, Revere, Medford, and in general areas in the Boston suburbs were fair game to all. As such, gangs tended to overlap in carrying out their illicit businesses: hijacking of trucks, fencing of stolen goods, numbers racket, drug dealing, bank robberies, horse race fixing, etc. Also, the fact that they were more or less in the same type of rackets was a source of irritation and friction among them. Members of the Irish gangs included Irish-Americans, Italian-Americans, Polish-Americans,

African-Americans, Jewish, etc. There was no oath to take, as with the Mafia, in becoming a member. This explained why a lot of Italian-Americans joined Irish gangs. Most of them were not "earners" as in the Mafia's view, which was to be able to generate illicit money steadily, to pay for protection to the Mafia capos (bosses).

The McLaughlin brothers controlled the Charlestown area. The leader of the gang was Bernie McLaughlin. There were more bank robberies in Charlestown than any other town or city in the world. The McLean brothers ran the Somerville gang. Later, Howie Winter took over that leadership role. It became known as the Winter Hill gang. In South Boston, the situation was somewhat murky, since both gangs, the Killeens and the Mullens, operated on the same turf. These two gangs were in constant turmoil between themselves. There was a bitter battle (more like a war) between them over heroin smuggling in South Boston. Whitey and one of the Killeen brothers fled South Boston, fearing they would be the next ones to be killed by the Mullens. In fact, they were the last two of the Killeen gang. Bulger, realizing that he was on the losing side, secretly approached Howie Winter and proposed that he could end the war by murdering the leader of the Killeens. On May 13, 1972, Donald Killeen was gunned down outside his home in the suburb of Framingham. Whitey then raised the white flag demanding a meeting with the Mullens.

The meeting, at Chandler's nightclub in the South End, was chaired by Howie. The Mullens were represented by Nee and King, and the Killeens by Whitey. He was the only one alive of the Killeens gang! At the meeting, an alliance was formed between him and Howie. In effect, Whitey was declared boss of the Mullens gang, although they were winners in the war against the Killeens. That was unusual, to say the least. Everything was split down the middle between Whitey and Howie's gang. All the horse and dog races, bookmaking, and loan sharking were now going to be under mutual control. The Mullens were allowed to run the heroin distribution in South Boston but paid protection money to Whitey and Howie. Wow, what a turnaround!

Besides the Mullens, every independent bookie, gambler, drug dealer, hijacking expert, etc. throughout Boston had to pay protection money to Whitey and Howie. The Mafia was to collect protection money from independents only within their territory—the North End. The decision was absurd. In particular, the losing gang consisting of only one person should dictate the terms of victory and rules to abide by, so that he benefitted at the expense of the winners, the Mullens. Unbelievable, but true! That did not sit well with the Mullens, but, for whatever reason, they had no choice.

How was it possible? One plausible explanation for the unusual outcome was that Whitey had the support of very powerful individuals, when he entered that meeting. This implied that he had the support, [6-5], of politicians, FBI, policemen and judges—the establishment. The link between the establishment and Whitey was none other than Billy, his brother, who ruled the State Senate with an iron fist, since he became President of the State Senate about that time. The establishment, the Irish gangs and the Bulger brothers, shared one common cause, the elimination of the Mafia in Boston and to avenge the Gustin gang.

Finally, it seemed like everybody was in charge of the West Roxbury, Roslindale, Mission Hill, Mattapan, Hyde Park and Dorchester areas. However, one person who exercised a lot of influence there was John Martorano, [6-7]. He often collaborated with African-Americans and Irish-Americans in drug dealing, prostitution and gambling. Martorano whose name translates roughly to grave digger. He inherited the business from his father who owned properties in the "red light district", prostitution houses, near downtown movie houses, theaters and Chinatown. The gangs in those districts were a bunch of disjointed groups who seemed to enjoy fighting each other more than collaborating.

The level of drug trafficking was rather low in Boston in the sixties when compared to the amount of cocaine smuggled into the U.S. by the cartels of Colombia. The South End, Dorchester, and the downtown red-light district were no-man's-land. That is to say, anyone could operate in those areas without paying protection money to anyone. The Mafia was also fragmented, as were the Irish gangs, with factions operating in East Boston, Revere and small pockets here and there in suburbia. Since factions located in the suburbs operated away from headquarter in the North End, they enjoyed some autonomy in terms of running their own illicit businesses: numbers racket, drugs, prostitution, shylocking, etc.

The Mafia's main faction in Boston resided in the North End [6-8]. It was often referred to by other mobsters as "In Town", in contrast to "The Office" in Providence. The Mafia in the North End extorted protection money from all the local businesses. Turiddu ran the Mafia like a banker.

He was the main shylock operating big-time in Boston and his main customers were bookies and gamblers. As in any gambling enterprise, profits were cyclic. When profits were down, bookies borrowed from Turiddu. He charged 1% interest per week. Also, he was in charge of a small operation trafficking in heroin. Any contracts for murdering were parceled out to the Irish gangs (Whitey Bulger, Martorano, Flemmi, etc.) who were very thankful for the contracts. This was a way for the Mafia to avoid attention from the establishment in Boston.

Stephen Flemmi, [6-7] lived next door to the Bulger family. Quite often the two families got together for Sunday meals. For years, he was an associate member of the Mafia, but he felt more comfortable working with Whitey. In time, he became one of many "hitmen" for Whitey. A "hitman" is one who kills for hire. The Mafia and Flemmi were incompatible. He didn't care for all that hogwash about blood rituals and omerta as was required to be a mafioso. Another Italian-American mobster, who joined Whitey's gang, was John Martorano, a second generation Italian-American. Again, he didn't care much about omerta, either, and did not want to be part of the so-called honored society. He became the most feared hitman in the Boston area. The charming thing about him was that he had that grandfatherly look that seemed like he would not harm a fly, yet, was responsible for more than 22 gangland murders, depending who is counting.

The two Bulger brothers cared for each other, as any other brothers. Whitey would often help Billy get elected, locally and State-wide. He performed miracles by having dead people vote for the first time in South Boston. In turn, Billy advised Whitey, at family get-togethers, about the lay of the land in politics. Both were not short on ambitions. At the very least, they were cognizant of their respective aspirations. The family would often have large Sunday dinners where the family, friends, cousins and uncles/aunts were invited. Sometimes neighbors were invited also: Stephen Flemmi, John J. Connolly, etc. Connolly's name was quickly shortened to Zip Connolly by Whitey. Zip was a classmate of one of the Bulger brothers in elementary school and he became an FBI agent in Boston, with a special recommendation by Billy.

Flemmi became Whitey's right-hand man in Whitey's rise in the Irish mob in South Boston. After dinner, Billy and Whitey often took long walks in the park. Billy has claimed for a long time, in the media, that he was not aware in all those years of Whitey's crime enterprise. However, the

Boston Globe reported otherwise. Clearly, something was amiss. There was no doubt that Billy urged Whitey to contact Zip at the FBI. After all, Zip owed Billy big time, since Billy helped Zip get the FBI job. Perhaps, Billy's motive could have been for Zip to steer Whitey away from crime.

Zip Connolly, [6-7,5], turned to Billy for three special favors during his career. When he graduated from high school, he asked State representative Billy for a letter of recommendation to the admission office at Boston College; secondly, after graduating from Boston College, he again asked State Senator Billy for a recommendation for a job opening at the FBI office in Boston. For this favor, Billy had to cash in one of his IOUs from Speaker of the House of Representatives John W. McCormack, [6-7,5], who, in turn, referred the application to J. Edgar Hoover, FBI director. Billy helped McCormack get re-elected by campaigning for him. The final favor granted to Zip was for Billy to help employ retiring FBI agents to State jobs. Yes, Zip owed Billy big time.

Like Billy, McCormack started out as a lawyer, doing favors for local thugs, defending them in court pro-bono. Thereafter, he entered politics by running as a State representative from a district that included South Boston. Basically, he was collecting all of the IOUs from people he represented pro-bono and easily got elected. With the help of the locals like Billy and Whitey at election times, he was able to make it to the position of President of the Senate in Massachusetts. McCormack's career extended for forty-six more years in US Congress as a Representative and Speaker of the House, third in line to become President of the USA. His special rapport with FBI director Edgar J. Hoover was instrumental in extending investigative and arrest powers across state lines and supporting liberal funding of the FBI. In some sense there was "I rub your back and you rub mine" mentality from Billy all the way up to Hoover, with McCormack being the conduit between them. For example, the US Air Force was about to dismiss Whitey with a dishonorable discharge for raping a woman, until word from Congressional investigations overruled the Air Force's decision. That was the beginning of things to come in the future from this special political connection.

Zip returned the favors or paid on the IOUs, when Billy was bucking to be Senate President. In the mid-1970s, Billy ranked number three in the Senate leadership. The FBI office in Boston opened investigations of bribery of senators who were positioned number one and two ahead of

Billy. Eventually, those two senators resigned, and Billy finally got his wish. In 1978 Billy became President of the State Senate. He took a page out of the President Nixon modus operandi. He made a list of his enemies and for the next 10–15 years made life miserable for them. In Cicero's time the enemy list was called the "proscription list". Nothing has changed in 2,000 years, except now the people on the list are not killed, but their careers were derailed or eliminated. Unbelievable but true, Billy asked Zip for only one small favor and that was to "take care of James" (a legalese jargon). This special relationship between the Boston office of the FBI and Whitey went beyond comprehension in modern times—that someone had a license to kill anyone in the streets of Boston and get away with it. It was unfathomable, but true. Not since Caligula, in ancient Rome, had an individual yielded so much power.

As President of the Senate, Billy yielded tremendous power in awarding state contracts and jobs. In effect, Billy had Zip Connolly by the balls. Billy had political IOUs as well as police (FBI) protection. This was a recipe for absolute power and absolute power corrupted absolutely, and at appropriate times, the Bulger brothers exercised that power. Billy walked around Boston as a little emperor without a toga. The emperor felt so powerful that he would dare to insult candidates (Dukakis) for the office of the President of the US on TV during his hosting of the Saint Patrick Festivities. That was unadulterated raw political power.

Billy created a novel scheme to secure protection from the establishment. IOUs were more potent than bribes, when it came to loyalty. IOUs bind both parties, as they are both equally vulnerable to the law. As for bribing, one can take or leave the money. This method of influencing people was developed to an art form in Cicero's time in ancient Rome. In those times, special connections, as in IOUs, were needed to escape the wrath of emperors or triumphant generals. These special connections established by Billy not only protected his career, but also Whitey's transgressions with the law and there were far too many of those to count.

In contrast to Whitey, the Mafia in the North End was in a very precarious situation in Boston. They did not have the needed connection or protection from the establishment, as Mafia syndicates did in every other city where they operated, such as: Detroit, New York city, Chicago, LA, etc. In those cities, bribing bought a lot of influence. The establishment in Boston was

Irish-American and "guineas" (an expression often used by Irish mobsters referring to mafiosi) were not welcome. Boston has always been known as an "Irish" town. So, the Mafia in Boston had to walk a fine line between legitimate and illicit business in order not to draw too much attention by the police, justice system and politicians. The Mafia could not afford to have these lingering wars between Irish gangs which eventually spilled over to them. On one hand, they liked the idea that the Irish-American gangs were fighting each other but, on the other hand, it eventually affected their business. There was a lot of interdependency among mobs. From time to time, "The Office" would call the warriors to Providence to investigate the cause of all those killings. Some killings had nothing to do with the conduct of illegal business, [6-7]. It had to do with a lover's spat, someone using foul language to his boss, or personal matters.

Politics in Boston has been the domain of Irish-Americans since the American Revolutionary war. Italian immigrants emigrated to Boston about 150 years later. The city has been mostly governed, from the police to the Mayor's office, by Irish-Americans. This is not to say that Irish-American governance was breeding corruption, but governance was seen through a green colored prism. Nowadays, roughly one-third of the population in Boston is Irish-American, one fifth Italian-American and the rest Latino, African-American and Jewish. Politically, today, it is wise for a candidate to take vacations in Ireland or Italy, or both, to garner both ethnic votes. Mayor Mandolino vacationed only in Ireland each year. He assumed that he had the Italian votes in his pocket. He was proven correct as he was Mayor for many years. The remaining votes were pretty stable and predictable. There has not been a Republican Mayor in Boston for more than one hundred years.

As Mafia syndicates in other cities have learned, they cannot survive unless they can bribe politicians, judges, and policemen (the establishment). Boston, at best, proved to be a difficult nut to crack for the local Mafia to bribe the Irish-American establishment. As such, the model for a big city crime syndicate, like New York or Chicago, did not apply to Boston. A capo was in charge of the New England states, and he resided in the city of Providence. In Rhode Island there has been, over the years, a much cozier relationship between the political establishment and the Mafia. Turiddu had to bribe capo Raimondo of Providence in order to be elevated to an underboss, sottocapo, position in Boston. This allowed for Turiddu to be boss over all illicit businesses in the Boston area. Raimondo would intervene only, when things got really out of hand, such as the out-of-control Irish gang wars during the 1960s. The 1950–1960s marked the best of times for the Mafia in the North End, as Irish gangs fought and killed each other at an alarming rate. It got so bad that capo mafioso Raimondo had to intervene to stop the bloodshed. The worst of times were just around the corner in the North End in the name of Whitey. After taking charge of all the Irish gangs in Boston, he was now ready to take on the Mafia and Turiddu. He was in a position to finally avenge the killings of the Gusting gang members in 1931.

SEVEN

Never Learned to Tap Dance

About this time when Whitey was making his power move against the Mafia in Boston, Vito was in the midst of changing his professional career. He asked himself over and over again: "What the f..k am I doing here?" His thoughts turned back to the warmth of his bed, as people walked gingerly across the icy airport runway to the plane. His language was always laced with foul words, but he couldn't help himself. He was raised in a shepherd family where everybody talked that way. Attending an Ivy League school did not curb his crude language. However, he reserved those foul words for himself and people who deserved them. It was early in the morning and the sun had barely shown its face at Baltimore Airport, where he boarded a plane to Boston, still sleepy, pursuing a job at a University in order to keep his scientific sanity alive and kicking.

It was not so much the lure of academia, but more like escaping from being handcuffed scientifically in classified research at a military government laboratory. Classified scientific work was not his cup of tea, as projects were predicated on military needs. It went against his spirit, as an academician. He felt that he was not put on this earth only to build a better bow and arrow for anyone. Thus, he was on a mission to search for another job in basic research anywhere in the world. However, there was a caveat to his search. He was not about to leave a secure job in government for an unsecured (untenured) one at the University.

In 1970, the aspiring researcher was employed as a physicist at the Naval Research Laboratory (NRL) after graduating from Yale University with a Ph.D.

degree in Applied Quantum Physics. There was nothing "applied" about the newly created research program at Yale. All the courses were in theoretical physics, although his background was in electrical engineering. As a young scientist, he was involved in the search for new magnetic materials, trying to understand the physics of magnetism. Soon enough, after employment, NRL asked him to come down from the "ivory tower" and get his hands "dirty". NRL management needed him to be more involved with classified work.

Obviously, there was a divergence of opinion about his usefulness to the Navy. By then, he had international visibility in the field of magnetism and magnetic materials in general. The Department of Defense (DOD) funded basic research on a short leash, meaning that tangible and practical results needed to be developed in a short time to be utilized in military applications, classified research. After all, that was the purpose of a military government laboratory. When NRL first employed Vito, management expected the time span between the initiation of a basic research project and the development of practical materials for military applications to be about twenty years. However, government military laboratories were under pressure from Congress to shorten the gap between the birth of a research idea and military applications. Ideally, administrators would have liked to reduce expectation time to months rather than years. Besides, it was easier for Congress to justify funding, since with devices it was easier to visualize possibilities and touch something real, rather than abstract ideas from basic research.

In the first two years, he pursued basic research in magnetic materials to his heart content. It all came to a crashing end, when Navy intelligence briefed him about some strange materials floating in the air in Northern Europe. Apparently, a Communist country in the Baltic Sea region had deployed particles in the air to disrupt radio communications between USA aircraft and land stations. These particles were referred to as chaffs or "snow-flakes". DOD made plenty of money available to military research laboratories in order to identify this strange material and utilize it for military purposes. NRL received funds on a flimsy proposal about utilizing these particles for the purpose of hiding or camouflaging Navy ships and planes from enemy surveillance by radar. One proposal called for particles to be dispersed in the air above a military ship to hide or camouflage it from radar surveillance.

The idea proposed by the NRL management team required the weight of the particles to be ten times the weight of a ship to be effective, according to Vito's simple calculation, often referred to as "back of the envelope calculation". Furthermore, there was no practical way to disperse so many particles from a ship into the air each time a surveillance plane flew over the ship. Surveillance from a satellite would have been impossible to derail. A satellite circled the earth roughly 15–20 times per day. This meant that the ship would have to carry roughly 200 times its weight of particles per day! Also, it wasn't possible to disperse that many particles in the air. Just the thought of deploying such a monumental number of particles gave one a headache. He informed the supervisors of his concerns. The penalty for exposing the fallacy of the idea was for him to defend it to the "brass": Navy captains, admirals, generals and funding agencies at the Pentagon. Yellow is the color of brass which they wear as stripes on their uniforms. The management's suggestion was veiled under the guise of a reward. "After all, you will get exposure to the brass." Reluctantly, Vito agreed to it, but he had no choice. In short, management needed a scapegoat and he was chosen for that purpose.

At the presentation, with tongue in cheek, he explained to the brass that if, by an accident of nature, a twirling wind (similar to the winds of a tornado) localized above a ship, the particles would land on the ship. As such, the ship would sink. Then, for sure, the ship would not be detected by radar surveillance. There was a sudden silence in the room, where one could hear a pin drop. One admiral stood up and said indignantly: "Our purpose in life is to save our ships from sinking by hiding from enemy's surveillances, not to sink the f...g ship ourselves." Vito's ears perked up as that was his kind of language. He thought, "Wow, now we are off this bullshit train". The admiral went on to say, "Do you have an alternative plan?" Vito had already prepared for that possibility. The "brass" accepted his plan on the spot and funded it right then and there, at a much higher level of funding than requested by NRL management. A sigh of relief could be felt from Vito's supervisors, but no thank you. Vito led a group of researchers to salvage the situation in a very short time for he was anxious to get back to basic research. For the following years, he split his time between basic research and classified work. However, as the project became more and more successful, the amount of time spent on basic research became less and less frequent.

As a scientist, the first impulse is to report new results to the scientific community and learn from their reaction or criticism. Yet, intelligence officers engaged Vito's group to talk about mundane conversations regarding publications in the open literature by them and others which, thereby, might accidentally reveal secret information to the outside world. According to the drift of the conversations, the Bible was going to be classified as a secret document. By this time, desperation was setting in and he needed to get out of classified work. He got to the point where he was ready to "jump out the window". A University position became more and more attractive to him so that he could spend more time in basic research. Since his job at NRL was more or less secure, he entertained the thought of a tenured position at the University. With a family to support and protect, job security was paramount. Thus, he finally decided to leave NRL on good terms. Many of his colleagues were good friends and later they often collaborated on publications. Furthermore, some of his colleagues participated in panel reviews at funding agencies that decided on the fate of future funding to universities.

The University of Notre Dame offered Vito a position in the Physics Department as an Associate Professor with no tenure. He was married by then. They had three children (two girls and one boy) and lived in a Levittown settlement called Belair, in MD, about fifteen miles from Washington, DC. He was not about to leave a secure job in government for an insecure one and, therefore, refused the position. He realized that universities did not grant tenure that easily upon employment and concentrated on beefing up his resume and climb that mountain once more and, as a former shepherd, that was a challenge that he welcomed. The turn-down disappointed him, but did not discourage him.

After a hiatus of ten years, he resumed the hunt for a faculty position. Lucky for him, the Navy had transferred him to another classified project so that he could spend a little more time on the research of magnetic materials. By then, his reputation as a research physicist became sufficiently noticeable in the Magnetics community that he was offered three full professorship positions without tenure, but he was not about to give up climbing that mountain. In a last-ditch effort to negotiate with a university about tenure upon appointment, he arranged for an interview with Fairmont University in Boston.

It was 5:00 am on a very cold February morning, when he boarded Piedmont Airline at Baltimore Airport to go to Boston for the interview. As the taxi emerged from the Callahan Tunnel on the way to the University, it came to a stop at a traffic light on Cross St. in the North End. A horde of people rushed past the taxi on the way to Haymarket Farmers Market. In the midst of this crowd, Ciccio, who worked in Johnny's bakery spotted Vito and waved. Vito had stopped by Johnny's bakery after attending Conferences in Magnetism in Boston, when he was a graduate student in New Haven. His parental duty was to bring home Neapolitan pastries to the family.

At his first attendance of the International Conference in Magnetism, hosted by Sheraton Hotel in Boston, he met most of the "who's who" in the field. They were the cardinals and popes of the field in magnetism, but what impressed Vito even more was they were "down-to-earth" people, with no airs. At dinner time, one illustrious and famous attendee shouted out, "Let's cut the bull shit; where is there a good place to eat?" "Wow, my kind of people", Vito mused. Since he was familiar with the North End, he directed a small group from the conference to the Zia Teresa restaurant and then on to Johnny's bakery on Hanover Street. Ciccio took orders behind the counter. Vito served as an interpreter, since Ciccio knew very little English. He spoke in a Neapolitan dialect which is foreign even to the rest of Italy.

There were three bakeries in the North End and all made the same type of Neapolitan pastries. That was because, at one time or another, they all learned to bake from Johnny, who was from Monteforte, Italy, near Naples, and a stone throw from Avella. Ciccio came to the North End on a tourist visa. After a couple of months, he married an elderly woman and they were divorced after six months. The whole thing was a scam. Osvaldo, owner of the "Gemelli" café in the North End, coordinated the scheme. His cousin worked in the Immigration Office in Boston, and was well aware of what was possible in terms of the timing for filing papers for citizenship. The scheme brought kitchen workers from abroad to the North End restaurants, cafes, bakeries, etc. The price to owners who trafficked in illegal immigrants varied between $5,000 and $10,000, depending on the kitchen experience of the worker. However, in some cases, the workers were coerced into doing "bookie work", as in the case of Ciccio. Bookie work was part of the number rackets, gambling on numbers, similar to lottery. At that time, there was no government sponsored lottery. All came to an end, when the Immigration Office uncovered the scheme. Both Osvaldo and his cousin faced prison terms and were cited for the scandal. Fortunately for Ciccio, the Immigration Office approved his application before the scandal broke out.

The taxi resumed the ride along Storrow Drive, from the North End, on the way to Fairmont University. The scenery and the friendly people of the North End convinced Vito that that was the place to raise his family. All that beautiful scenery along the Charles river came to an abrupt end, when the taxi dropped him at 923 Belvedere Ave, in front of a white/gray brick, non-descript building. Vito asked the driver where the University was located, as he exited the taxi. No sooner had the question been asked that the taxi took off. There was no building with the Fairmont logo on it. Vito wondered whether he was in the right place, shivering and standing on the sidewalk. He decided to investigate the campus by walking around.

The campus was not a typical one, like those at Yale or Toledo Universities. Brick and cement all over and no greenery to be found. It looked more like downtown Washington, D.C. with all the government buildings spread all over the inner city. Today, the campus is five times larger with lush greenery courtyards spread uniformly over the campus. To stay warm, Vito entered one of the buildings, not knowing where in particular he was going. He rationalized that if he didn't see any students soon, he might be someplace not associated with the University. He was having second thoughts about applying for a job there and then surmised that, perhaps, morning classes haven't yet begun. He tried desperately to stay calm.

All of a sudden, students showed up on campus for the morning class, pouring out of the Green and Orange lines at the subway stations. What a relief! After breakfast in the Student Union, Vito drifted toward the Chairman's office for the 9:30 am meeting. This was followed by meetings with senior faculty members of the tenure and promotion (TP) committee; the people who decided on tenure upon appointment, with the consent of the chairman. All of them were non-committal about tenure. It was like playing a poker game. No one revealed his cards.

In the afternoon, Vito gave his presentation to students and faculties on "magnetic super-lattices", a terminology that he coined in his publications. Students participated in the questions and answers period after the lecture, although the subject matter dealt also with rather novel mathematics. This meant that the presentation included a lot of "pretty pictures" describing the phenomena to complement the formal mathematics. Vito didn't know at what level to pitch the lecture. So, he had to ad-lib by encouraging students to ask questions. Surprisingly, the students seemed to digest the material and, after the talk, half of the audience wanted to hear more, until the chairman intervened.

Finally, the schedule called for meetings with the Dean and Provost in the afternoon. The Provost was the person who ultimately approved all academic appointments. But, Vito loved to roll his dice and try his luck. He convinced himself that he had nothing to lose by asking for tenure and was happy either way as NRL treated him very well, salary wise. NRL had just promoted him within two weeks to a very high grade level as soon as the directorate got wind of his being considered for a faculty position. Usually, it took about a year for a promotion to be processed through the Human Resource Office. This time, Human Resource rushed the promotion through in two weeks! The new position at NRL called for Vito to be an adviser to the Division Head in charge of more than 200 scientific researchers.

The conversation with the Provost started in a friendly tone, about living conditions in Boston and Washington DC, family's interests, etc. Vito was desperately trying to remember what he had rehearsed to say to the Provost. Before he could blurt out his thoughts, the Provost went on the attack by asserting that Universities rarely grant tenure upon appointment. However, he would consider a full professorship with tenure after one year. That was nothing more or nothing less than a pre-emptive shot to disarm Vito, who was flabbergasted. Vito was not about to explore the crumbs thrown at him by the Provost. He was too proud for that. However, he stayed calm. He had seen worse up in the mountains confronted by a wild boar, and this one behaved like one.

He had had the pre-conceived notion that academia was a bastion of collegiality and civilized behavior. However, this stalemate was nothing compared to when his neck was on the line when confronted by the brass at the Pentagon. That episode prepared him well for this type of mental confrontation. He re-gained composure and came out like a wild bull protecting himself and his family. The same determination was oozing out of him as when he was up on the mountains trying to corral wandering sheep. Vito was slow and deliberate in delivering every word so that it resonated in his f…g ears, "With due respect, I have never learned to tap dance and I am not about to learn now". He also added, "I am perfectly happy to return to working with the Navy which just approved a promotion, on hearing of my possible departure. I will be happy either way, whether or not you employ me". The Provost chuckled and knew that Vito was digging in his heels. The stalemate was like the confrontation between the bull and the matador eyeing each other to see who blinked first. After a short interval of silence, the Provost wanted to know exactly what Vito could contribute to the University.

At this point, Vito knew he had the Provost by the balls. From previous conversations with senior faculties on the TP committee, it was shocking to him that they were more interested in the classified work than Vito's publications in the open literature. Only one classified patent resulted from all the classified work by Vito's group, and it hadn't seen daylight for more than ten years. Yet, they were impressed with something that they hadn't seen. Vito's reaction may be summarized by a comment to himself: "They are out of their f...g minds. Imagine they wanted to establish classified research on campus?" After a short pause, Vito explained to the Provost what was entailed in establishing a classified laboratory on campus. Stanford University and Georgia Tech had established elaborate classified laboratories operating just outside campus. The laboratories were managed by private companies but, somehow, subordinate to the two universities. Funding to the two universities was funneled through DOD as legislated by Congress. DOD charged 10–15% for the ombudsman work [7-1].

However, Vito did not relate the fact that unless and until Congress legislated another arrangement like for the other two universities, it was a waste of time for all concerned. It would have been easier to fly to Mars on a broom stick than to get Congress to do anything new. He did not have the heart to explain how the "cards were stacked" in Congress, needing lobbyists and a cadre of politicians to pass legislation. Vito wanted nothing to do with that world. He did not want to get stuck in a quagmire of bullshit artists and politicians. Fairmont University had no experience with the political world. They didn't even employ a lobbyist. In the political world, merits of science have nothing to do with securing a classified laboratory at a university. Conversation went on for another ten to fifteen minutes and, finally, the nightmarish meeting was over. He honestly couldn't care less about the outcome of the interview. His body language told the Provost as much.

On the way back to the airport, Vito stopped by Ciccio's bakery in the North End to say hello and buy some pastries for the family. Vito surmised that he could kiss that job at Fairmont goodbye. Back home late at night,

Vito announced the good news that the pastries were still warm. Apparently, Ciccio prepared the pastries for Vito just before departing Boston. By that time, Vito had already forgotten about the interviews and was at peace with himself, knowing that he gave his best. At the meetings, he was determined not to be awed by academia and was ready to accept any outcome. As such, he decided that there would be no more scaling of the mountain to secure a tenured position.

In the spring of 1985, Vito's wife called him at work to read the letter from Fairmont University. Basically, tenure was granted upon appointment as a full professor. Vito later learned from the Chairman that eight faculty members in the department voted in favor of tenure and two were against it. He never bothered to inquire about those two, as he felt that he had nothing to prove to them. He had more publications than the entire TP committee combined! However, his salary was slightly below the average salary of a full professor. Apparently, Fairmont University still wanted Vito to learn to "tap dance". As far as Vito was concerned, getting back to basic research was alive and kicking. As in any family, there were many questions to address: where to live, school system, effects on the children, etc.

After settling down in a rental apartment in Newton, he established an open laboratory for anyone on campus to conduct fundamental research in developing new magnetic materials. He put his heart and soul into that project as that was the only reason or motivation to apply for a faculty position in the first place. Also, he wanted to demonstrate to the University administration that funding could be generated from basic research. To administrators, money spoke louder than peer-reviewed publications or scholarly research. A research group was organized and the laboratory equipped with the latest technologically advanced instrumentation funded by government agencies. A world class laboratory was established in a very short time, but no one else at the university knew or acknowledged anything about it. Funding and scholarship derived from it was not enough to appease the administration. Apparently, the administration was still hell bent on establishing a classified laboratory. At this point in time, Vito just ignored their silent protestations as it had nothing to do with scientific arguments or with rational thinking. Thank God for tenure.

The family bought a house in Newton, a suburb of Boston, and sold all the properties in Maryland. Adjustments to academia with its internal politics were rather mild compared to funding squabbles at government agencies, although the teaching load was heavy in the beginning. The university wanted to remind Vito about the classified laboratory on campus, but he welcomed more teaching loads. He needed the teaching experience. Fortunately for Vito, he broke away from these petty academic spats on weekends. Festivals, playing bocce, restaurants, cafes and bakeries drew tourists, as well as Vito's family, to the North End. This meant that the family didn't have to wait for Vito to go to a conference to secure pastries.

It took only a couple of visits to the North End for him to understand the locals, who were first and second generation Italian-Americans, as he was well steeped in their lifestyle, culture and dialects. The few university and professional students who lived there did not mingle much with the rest of the residents. Initially, it shocked Vito to discover such a community in America. He was coming full circle. After adopting American cultural ways from the mid-west to the East coast, he found himself in an oasis of Italian immigrants who never adapted to anything outside of their community. By their dialects, he could place them in the region of Italy from where they came.

EIGHT

Dizzy Blondie

Vito's family lived on Commonwealth Avenue, Newton, for five years near "Heart Break Hill". The house marked the 19th mile of the 26.2 mile annual marathon race in Boston. Up to that point in the race, the racers ran, more or less, on flat ground. Just about when the racers were exhausted, they were staring up "heartbreak hill" toward the Boston College campus. Usually, the race was held in mid-April on Patriots Day, in honor of the heroes of the American Revolutionary War of 1776. Students affiliated with Vito's research group and colleagues from Fairmont University celebrated the festivities at Vito's house, where the racers passed by. They manned a water stand, handing out cups of water to the racers. Though the race started at 11:00 am, some racers were still at it until early evening. Most of the spectators, as well as Vito's guests, left by that time. Remarkably, the spirit of the last few remaining racers was truly amazing. By then, Vito's children manned the water stand until no one showed up, running or crawling along. This yearly get together ended soon after the family moved to the North End district of Boston.

The North End today is a destination for many tourists in search of historical sites dating back to before the American Revolutionary War. They often walk along the Freedom Trail to the North End, Faneuil Hall, Paul Revere's house and other historical sites.

Paul Revere's house.

The house and statue of Paul Revere are located in front of the Old North Church.

Old North Church can be seen behind the statue of Paul Revere.

Colonial Governors and British artisans are buried in Copp's Hill Burying Ground overlooking the Atlantic Ocean and the bocce courts.

Copp's Hill Burying Ground overlooking the bocce courts and Charlestown

During colonial days, the North End occupied a small parcel of land. It was not until after the Revolutionary War that more land mass was made available to supplant sea water for new settlements. Water was displaced with dirt from hills in the suburbs. Some houses were built on wooden stilts. Other attractions for tourists are Italian restaurants and festivals.

Map of the North End during colonial times.

Most Italian immigrants in the North End appear to be curious and confused about why so many tourists and all the fuss about the monuments, as they have been exposed to monuments all their lives in Italy. They shrug their shoulders in wonderment and feel resigned to the hordes of tourists. Even in small towns in Italy there are Roman statues and/or monuments that most locals rarely pay attention to. The only time that they honor a monument is when city hall organizes a special occasion to commemorate a statue or an historic event. Most often, they had no clue as to what the statue represented, except for city officials or literati. Clearly, there was a disconnect between the locals and the historical sites ever since they emigrated to America.

Long before the arrival of Southern Italian immigrants in the twentieth century, Northern Europeans had come to the North End since the pilgrims landed in Plymouth, MA. Boston changed dramatically in the 19th century with the arrival of Irish immigrants, especially following the Great Irish Famine. Originally, the Brahmins (British settlers) of Beacon Hill represented the upper-class society. They held political, police and financial control of the city of Boston and the suburbs. The Irish immigrants held menial jobs, such as maids, street cleaners, etc., but there was little social interaction between the two groups of English speaking immigrants. By 1900, the Irish became the establishment. They displaced the Brahmins in Boston City Hall. Irish immigrants were elected or appointed to top positions in the political, police, and legal systems.

The most prominent Irish politician in Boston at the beginning of the 20th century was John F. Fitzgerald, [6-2], known as "Honey Fitz" for his charming personality. During his two terms as Mayor, Fitzgerald made major improvements to the Port of Boston; an investment that brought increased imports from Europe. His daughter Rose was born in the North End. In Boston, Rose's son, John F. Kennedy, started his political career. In his later years Honey Fitz taught his grandchildren how to succeed in politics. One of them, John (Jack), went on to become the 35th president of the United States.

Rose married Joseph (Joe) Kennedy at the age of 24 after a courtship of seven years. After marriage, they moved to Brookline, Massachusetts, now the John Fitzgerald Kennedy National Historic Site. Joe's father, P.J. Kennedy, was a political rival of Honey Fitz. Joe provided well for his family, but rumors in newspapers claimed that he had affairs with actress Gloria Swanson and other women. Her father told Rose before marriage that divorce was not an option, since the church did not recognize divorce then. She was a devout Catholic throughout her 100th birthday, not missing Mass once. Later in life, Rose retired to Hyannis port on Cape Cod, MA.

James Michael Curley [8-1] succeeded Honey Fitz Boston's mayor. By 1900 he was Boston's youngest ward boss and went on to serve three terms in Congress, four terms as Mayor, and a term as Governor of Massachusetts. He also spent time in prison for fraud, after which, he was re-elected Mayor. Curley was more popular with the newer immigrants, such as the Italians and Jews, than he was with the Irish immigrants.

In the early 1900s, Jewish, Irish and Italian immigrants arrived and settled in the North End [8-2]. Most of the Italian immigrants came from Sicily. They were attracted by the area's low-rent housing and its proximity to downtown Boston.

Tenements in the North End built in early 1900s.

It was a natural choice for poor, working-class Italian immigrants. Also, during this time, the city of Boston upgraded many public facilities in the neighborhood. Christopher Columbus High School, a public bathhouse, and a public library were built. This wave of immigrants, mostly from Sciacca, Sicily, was very resourceful in creating new factories on the waterfront. Italian immigrants founded the Prince Macaroni Company and small fishing companies. A large number of Jewish immigrants had also settled there, started businesses, and built synagogues.

Italian immigrants were at the bottom of the social totem pole, but they worked their way up. Some of them realized their American dream of a house in suburbia. Nevertheless, the population of the North End reached a maximum of 45,000 people within a square mile, denser than Calcutta, India. Irish immigrants, who had settled there during the Great Famine, numbered 15,000 in 1880; ten years later, only 5,000 remained. By 1905, of the 27,000 people living in the North End, 22,000 were Italian immigrants.

As the neighborhood became increasingly Italian, other ethnic groups began to move out. Irish immigrants often clashed with Italians, despite the fact that the vast majority of both groups shared a common religion and political party. The two groups were in competition for jobs as well as housing, and there were cultural differences, including different styles of Catholic worship, that caused additional friction. Whereas Irish immigrants displaced Yankee residents from the North End in the 19th century, Italians crowded out the Irish settlers later in early 20th century. Jewish immigrants stayed longer than the Irish but, eventually, they too were crowded out.

Another wave of Italians emigrated to Boston following World War II which lasted about 15 years, and brought immigrants from Sulmona, Avellino and elsewhere in Southern Italy. Several of these new residents opened Italian restaurants, cafes, and bakeries in the North End, which helped keep the Italian traditions and culture alive into the 1970s when the neighborhood began attracting yuppies and other young professionals working in the financial district. Today, the population of the North End is roughly 7,000–8,000, in which Italian-Americans make up about 50%. Most Italian immigrants have moved on to the suburbs. Small group of immigrants who came from the same region of Italy formed small enclaves within the North End, Abruzzesi on one block, Sicilians on another, and so on. Original Italian immigrants are slowly becoming a vanishing breed in the North End.

This latest wave of immigrants relied on each other for support. A strong bond developed among them over the years. As in most close-knit Italian immigrant communities, they did not assimilate very well with surrounding communities. in fact, they were completely oblivious to the American diversity of cultures. In all those years, they never made peace with or adapted to changes in their lifestyles. Their support system prevented them from participating in or engaging in new trends of American lifestyles. They adhered to an artificial enclave where their lifestyles were stuck in the ninety-forties and fifties, even though the world around them changed. They were frozen in time. Basically, the Mafia took advantage of the isolation which was self induced. Mafiosi were able to operate freely in the neighborhood, like fish in a pond. Similar enclaves of Italian immigrants could be found in New York City, Philadelphia and other cities along the East Coast at about that time, as well.

Over the years the North End gained, through newspaper stories, a horrendous reputation for gangland killings and notorious thugs. However, the locals that Vito met were just ordinary people going about carving a life in America as in any other town in the USA. In fact, by the time Vito arrived in Boston, the Mafia was leaderless and in turmoil. A new boss of all the Irish gangs had emerged by the name of James "Whitey" Bulger as the kingpin of crime in Boston. The outside world was not aware of the change, but the old reputation about the Mafia stuck in people's minds, especially outside of Boston. Also, unbeknownst to Vito, Guido Alvaro, a childhood friend, lived in the North End managing a pizzeria and trafficking in cocaine.

By then, Sonny or Guido had lived in the North End for about twenty years or more. His apartment was located on Quarter Street in a cozy, surreal courtyard. Within the courtyard, there were two families connected with the Mafia and one other family, affiliated with the Boston Police Department. These two families, on opposite sides of the law, were related by marriage. Guido's apartment was located between these two apartments. They all lived in harmony, throwing parties during festival times. One police officer who lived there quit the department with the aspiration of becoming an actor in Los Angeles. His claim to fame was his appearance in a minor role in the movie, "The Godfather". Being connected with the Mafia presented some risks, such as shootouts from rival Irish gangs, even in the courtyard. From time to time, Whitey's gang would take pot-shots at Mafia groups wherever they lived.

At the time of Vito's arrival in Boston, the Mafia was fragmented because their capo, Turiddu, Ref. [6-8], was incarcerated in 1983. Mafia factions operated in East Boston, Revere, Medford and other parts of suburbia. However, in Boston, Whitey, [6-5], controlled the heroin and marijuana trades, although he claimed that South Boston was clean of drugs. Principally, Sonny worked with a young man, Alessandro (Alex), in a pizzeria on Hanover Street, North End. Alex just graduated from Christopher Columbus High School and was the son of Lorenzo (Larry), who lived in the same courtyard as Sonny. Lorenzo had been connected with the Mafia for over thirty years. Alessandro aspired to learn from the master pizza maker and also learn about cocaine trafficking from him, Sonny. Obviously, Alessandro's operation fell below "radar" detection by Whitey. Besides the pizzeria in the North End, Sonny helped his brother Davide in Medford to run the pizzeria, when the brother was traveling, which was often. Sonny assisted other mafiosi in expanding the pizza business to the Charles Street area, across from the Massachusetts General Hospital, MGH. In essence, Sonny was keeping a low profile and being no threat to Whitey by moving around from place to place, laying low until the nightmare of Whitey's dominance in Boston would end.

Colleagues of Vito at the University tended to equate living in the North End with living in the throes of a Mafia war, as in Sicily during the 1970s. In fairness to his colleagues, there is nothing to admire about the Mafia, although glorified in movies like the Godfather. Basically, the Mafia is a secret cult, divorced from society, whose main purpose in life is to make money by any means, including murder. There is nothing to prevent a respected member of society from being a mafioso. There are many such examples of mafiosi who remain incognito all their lives, although highly respected in their communities. Omerta (secrecy) within the cult itself insures their privacy. One of the main beliefs of this cult is that it is a sin to pay any form of taxes, because that is their main source of money. They invented a form of taxation, long before governments woke up to the idea, by extorting money out from their members and business people. Thus, the Mafia does not play by the same rules as everybody else. They make the rules for their members to adhere to. Otherwise, there are consequences.

The word Mafia is rarely, if ever, mentioned by the cult members to describe themselves. It is not in their dictionary. They use words like "cosa nostra"/ "our thing" and refer to each other as "our friend"/ "amico nostro". The Mafia is sub-divided into small groups in which illicit operations within a group are guarded with their lives. However, each group contributes financially to the capo. The murder of a member can be approved only by the capo. Otherwise, it may result in a Mafia war between groups or factions as in the 1920s and 1950s in New York City, and in the 1970s in Sicily.

University colleagues were influenced by newspaper stories embellishing Mafia connections to the North End. Most stories were not true, but it sold newspapers. It is remarkable how opinions can be formed by people in general about a place without ever visiting there. For example, from 1985 to 1993, no one was aware of the fact that the Mafia in the North End did not control its own affairs. Mafiosi were dispersed all over Boston and the suburbs. Their capo and the sottocapi, underbosses, were running for their lives to avoid indictments and jail, with Whitey's assistance. Colleagues at the University advised Vito not to settle there.

The bad reputation was based on two horrific incidents that involved University students and were reported nationally in the media. One incident that terrified the whole North End was that Andrew P. Puopolo and his Harvard University classmates and football teammates spent an evening running around nightclubs near Faneuil Hall. In the early morning of November 16, 1976, Puopolo's friend, Charlie Kaye, was accosted by a prostitute on Cross Street. The prostitute stole Kaye's wallet and ran away with it. Puopolo chased after her. Unbeknownst to Puopolo, three African-American men came to the aid of the prostitute and stabbed him to death. Initial reports insinuated Mafia involvement in a drug deal gone bad, but the Mafia had nothing to do with the incident. After many court appeals, the case was eventually settled out of court and all the men were found not guilty. The athletic fields in the North End, including the bocce courts, were named thereafter as Puopolo's Park.

In another story reported nationally that year was the annual fracas between the North End and Charlestown High School students. During one of the festivals, there was a free-for-all in which one youth was shot five times, but survived. One bullet is still to this day lodged in his body. Again, initial television reports claimed that a drug deal, orchestrated by the Mafia, had gone bad. Clearly, the Mafia has never been a holy institution, but those incidents could have occurred anyplace in Boston or in any other city at

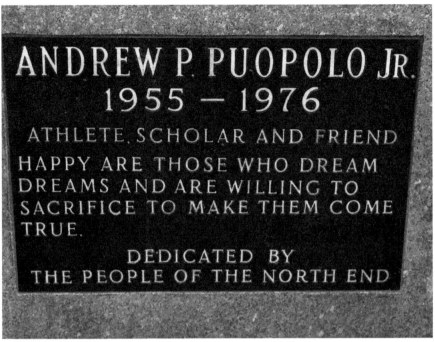

The plaque is found at the entrance of the baseball field next to the bocce courts.

any time. The feeling among residents of the North End was that it was the quietest and most crime-free district in Boston and vicinity. Besides, they really had no choice as to where to live. They were poor and stuck there. They did the best they could under the circumstances. Residents were proud of this reputation and were keen to maintain that peaceful appearance.

A married couple with an adorable child from Chicago moved into a basement apartment in the North End. They often visited the bocce courts and enjoyed the outings and mingling with the locals. The husband was a young litigation lawyer working in the financial district. To the couple's consternation, every morning between 3:00 and 4:00 am they were awakened by the ruckus next door in a deli/grocery store. When the bars and night clubs near Faneuil Hall emptied out, drunken customers would rush out to get a bite to eat. The deli was open for business twenty four hours daily. The noise every morning was unbearable. What to do? Surprisingly, the couple did not turn to the police. That seems to have been the logical thing to do, but that would have taken too long for the problem to be addressed, if at all. They took the advice of their friends at the bocce courts. The husband turned to a friendly neighbor who owned a shady loan shark store at the end of the street nearby. In less than a day, the noise went away, as the deli closed the shop for business at 11:00 pm sharp every day. Needless to say, that lending store was a crooked one. It loaned money at 1% per week. It was advisable for clients to pay back the exorbitant interest rate.

Rumors circulated around town speculating that mafiosi kept tabs on muggers and steered them away from the North End. Hogwash! The real reason was that if a mugger hit on a mafioso or his relative, there would have been serious repercussions. Hence, there was too much risk for a mugger to hang around the North End. Nevertheless, Vito's family bought an apartment there even though traffic from the North End to Fairmont University was unbearable, especially in the mornings. In summary, Vito was not overly concerned with stories about Mafia stories in the newspapers.

As a teen-ager, Vito had lived in a Mafia neighborhood in Aliquippa, PA, although he had not been aware of it. Residents have never felt immediate danger for their lives or any kind of intimidation, as long as one minded his or her own business. Besides, mafiosi do not advertise who they are and do not appreciate being singled out. It would be dangerous to expose the identity of a mafioso publically. There is an old saying in such neighbor-hoods: Fatti i cazzi tuoi/mind your own fucking business. In some sense, the neighborhood in the North End exercised some form of omerta, a code of silence or secrecy. Other than that, living there was no different from any other district in Boston, except that there was a large presence of Italian immigrants. Vito reasoned that this place should be no different from other places with similar reputations about the Mafia: New York City, Chicago, etc., and people still lived there. Although he felt at ease with colleagues in academia, he was equally comfortable among Italian immigrants and North Enders in particular. The family was excited about the new cultural environment so familiar to papa.

After residing one week in the North End, a murder, arson and explo-sion occurred during a festival. Naturally, the family was apprehensive. The murder involved two vendors, who were out-of-towners, jockeying for space at a festival site. Each vendor rented approximately one to two square meters of space for $500. It is interesting to note that the space, or sidewalks, belonged to the City. Yet, the City did not profit from it. The organizers of the festival did! Perhaps, the collected money was used as pay-offs for police protection. Usually, the location of the space was assigned on a first-come-first served basis. The money was paid to the organizers who assigned the space. Space assignment was not always discharged fairly; some vendors occupied the same space each year without paying. In this case, the two vendors were from out of town and had no special connection to the organizers. Hence, they were trying to establish their turfs right from the start. Obviously, there was some hanky-panky business between police and the organizers.

In regard to the arson, a restaurant owner hired someone to set fire to his place in order to collect money from his insurance company. The purpose of the ruse, of course, was to upgrade the restaurant. Actually, the loud explosion was due to a large underground electrical transformer which overheated, blowing up next to a condominium. Nothing to get excited about. These incidents were dismissed out of hand by the family, since it could have happened any place.

Slowly but surely, Vito's family was assimilating into a new and ethnic culture that the rest of the family was not aware of before, that of the Italian immigrants. Previously, he was exposed to the lifestyles and cultures of the Midwest, and East Coast and easily blended into them. It was important for Vito to introduce the family to the flip side of his life, that of an Italian immigrant. At this point in time, he made peace with politics in academia. He chose to ignore it, since he was a senior professor. He was a man of multiple cultural traits and able to switch from one to the other depending on whom he was dealing with. Much like a chameleon, he morphed into whatever culture, depending on whom he conversed with. However, he was mostly at ease with bocce players, who were there to unwind from the hustle and bustle of the city.

By this time, the whole family had acclimated to the new city. The children met new friends and attended local high schools and universities. Anna was involved with the local PTAs and libraries. Vito made peace with the weather in Boston and organized the largest research group at Fairmont University. For once in his professional career, he was free to choose the type of research to engage in. This meant that, in order to fund his research, Vito often traveled to Washington, DC, submitting research proposals to government funding agencies: NSF, DOD, ARO, NASA, etc. It had taken many years to build the network of government contacts in Washington

DC to plant "seeds" for funding. As far as the University was concerned, the nature or type of research didn't matter as long as the money was green. Thus, the axiom of "publish or perish" in academia is a misnomer.

Not raising funding for research can lead to a miserable life at a university, even for a tenured professor. For example, a colleague of Vito, who was well regarded in the scientific community as an expert in the theory of relativity with over 500 peer reviewed publications, never raised a single dollar for his research. He paid a price for his "freedom" to behave like a butterfly, to jump from one project to another on a whim, with no consideration for generating funding in 30–40 years. The "penalty" was to be subjected to teaching freshmen physics laboratory courses instead of high level theoretical physics ones. His academic scholarship didn't matter much to the University even though this professor was nominated for the Nobel prize in physics for his research on the helium atom.

On weekends, Vito and Anna took time off to unwind from the demands of academia and settling in the new home. They invariably went to a restaurant or a festival or just sat on a bench at the bocce courts. At the courts, Vito would enjoy hearing the exchanges between bocce players. The players were not amused that Vito would understand every word they said in their dialects. In their small-town backgrounds they were suspicious of any stranger appearing on the scene, one that smiled or laughed at what they were saying and, especially, from one named Vito. For them, it was like being nakedly exposed.

They knew that Vito and Anna were not "mere" tourists, since they were very familiar with the game of bocce. For the players, it was an uncomfortable feeling to have someone to look at them as if they were in a zoo. However, it did not take long for Vito and Anna to get acquainted with the bocce crowd, especially when Vito started conversing with them in his Neapolitan dialect. Vito wanted to convey to them that he was one of them. The bocce players' mood simply perked up. "Hey, hey, fetente, sfaccimmo,…", meaning " you dirty smelly rat…". They shouted in unison smiling and came toward Vito and Anna engaging both in conversations in Italian and English. One of the bocce players, Iaccarino, was somewhat amused but skeptical, since he could decipher from Vito's distinct Neapolitan accent where he was from. Iaccarino was a typical Neapolitan, suspicious of any stranger and superstitious.

Scene at the bocce courts.

Iaccarino was born and raised in Afragola, a town a stone's throw from Naples. "Cum ti chiam a Avella?", "What do they call you in Avella?" He asked. Afragola and Avella are located on opposite sides of Mount Vesuvius. Vito blurted out, "Vituccio." A brief moment of silence was broken by loud laughter from all the players, since the name implied a diminutive of Vito, confirming the physical stature of Vito. Onofrio, a friend of Iaccarino, came forward embracing, not Vito, but his wife. Then, Onofrio, said, "Your wife is welcome here, but you, I don't know". Vito retorted, "Tu si nu fetente"/"You are rotten to the core" and all started laughing. The implied meaning was "Get your dirty hands off my wife". That was the beginning of a wonderful friendship. It was clear to Vito and Anna that they were welcomed with open arms. Of course, Vito was pleased to be accepted as one of their own. Obviously, the gathered crowd surrounding the couple preferred the name Vito, because they were comfortable with it and reminded them of the place they came from.

Sonny spent a lot of his time at the bocce courts. He enjoyed life to the fullest being the entertainer, the bullshit artist, and just having fun with the old-timers and friends. In particular, he loved to kibitz at Caffe del Calcio (soccer cafe) on Sunday morning after church, holding court with wannabes (potential mafiosi). On a sunny day, surrounded by wannabes, he would sit in front of the cafe enjoying the sun and looking over tourists and newcomers, as if he had to approve of their entry into the cafe. However, he protected his privacy fiercely to strangers due to his association with the Mafia. That was the main reason Vito was not able to single him out at first, when he visited the bocce courts.

The pride and joy of Sonny was his son Salvini (Sal) who finished High School at the same time as Alessandro. Sal was tall, handsome, dark haired, and a football player. He was a lineman on the football team and popular with the cheerleaders. His daughter Carmela, two years younger than Sal, was aggressive and motivated and had plans to go places and be important politically. She resented Sal, because he got all the attention from her papa. She was determined to prove to her papa that she was going to be a better "man". Sal aspired to follow in his father's footsteps which his mother, Jesse feared the most. She kept reminding Sonny that he was too soft on Sal and he should sit down with Sal and plan a future for him, away from pizza enterprises. There were local colleges offering him a football scholarship, but he showed no interest in them. In effect, each member of Sonny's family headed in separate ways, a fiercely independent bunch.

One tradition, frozen in time, which was carried over from the latest generation of Italian immigrants in the ninety forties and fifties, was the cafe scenes. On Sundays, the cafes serve espresso and freshly baked pastries in the morning. The choice of cafes is whether or not one wants to see Italian soccer televised live or to watch popular RAI television programs from Italy. The soccer audience in the cafe was split into two groups. One group favoring one team and the other the opposing team. The ribbing between the two groups was friendly and engaging, since they all knew one another very well or they came from the same region in Italy. For both Vito and his wife, it was quite entertaining watching the people having fun kibitzing or ribbing each other. It was like being in a special theater where the actors and audience were one and the same.

Sometimes there were unexpected surprises. On one particular Sunday, the mood was festive as usual and full of anticipation as customers were enjoying their pastries and espresso. The talk was so loud that it drowned out the TV audio. A customer shouted to a friend across the café, "Here comes Dizzy Blondie". For the lack of a real name, people in the cafe referred to him as Blondie. Vito and his wife expected some blonde woman to step into the cafe.

Cafe scene where people are watching a soccer game.

Dizzy Blondie was a tall, sturdy young man with streaks of long blonde hair over his shoulders and tattoos all over his arms, carrying a 1'x1'box to the cafe. There was nothing "dizzy" about Blondie's behavior. He was strictly business in selling fenced material, except for the one time, he tried to sell to a policeman. Thereafter, he took precautions in avoiding such embarrassment. Lucky for him, the cop was also looking for a deal, like the rest of the customers. Dizzy Blondie plopped the box on the counter as there was no open table. He pulled Rolex watches out of the box and shouted at the top of his lungs that a Rolex watch could be had for $500, cash only and no receipts. Typical Rolex watches sold in a jewelry store for about $20,000 or more. Further examination by people there revealed that indeed they were the real McCoy. Vito had seen many shenanigans before in Aliquippa, PA, but this one topped them all. He simply exited the café with his wife as he "smelled a rat". He didn't want to be witness to a potential crime. Blondie made these trips to the café about once a month, and, each time, Vito would leave the café. Blondie represented the Winter Hill Irish gang headed by Whitey in South Boston and Somerville. Obviously, Blondie had no qualms about operating his business in the North End, since Whitey was in control of Boston including the North End. The Mafia boss was in jail at that time, so there was no mafioso challenging Whitey.

Sunday morning was a special time. Tourists were nowhere to be found. No guided tours to Paul Revere's house and statue, the walking path to Bunker Hill, North Church, or maddening crowds asking numerous questions about Italian restaurants in the vicinity. On that day, one could walk on Hanover St., the main street, without being bumped into by tourists. Vito and his wife attended church service and afterward enjoyed walking around to look at the historical sites, uninterrupted. As Vito looked over the housing during these walks, here and there, they were in bad shape. The buildings were old and usually the rooms small compared to newer apartment buildings. However, few buildings were renovated in view of the upsurge of real estate prizes. He thanked his lucky stars that he didn't buy within the North End, but bought into a nearby waterfront modern apartment building, a remodeled fishing wharf.

One fellow who often offered to buy an espresso for Vito and his wife was Donato. He would often sit at their table and loved to talk incessantly about anything and everything. Without invitation, he joined the table where Vito and his wife were about to order espressos and offered to buy. He started saying, "I have noticed that you have been coming here regularly and I want to welcome you to the North End, although I am from Medford. I used to live in the North End. My name is Donato, blah, blah…". The locals referred to him as yakkity, yakkity and for good reason. Once he sat down, Vito and his wife could not shut him up. He continued talking about his job in construction and his involvement with politics of electing the Mayor in Redford. The current Mayor's house was next to his house, blah, blah…

Vito was wondering who in the hell wound his clock and what this had to do with the price of rice in China. He talked about everything under the sun except what he was doing with Sonny in Fla. Inadvertently, Donato let it be known that his first destination in the USA was Hollywood, FL, where he worked in the same pizzeria as Sonny in the mid 1960's. The only problem with that conversation was that Vito didn't know who Sonny was. It was exasperating for the couple. Again, Donato continued his conversation. Was Donato trying to impress Vito that he knew Sonny? Hard to tell. Anyway, he claimed to have been employed by Sonny back then. Vito did not connect the name Sonny to his childhood friend Guido Alvaro.

Nevertheless, Donato was an interesting fellow. If he had stayed in Italy, he would have been referred to as a "hillbilly", since he spent all his life being a farmhand and on the mountains. His family and ancestors lived on various farms as a farmhand and as a shepherd. He may have been a peasant or a farmer but definitely not boring. He had a down-to-earth philosophy about life in general and was a brilliant conversationalist who drew attention to himself. Most importantly, he had a good heart. These were all the qualities that Vito admired most. He was born in a town near Avellino, Italy, and, at the age of twenty, he emigrated to Hollywood, Fla. For generations, since his family toiled the farms of Avellino, he had little formal education. Obviously, he learned a lot on his own, in view of his ability to express his opinions. The area where he farmed was wine country, where one of the best red wines in Southern Italy are produced. The wine is being sold in the USA under the name of Taurasi and costs about $30 or more per bottle.

In Avellino, he worked on the farm owned by Aniello, who emigrated to the USA before Donato. Mainly grapes and hazelnuts were cultivated on the farm. Grapes and hazelnuts were sold to only one distributor who then produced and exported wines and hazelnuts worldwide. In those days, financial transactions between farmers and distributors was totally controlled by the Camorra, the local Mafia organization. Farmers were not allowed to negotiate for higher prices by taking their business to other distributors, only the one chosen by the Camorra. This practice had been in place for many generations in the Campania region of Southern Italy. Aniello learned, early in life, the nature of doing business with the Camorra, legal or otherwise.

By the late 1960s, Donato moved to the North End; he was a part-time bookie working for Sonny, dealing in the numbers racket. Vito introduced himself as a custodian of the library without specifying what town, working flexible hours. Donato didn't have a clue as to what being a custodian entailed, and neither did Vito. He pretended to know the meaning of the word. Vito explained to Donato that a custodian sets up security systems at a new library and was in custody of important financial documents. When in the mood, Vito could bullshit as well as Donato. Of course, Vito was shocked that Donato made sense of his gibberish talk. Vito was not about to tell Donato about himself for, within a millisecond, it would have been "blabbered" all over town. His privacy meant more than socializing with Donato. Obviously, he was too curious about this new couple. It was important to Vito to come across as just a "working stiff", and he wanted to be accepted as one of their own, not as some nerd. He just wanted to enjoy a relaxed relationship as in the old days in Avella. He was in the world of bullshit artists including himself. He started a simple life as a shepherd, assimilated into the American culture, and now had returned home full circle to bullshit artists.

Donato introduced Vito to his friends as the "Dottore" of housing. People at the cafe did a double take and had a peculiar look as if to say, "What?, did I hear that right?" Donato was of the typical mind set of the old generation when anyone associated with books or had special skills or something that he didn't understand, he or she was referred to as a "Dottore". Vito did not correct him. Donato introduced Anna and Vito to the godfather of his first child as Aniello. He was a former landowner from the Avellino area who, at one time, employed Donato on his farm. Donato was sponsored by Aniello to emigrate to the USA. Aniello imagined himself to be a great hairdresser and stylist and changed his name to a French-sounding name, Jean-Claude Sassoon, thinking that he, too, could be as successful as the French hair stylist, Vidal Sassoon. For all those years that Vito was acquainted with Aniello, he did not have the courage to tell him that Vidal was not a Frenchman, but an American, and he could change his name back to Aniello in the Salon. However, Vito did not want to interfere with Aniello's mind set. His haircuts were all of the same shape or style. Women looked like sheep after his cuts.

Aniello's mother died when he was born. That created a difficult relationship between father and son over the years. His father, Girolamo, was distant from his son and very strict until the father died in the North End. He was an earner and, in the parlance of the Mafia, he was a "made man". An earner in the Mafia is different from a wage-earner in that a wage-earner holds a 9–5 regular job. Thus, a regular worker earns his money, whereas a Mafia earner has no regular hours and is, of course, involved mostly in illicit activities, extorting money out of people one way or another, mostly by violence and threats. Girolamo was involved with prostitution, gambling, pin ball machines and racketeering. In Italy, he was a Podesta, Fascist Mayor, before and during WW II in the town of Montefalcione, in the Avellino area. As a crooked Mayor, he accumulated wealth and farmlands, although his monthly stipend was no more than $100.

As the Allied Army advanced in WW II, toward Avellino, Girolamo crossed the battlefront between the German and Allied armies into the "liberated" zone of Naples. Had he stayed behind in the German zone, he would have been shot by the Communist partisans once the German Army left town. In the liberated zone, he was able to mingle with the locals and hide from the Communist partisans until law and order was established in his hometown. Basically, there was a civil war in Italy soon after the War and it was extremely dangerous to reveal one's identity, especially a former Fascist. Fascists were rounded up all over Italy and indiscriminately killed by Communists, without trial.

This period of time was no different from the times in ancient Rome when a triumphant general would issue a list of people to be massacred, referred to as the proscription list. Whoever did the killing had first right to assume all the riches and properties of the person on the list. In order to avoid being killed, a person on the list would travel to a foreign country and wait until things calmed down or wait for another ruler to take over before returning to Rome. Similarly, a Fascist mayor could ill afford to be in the welcoming party to an advancing Allied Army into his town. The partisans or the Communists would have shot him right on the spot. Hence, he left town before the Allied Army entered City Hall.

When things did calm down, Girolamo returned to his hometown and assumed ownership of his farms and villas. To add insult to injury, he was elected Mayor again, but this time under the banner of the Democratic party after WW II. He then set his sights on to the USA, and left Aniello in the care of Donato's family on the farm. Girolamo lived in a boarding house in Boston's North End and behaved as if he were the Mayor of the boarding house. The rest of the boarders were, one way or another, associated with the Mafia. He soon became group leader of the boarders and was deeply involved with Mafia organization. The father sponsored his son, Aniello, to emigrate to the North End and employed him as a bookie selling lottery numbers. The winning number was based on an artificial number that produced the most revenue for the Mafia. A delicate balance was reached such that sufficient numbers of people hit the jackpot and at the same time the Mafia profited. At times, the number was based on a combination of numbers resulting from winners of the first three or four horse races at Suffolk Downs in East Boston. However, the Mafia reserved the right to choose any combination of races to maximize profits.

Aniello had a wild life as a young adult. He was both a bookie and hair stylist. His business was doing rather well, and he was becoming an earner.

It didn't take long for him to invite trouble, since the word around town was that he was an up and coming star in organized crime, a wannabe. He was framed by another competing and upcoming star. A woman accused him of sexual advances in his salon. The charge was bogus, but no matter, he was blackmailed by the competitor. As a result, Aniello bowed out of both the salon and bookie businesses and his competitor took over both. Finally, he landed a job in the Boston subway system. It took powerful influences from corrupt politicians for him to land that job. He was demoted to being a clerk selling train tickets after he rammed a subway train into a dead-end station at Cleveland Circle, Boston.

One topic that seemed to preoccupy Aniello was the farms that were left abandoned by his father when he came to America. In Italy, there are too many incidents in which squatters were taking over abandoned farms. Albanians, who emigrated to Italy, specialized in taking over abandoned farms owned by farmers who emigrated to the USA, as reported frequently in Italian newspapers and RAI radio. After occupying a farm for a certain number of years a squatter could claim the farm legally, according to new laws enacted in Italy.

Aniello worried that someone would take over the farms and properties and, therefore, he put his cousin, a lawyer, in charge of everything. Unfortunately for Aniello, his cousin was a bigger crook than the Albanian squatters. Unbeknownst to Aniello, the cousin put his name on the deeds. Donato tried to be helpful by telling him that lawyers know how to f…k you over legally. According to Donato, "If Albanians took over your land, at least, you have a legal chance to recover the farms before the law takes effect. You can claim that you never left the farm. As such, squatters can be charged with theft". That was not what Aniello wanted to hear. He wanted to be re-assured by his former hillbilly about his cousin. That was the role designated by him to Donato in the past. Aniello retorted, "I am going to have you deported back to Italy as an undesirable by the immigration office like Lucky (Luciano). What you don't realize is that unlawful squatters can take over properties by demonstrating occupancy even for a short time." Aniello got up from his chair and bolted out of the café, visibly upset. Vito was grateful that Aniello had monopolized the conversation. He didn't know whether to console Aniello or blame him for sloppiness in handling the deeds. These two friends bickered anytime they got together for any occasion, but they always managed to patch things up.

Thus, a new relationship was forged between these two friends. For the first time in his life, Donato enjoyed the new gained freedom in America of being able to speak his mind without being admonished by his former landlord and get away with it. In the old country, he would have been hung from the highest tree, if he spoke in that manner of style or tone to Aniello. Girolamo probably turned over in his grave hearing the temerity of one of his former farm worker giving legal advice to his son. This mind set is reminiscent of the feudal system whereby a serf could not speak to his landlord unless spoken to.

NINE

Out of Las Vegas

Besides the beloved culture-rich cafe scene, the North End has a substantial restaurant presence. There are about 100 restaurants squeezed into one square mile, featuring a variety of Italian dishes sprinkled with new herbs or condiments and, therefore, reflecting the new trend in Italian recipes. In the 1950s, restaurants were family owned eateries which featured foods reflective of the regions, where they came from in Southern Italy. Over the years, the recipes have been bastardized in the sense that the original ones have been modified, since a new generation of chefs have appeared on the scene. The basic difference is that traditional recipes were prepared with condiments, herbs and cuts of meat that cooks were familiar with in Italy, recipes handed down from past generations. Since the mom and pop eateries, many more varieties of herbs, condiments, fruits, vegetables and meats have become available. The new generation of cooks have strived to experiment with new recipes. Some new ones have improved the taste over the original recipes, but others are a disaster. Fortunately for the restaurants, most tourists are not able to discern the difference. A visit to the North End is a culinary experience not to miss.

This evolution of new recipes is unavoidable. Nowadays, a chef would have to go an "extra mile" to cook anything in the authentic Italian way. Original Italian recipes call for at most three to four ingredients. However, the real purpose of the so-called new trend in Italian cuisine is to market cook books which often sell very well. As such, it has a lot to do with appearance rather than taste. Unfortunately, one cannot eat appearance for it only exists in the mind, not in the taste buds.

In addition to restaurants, only two bakeries remain today. At one time there were as many as six. These two bakeries have remained faithful to the old way of preparing pastries in the traditional way, even though there is a new generation of bakers managing the two bakeries. Examples of the old recipes include sfogliatella, parigina, cannoli, baba-rum assorted pastries, farro-ricotta pies, marzipan-base cookies, almond-base cookies, napoleons, etc. Farro-ricotta pies date as far back as ancient Rome. Nowadays, they are usually baked at Easter time together with variations of the recipe that include rice, for example. Initially the clientele was mostly the local Italian-American. Nowadays tourists, locals and suburbanites have grown to love the traditional pastries so much so that standing lines can be seen any day of the week at bakeries. It is proof that traditional pastries have hit a "home run" with customers.

Assorted Italian pastries

There is no supermarket in the North End but, on Friday and Saturday, there is an open Farmer's Market, referred to as Haymarket. During the 1950s, Haymarket sold fish, meats, clothes, shoes, fruits and vegetables, spaghetti, etc. and it spread over Salem, Merrimac, and Cross Streets, as well as at City Hall area.

Today, Haymarket is a lot smaller in size occupying Hanover, North and Blackstone Streets, across from City Hall. Vito's uncle from Everett, like many others who came from Southern Italy, carried on that ritual of

Haymarket on Salem Street in the 1930s.

shopping at Haymarket from as far back as one can remember. It was more of a cultural thing that carried over from the old country, where the farmer's market was available once a week. Fish, fruits and vegetables from all over the USA and South America are sold there in the North End. Vendors buy wholesale from warehouses in Chelsea and sometimes from local farmers. The quality of produce is typically not of the same standard as that of a supermarket. Price varies depending on one's ability to negotiate. Thus, shopping there becomes a hit or miss proposition.

Food recipes at restaurants and produce at Haymarket may have changed with time, but institutions like the historic Protestant Old North Church, Catholic churches (Italian and Irish) remained pretty much constant. In the 1990s, there were about ten Catholic churches; some qualified as chapels. The two main Catholic churches on Hanover St., Saint Stephen and Saint Leonard, practiced their Catholic religion very differently. Saint Stephen (where Rose Kennedy was baptized), affiliated with the Saint James order, employed Irish priests who spoke with a strong Irish brogue.

The subject matter and religious implications in their sermons were significantly different from Saint Leonard Church. Saint Leonard was affiliated with the Franciscan Catholic order, and employed mostly Italian speaking

Saint Stephen Church on Hanover Street.

monks. It was rather difficult for Italian immigrants to understand the Irish brogue, especially since they barely understood English. This difference in religious practices segregated local Catholic worshippers even more.

Most locals belonged to religious societies whose sole purpose was to raise money for college scholarships and festivals. Typically, a society held a banquet in the fall, charging members a substantial entrance fee to attend. Non members attended only by invitation of a member. The biggest society was the Tizio club of Sulmona, a province of Abruzzo. Most of the members were first, second and third generation Abruzzesi from the Sulmona area. The dinner featured a six course meal: antipasto, polenta, pasta, meat (grilled rabbit or pork), a vegetable dish or salad, dessert, and, of course, locally produced wine. The food was farm food typical of that area. Attendees voted on which home-made wine was the best. Competition among home-made winemakers was fierce. Wine-making dated back to the days when they emigrated to the North End in the 1950s and has been kept alive to this day.

At the banquet, besides the dinner, old Italian tunes and, in order to appease the young generation, American popular music was mixed between dancing breaks and dinner. Contacts with local butchers, bakers and deli owners were very important at the banquet. The butchers were known for making the best sausages and each resident wanted to make sure that a particular butcher saved some for him/her. There were three butchers from Sulmona attending the banquets. Ciccio, the baker, who came from near Naples, was a loyal friend of Vito, and would inform him when the farmer's bread was available fresh in his bakery. Vito relished the bread. He was raised on it back in Avella. Ciro, who owned the only deli in the area, featured cheese from Siena, Italy. Ciro would proudly say, "If you have to ask for the price of Siena cheese, don't buy it." People wouldn't dare ask for the price of anything in his deli. The Siena cheese was shipped from New Jersey and only through special Mafia connections. All of these special characters were regulars at this banquet and people made their queries to these merchants.

Each society was named for a Saint. However, membership in each society was totally segregated according to where one came from in Italy. One society, for example, consisted of only Sicilian members, another from the Avellino-Naples and Abruzzo Provinces. Of course, local businessmen were welcome to contribute to the coffer. Elena Santuzzo was one of the organizers and, as such, she could invite anyone, including her good friend Anna, Vito's wife. She was owner of a large apartment complex, with thirty rental apartments, and had been born in the North End. Her marriage had been arranged with a shoe salesman, Danilo, from Sulmona. Her family planned and organized the Tizio banquet each year.

Anna met Elena one summer evening at the bocce courts. Elena usually accompanied her husband Danilo on his nightly walk to play bocce. She was there not so much to keep him company, but to see with whom he was flirting. The bocce courts were well attended by many older and some younger, good-looking Italian men who had roving eyes for the many young, mainly Irish girls living in the neighborhood. These young women were very friendly with the men, flirting and befriending these seemingly harmless older men, but it was not so innocent with the men. They, including Danilo, had different intentions. Sometimes, he could be seen walking away from the court with one of these young women towards the dark waterfront. The gossip in town was that he frequented a Sicilian mistress in Charlestown. On his way home from his factory job in late afternoon, he pretended to his wife that he had to stop over at Johnnie's supermarket in Charlestown to pick up so-called needed groceries before getting home. Elena lamented to other women about all the groceries her husband would bring home besides those of their weekly shopping days.

Typically, while the men played bocce, the wives socialized. During a conversation between Barbara, a neighbor, and Anna, Elena broke in and said she would love to come along shopping downtown with them. It was not easy to get to know the wives of the bocce players; they kept to themselves, isolated by the male oriented society. Elena had a wild streak in her; she could be impulsive. She loved to get out, if she could find someone to pair up with. At that time Barbara and Rie enjoyed going downtown to Filene's' basement to poke around and try to find some good bargains. So, the next day at lunch they met up and that started the outings of bargain hunting. Anna noticed that whenever Elena purchased something, she would pay in cash, even though she had a credit card. It came out later that she did not want her husband to find out about her shopping sprees; so, she always carried a lot of cash with her.

Her four boys were happy that she was getting out of the house, instead of just sitting at the windowsill watching people pass by. She also joined the exercise classes being organized in the Community Center at the suggestion of Anna. Once a year Danilo organized the polenta dish, customarily prepared by men from Abruzzo, at the Tizio Club banquet. Elena made sure to invite Anna's family to the banquet, although her husband did not encourage the invitation. It was all part of him ruling the roost and controlling her venturing into a new life of socializing and meeting people outside of her immediate family circle. Her husband could not cope with the changes in her life though his extra-curricular activities with other women were well known. Danilo would disappear and was more and more absent for no reason, which drove her crazy. Rumors about her husband started her drinking binges which eventually killed her before she turned 50. Elena was such a sweet and loving person, and it was a tragic loss to her four boys and her friends.

Danilo moved in Medford, MA, with the mistress and her mother the day after the funeral. However, that situation created an untenable position for a Mafia mobster who had been married and divorced from the mistress. It did not look good to other mobsters that his former wife was frolicking around town with Danilo. Only through the mediation of Danilo's good friend, Lorenzo, did the situation settle peacefully between Danilo and the mobster. Danilo was advised to marry the mistress with" good" respectful behavior or else.

Competition among local wine makers was the highlight of the evening at the Tizio banquet. Locals made their own wine and stored it in their basements. After a year, the wine was served to be evaluated by the banquet attendees and voted upon. A unique dish of polenta prepared in the Abruzzese style was served as well as many other gourmet dishes. Tomato meat sauce and Parmesan cheese were spread over polenta. The banquet was attended by a thousand or more people. By the time guests hit the dance floor, after that sumptuous meal, they were drunk and happy to move around dancing. Guests of honor were not politicians, but local wiseguys like Alex, Sonny, etc. Scholarship money was awarded to high school students who were either related to the organizers or friends of the organizers. No one complained, since they all thought that it went for a good cause regardless of who the students were. Unfortunately, some recipients never attended any college. In addition, about $100,000 was raised from the evening's festivities, to be utilized for festivals in the following summer.

Naturally, there was competition among the societies as to who would sponsor the biggest name in the entertainment world. However, only four festivals were considered major and were spaced one month apart in the summer. For minor festivals, a statue of the Saint was carried through the streets on Sunday at noon, led by the Roma band, while collecting donations for the church. For major festivals, the procession and live entertainment was scheduled for Friday, Saturday and Sunday. Live entertainment with nationally recognized entertainers from Las Vegas were featured on stage. Most of the money raised at banquets was spent for the expressed purpose of inviting well known entertainers who would draw as many people as possible. It drew tourists from New York City and New England. Today, it is wall to wall madness with people from all over the world as far away as Australia. Hence, life is beautiful for local businessmen during the festivals.

It is not clear to what extent local merchants contribute to the coffer, since they are the ones primarily benefitting from large turnouts.

This craze didn't catch on until the turn of the century. In the 1980–1990's, the festival scenes were rather glum attended sparsely by locals. Entertainment was provided by the local band that played mostly old Neapolitan songs that locals adored and sang along with. It was not unusual to have a local performer on stage singing his or her "heart out". The atmosphere was casual and the band members relaxed passing around jugs of wine; by night time, they were drunk out of their minds.

Typically, the stage was placed at one end of Hanover Street or North Street. Other festivals took place on West and Somerset Streets. Vendors sold food like lasagna, macaroni, grilled hamburger and other meats, shucked oysters, as well as selling toys for children. There was also a BB gun shooting gallery with figurines as targets, a display of the statue of the Saint. The scene is reminiscent of a middle-east bazaar. Tourists enjoyed tasting the ethnic food. Vendors lined both sidewalks of the streets selling their wares and food. Tourists attended in huge numbers so the streets were totally congested. These rituals have been going on for about seventy-five years and the routine is exactly like the ones celebrated in Italy in the 1950s. Interestingly, religious festivals are no longer in vogue in Italy today. The immigrants who came over in the ninety fifties, and their offspring have been organizing these festivals in the exact same style as in the past. Nothing has changed since then.

No one wanted to hear the local talent, usually performed on Friday evenings, but, on Saturday night, more vendors came to squeeze into whatever little space was available on the sidewalks anticipating bigger crowds. Famous entertainers were going to perform on stage at night. The people were jammed onto the street, but thieves didn't mind. Tourists and locals alike anxiously waited for the big show to arrive. In front of the stage, space was set aside for dancing while entertainers performed. Over the loudspeakers raffle tickets were sold during intermissions. It was a somewhat surreal scene to be there listening to a Las Vegas entertainer in the middle of a dead-end street with tourists munching on Italian sausages and pastries.

On Sunday, the priest gave the morning Mass to those congregating in front of the stage. After the Mass, the statue of the Saint was carried through the streets on the shoulders of burly young men. The statue was followed by the priest, important dignitaries, the faithful, and the local band. The band played old, popular Italian tunes that only the old timers would recognize. Unfortunately, the priest also recognized the tunes as well, and he didn't think that they were appropriate. There was constant bickering between the priest and the band leader. The scene is depicted very well in the movie, Godfather II. It was somewhat comical to see some "wannabes" dressed in their $2,000 suits following the procession and some of them being pall-bearers in carrying the statue of the Saint. They would pull out C-notes ($100 bills) to donate to the Saint, making sure that everybody saw them. Yet, they would kill over a one-dollar bill, in their endeavors. The statue made stops at places where store or restaurant owners would donate money. The money was clipped onto straps of cloth wrapped around the statue. The procession continued for the whole day until they had visited all the streets. By late evening, the procession made its way back to the stage while entertainment was still going on. At this juncture, confetti was dropped from the roofs and fireworks began. All the while, it was pure bedlam, as people started to dance with strangers, and tossed confetti at each other. It was a scene reminiscent of Mardi Gras in New Orleans.

Festival scene in the North End.

As mentioned, Italian immigrants of the North End came from different regions of Southern Italy, and, therefore, their customs differed, in some cases, like night and day. It was these differences that were the source of friction and discord among them. However, the common denominator among them was that they had to have a festival in each one's own style. In Sciacca, Sicily, they celebrated "Madonna del Soccorso" (Madonna of the Sea Rescue). The literal translation does not do justice. It is better known as the Fishermen Feast. That tradition has been imported to the North End by those who emigrated from Sciacca to the USA in the early 1900s.

Sicilian-American religious societies often invited well-known and established Las Vegas entertainers to perform at festivals, such as: Fats Domino, the Drifters, the Supremes, Frankie Valle, rock and roll bands, sometimes comedians from New York City night-clubs, etc. Frank Sinatra was invited every year. One year, his name was listed in the program, but he bowed out at the last minute. The obvious question that begged to be asked was: where did the money come from to pay for entertainers like Sinatra? Raffle tickets covered only about 10–15% of the cost of an entertainer. Perhaps, another 15% from banquets. Where was the rest coming from? Either local merchants contributed the money or someone in the Society had special connections with some entertainers, like collecting on IOUs or favors.

Apparently, by not specifying which Madonna, Sicilian fishermen believed that they had a better chance of being rescued at sea when in danger. There are many female Saints in the Catholic religion, and all are referred to as a Madonna. Fishermen are not particular as to who comes to their rescue, when they pray for help, as long as it is one of the Madonna. Thus, the concept of Sainthood to Sicilians is different from traditional understanding of a Saint to other Catholics. In some sense, Sicilians appear to be very democratic in choosing a Madonna at a critical moment, as long as a Madonna comes to the rescue. For most Catholics, a miracle must be performed by a religious person before becoming a Saint. That is not the case in Sicily. Sicilians have discovered a way by which to bypass the Curia in Rome and be able to celebrate whatever and whenever they like by not specifying the name of a Saint, like the Madonna Della Cava (Madonna of the cave). The person may have been a good woman or performed a good deed, but the church did not consecrate her as a Saint. That attitude does not sit well with other immigrants who may be devoted Catholics, used to conventional names of Saints condoned by the Church.

Neapolitan immigrants were no different from Sicilians. In New York City, the biggest Italian Festival, was the feast of San Gennaro, patron Saint of Naples, who was never consecrated as a Saint by the Curia. By and large, Neapolitans tend to be somewhat mischievous in their regard to Saints. The Roma band, important dignitaries, and the priests followed the statue of Saint Mary during the Sunday festival procession. The band leader, a Neapolitan immigrant, would play the song "Mala Femmina", a famous Neapolitan song composed by the comedian Toto, which means roughly, "the woman whore", trailing the statue. Naturally, the priests and some immigrants were offended. They thought that it was blasphemy and that a different band leader should lead the band.

The feast of Saint Anthony was sponsored by immigrants from the Avellino area. Local talent was invited to perform at the Saint Anthony festivals. For some unknown reason, the New York crowd came to this festival in droves, and, especially, tourists from Italy made the trek. They marveled at the fact that, in Italy, nothing as big as this was taking place. This tradition was truly frozen in time and entrenched in the younger generation. When Vito's family first moved to the North End, Saint Anthony Festival was so poorly attended. Vito's dog, a golden retriever, was welcomed on stage to be fed a hot dog or hamburger by one of the band's member and he drank beer along with members of the band. All the while, the band leader sang Neapolitan songs together with the locals. It was truly beautiful to be there.

The Avellinesi (immigrants from Avellino area) were no different from the Sicilian and Neapolitan immigrants. The organizers of the Saint Anthony Society's claim to fame was that Saint Anthony is the patron Saint of Monteforte (Southern Italy), where most of its members were from. Their claim defies history, since the rest of the world knows otherwise. Saint Anthony is the patron Saint of the city of Padua (Northern Italy). Their response was that Saint Anthony vacationed in their town, when he was a child. Obviously, there is enough logic in their argument to kill a horse. They were hell bent in putting on a spectacle, no matter where Saint Anthony came from. After all, it is all in people's mind what to believe. Today, this festival is the biggest one in the North End. Bocce, softball tournaments, and talent shows are scheduled at the same time. Although Italian immigrants had their differences, they were unanimous in maintaining their attachment to the old customs.

Saturday night at the festival of Saint Anthony in the North End.

Interestingly, Vito and Anna have made numerous trips to the town of Avella, Italy. Today, the festival scene is nothing like the one that he remembered as a child. After WW II, festivals attracted people from nearby towns and the streets were full of vendors, and young and old people abounded. Music by local bands blared throughout the streets. Opera productions or classical music which was highly popular with the people then was long discontinued. In their recent visit, the festival was sparsely attended, with only a handful of vendors. The ceremonial procession was led by a priest, but no band. It was hard to distinguish it from a procession at a funeral. The rest of the world has changed with time, but not the festival scene in the North End.

TEN

Movers and Shakers

As Whitey was making his power move to take over the Irish gangs from the mid-nineteen sixties to the eighties, Sonny and Lorenzo (Sonny's best friend), were enjoying the best of times. They lived in a cozy housing complex resembling a castle or a large villa near the Cobb's Hill Burying Ground. Their children attended private Catholic schools in Newton, MA, their illicit business was thriving and Turiddu was showing more trust and confidence in both of them. In short, they were the movers and shakers of the North End. Fortunately for them, the long arm of Whitey did not yet reach there during his power moves.

By the late 1960s, Sonny and Jesse had two children, Carmela and Sal. They attended kindergarten and driven to school by a person Sonny would often call "half-a-day". That was because "half-a-day" worked at Boston City Hall for a half-day and still got paid full-day wages. There were benefits in Sonny's bribing City Hall commissioners who employed "half-a-day". The car-pool driven by "half-a-day" included Sonny's children plus Alex and his two sisters, who lived in the courtyard complex. From the day they were born, Alex and Sal were the apples of their fathers' eye. They could do no wrong. The sisters played second fiddle to the boys. Over the years, this special attention built resentment between the two gender groups. The girls had to work harder to get the attention from their papas.

At a very young age, Sal and Alex served as altar boys at the Sacred Heart Catholic Church every Sunday. They looked so adorable up at the altar, so intense and focused. Both fathers were so proud of the boys beaming from ear to ear. These two boys were no angels. They were full of mischievous behavior. They would organize a group of kids running around town looking for any excitement: stealing fruits at Haymarket, disrupting other kids at playgrounds, hassling tourists, etc. No one dared do or say anything about it. After all, who was going to bring it up to two mafiosi. Sonny was the usher collecting money for the church and at festivals times, Sonny led the charge in collecting money from businessmen during the procession of the statue around the streets.

Father Cucu, short for Cucuzzilo (little zucchini), was born in Naples. He was the priest at Sacred Heart Church and was ordained in the Salesian order. With a name like that, certainly, he must have heard many derisive comments. However, that is not what drove him into the priesthood. He had a passion for bringing old scriptures to modern times and making them relevant to parishioners. He was an exceptional orator and gave excellent sermons, well thought out and philosophical. He was truly a theological giant who did not belong in a small town setting, but more in a theological institute or a divinity school. He related to and loved the parishioners so much that he was involved in a personal way with them and the feeling was reciprocated. He could be found walking the streets where people would come up to him with their problems to get guidance mainly in family problems.

He knew everyone in town by first name. Without his assurance, no real estate deal would be consummated. Cucu was instrumental in Sonny's purchase of his apartment at a ridiculously low price. Buyers and sellers consulted him because he could be trusted. Being from Naples, he was well aware of the superstitious and suspicious feelings of the locals and the ways of mafiosi. Not surprisingly, he got along very well with Sonny and Lorenzo, convincing Sonny to be an usher and Lorenzo to be the ombudsman who overlooked the festivals for the church. He saw Sonny to be a hustler who could be helpful in raising money for the church. It paid off for Sonny to be an usher. He would have hustled Mother Mary for money, if asked by Cucu. Sometimes, faith worked in mysterious ways. Sonny, Lorenzo and Cucu formed a strange threesome. Father Cucu, of course, attended to religious matters, Sonny was in charge of collection and Lorenzo was the custodian of traditions. Lorenzo would warn band leaders to keep the music "clean" during processions of the religious statue.

Come winter, around February, they absolutely had to leave that cold and dreary weather of Boston. They stayed at Lorenzo's house nearby Boca Raton, Florida. Father Cucu's mistress did the cooking. He assumed a completely different personality there. He was at ease in the company of mobsters and conversed on equal footing in their dialect. In Naples, he had seen it all, being in a rough neighborhood of Camorristi. He could have survived then only by taking Camorristi on at their game of one-upmanship.

Their fourth partner in golf was none other than a former North Ender, Mr. Williams, who "retired" from the Mafia. His real name was Gusmano which does not translate to Williams, but the name Williams improved his image. His accent was revealing, no Irish brogue. He was one of the lucky ones to retire from the Mafia and still be able to tell about it. He socialized with people like Meyer Lansky and Bugsy Siegel in the 1930s.

As teenagers, Alex and Sal were getting to be quite a nuisance in the neighborhood. Sonny and Lorenzo decided to cool their asses by putting them to work in Sonny's pizzeria. Sonny opened another pizzeria on Hanover Street within a stone's throw of the Mafia headquarters. However, unbeknownst to Sonny, the capos had plans to open three more pizzerias nearby in which Sonny would train others in making pizza. More importantly to the capo, it meant more protection money coming in to him. In addition, it meant that Turiddu would be in a position to lend money to open the new pizzerias or more shylocking business for him. It was a win-win situation all around. There was no competition from the Irish gang, since they were busy pushing heroin and, perhaps, some cocaine and marijuana, in their neighborhoods. For Sonny, it was a simple case of piggy-backing onto Davide's contacts. From his perspective, he and his brother were collaborating in joint businesses with friends from the Avellino and Miami areas. Davide was more than willing to share his contacts and getting back to what he always enjoyed doing, making pizza in Medford.

As a teenager, Sal attended Columbus High School in the North End. He was hell bent in pursuing his father's career. Sonny recognized early on where Sal was headed and was heartbroken. Another reason that he moved from Miami was to gain as much distance from the drug scene as possible. He didn't want Sal to be exposed to that. Sal was just a brat who needed hard discipline. In a brawl with Charlestown teenagers, there was a shootout in a small park across from the bocce courts. In the shootout, one boy was seriously injured with five bullets in his body. Four bullets were removed, but the last one was left intact near a vital organ. The boy survived, but Sal was caught with a handgun by the police. Thanks to Sonny and his friendly police neighbors, the report was never made official. Sonny wanted to clear the police record as he had a dream for Sal to pursue books and sent him to private school.

However, trouble seemed to follow Sal. After school, he was nowhere to be found. He hung around with the wrong crowd and was basically raising hell in the neighborhood: petty theft, fighting and pushing drugs to tourists. The only activity that Sal participated in high school was on the varsity football team. He was good enough to be voted by coaches on the all-city select team. However, his grades were so poor that the likelihood of a college scholarship was virtually nil. Sonny took Sal out of Columbus High and placed him in an expensive private school run by nuns in Newton. Again, "half-a-day" drove Sal to the school in order to insure that Sal would arrive on time. Also, Sonny hired a tutor to help Sal with homework. It was a painful time for the family. Sal was up to no f…g good at any place.

Carmela was a different story. She was papa's girl and adored her papa. She was quiet and unassuming and loved to work in the library. She was everything that Sal was not: a valedictorian in high school, a 3.61 grade average (maximum of 4.0) and a superb cook like her father. After graduating from Suffolk University, she was hired at City Hall as a mediator between minority people and the Mayor's office. Unbeknownst to Carmela, Sonny opened the door to this golden job opportunity for his daughter. A lot of friends there "owed" Sonny a favor or two. Sonny loved to throw parties at his pizzeria for potential candidates to City Hall at election times. He was influential in getting the votes from people of the North End and knew the art of greasing the palms of candidates. Needless to say, Sonny loved his children immensely. Of course, he was happy for Carmela, but at the same time his heart was aching for his Sal. He had a dilemma. It was obvious to the family that Sal's behavior could lead only to a point of no return. It reminded Sonny of the times when he first joined the Mafia. After all, the son was just emulating his father.

Alex, Sal's friend, worked in Sonny's pizzeria after school and on weekends. School was not his forte, although he had the smarts to become an excellent student like his father, Lorenzo. He put all his energy, into following Sonny's footsteps in making pizza and helping out in the cocaine network. Needless to say, he also rose quickly in the eyes of the Mafia. Sonny took him under his wings. The late seventies could be characterized as the "Golden Age" for the pizza business in the North End and vicinity. However, clouds were looming over the horizon in the name of Whitey. He consolidated all the Irish gangs under one umbrella, the Winter Hill Gang, led by Whitey and Howie Winter. Whitey was beginning to flex his muscles by keeping an eye on Mafia heroin smuggling in the North End and at other Boston districts. He may not have been aware of the connection between the pizzerias and the large cocaine trafficking.

Alex barely finished high school to join the school of hard knocks. He learned to make pizza and eventually, with the help of his papa, Lorenzo and Sonny, took over from Sonny's drug enterprise. Over the years, he made a steady rise among the ranks to become one of the leading figures in the Mafia in the North End, even during Whitey's heydays. For one thing, he fell below "radar" detection for Whitey to notice him. Whitey was allergic to competition. Alex was an up-and-coming starter not well known by his own peers, let alone by Whitey. His operation extended beyond the North End and South Boston, away from Whitey's attention.

Even during the 1980s, at the peak of Whitey's reign in organized crime in Boston, Alex expanded his business by acquiring real estate offices in the North End and in Naples, Florida. In addition, he became the owner of a steak house in downtown Boston. The relationship between Sonny and Alex was like father and son. Every time Sonny won a Bocce tournament, he and the rest of the team would be invited to the steakhouse for a stupendous meal. In addition, he sponsored Sonny's bocce teams in every tournament entered in Boston or elsewhere. As much as Sonny was mentoring Alex all those years, he did not want the same for his son Sal. Jesse, by then, was well aware of Sonny's friends and she forbade Sal to go near any pizzeria managed by Sonny. Alex's older sisters, Teresa and Silvana, were a carbon copy of Carmela, as they socialized together. Both were excellent students in high school. They went on to become teachers in private Catholic schools which paid measly salaries. Alex hired both of them to manage the real estate agency, including rental housing in the North End.

The majordomo of the family was Lorenzo, papa. He and Father Cucu enjoyed reciting poetry in Latin as both were fluent in Latin, Italian and

Greek. Lorenzo was an interesting character. He was well educated in Italian, Latin and Greek literature in the Lyceum school in Abruzzo. Like his friend Danilo, his marriage was arranged to a woman from the North End. He worked in a candy factory in Belmont and the Navy shipyard in South Boston and also operated as a bookie. His wife inherited rental properties in which one apartment was rented to a family whose male residents worked for the Boston police department. The apartment next to it was rented to a Mafia family. Both families emigrated from the same town in Abruzzo and co-existed peacefully for years. It must have made for a very strange relationship between the two families as it was inconceivable that they were not aware of each other's affairs.

Lorenzo was smooth as silk. Much as in the movie "The Godfather" where the godfather was advising Michael, Lorenzo was advising Alex. Tall and handsome, Lorenzo was a cultured man, suave, sophisticated and witty. His pronunciation of the Italian language was exquisite and merciless to anyone who spoke with a dialect. At the bocce courts, he would often entertain tourists with his charm and poetry. His other love was gambling and running a numbers racket for the Mafia in the North End. To the bocce players, he was a pain in the ass, but they welcomed him with his humor and levity. Lorenzo and Sonny would get into arguments about their Italian dialect. He would say: "I don't understand a word you are saying. What language are you speaking?" Sonny would reply in pure dialect: "Parl cum te fat mammat"/"talk like your mother made you." Of course, these conversations were all in jest to tease each other. The annoying thing about him was that in the middle of a bocce game, he would cite poetry in Latin gesturing with his hands, as if he were in the Forum Romano. He had an audience for sure. Most bocce players would like to have thrown something at him to stop his poetry recitals as they were painful to hear. Nobody could understand a f..g thing.

Although Lorenzo loved to compose poetry, he was also a brilliant negotiator. Turiddu recognized that and promoted him to a "Consigliere" position, adviser to the capo. His negotiation abilities helped a friend out of a possible life or death situation. His friend, who emigrated from his town, was carrying on an affair with a woman who had just divorced a mafioso. In ordinary circumstances, it was not unusual, but the problem was that the affair embarrassed a mafioso in the eyes of his colleagues. That was a "no-no". Lorenzo knew both individuals very well. When the affair became public, he explained to his friend, in a very nice way, that he had two options: commit to the woman's family and marry her, or make no commitment. The first option was reasonable according to Lorenzo, but the other option, most likely, would end up with your balls served on a plate at a restaurant in the North End as a special gourmet dish. Lorenzo explained to the mafioso that he could not control other people's affairs, when they were about to get married. Besides, there were practical things to consider: "How are you going to support her high maintenance lifestyle, children and condo fees? If anything you should be paying for the church fees, when they get married". The situation was diffused without consequences. The friend married the woman.

Turiddu put Sonny in charge of all the pizzerias and people working there. The Mafia forced a flower shop owner to sell his place to Sonny at a ridiculously low price to make room for a pizzeria and a tiny space for a carry-out Chinese restaurant. The Chinese restaurant was the size of a closet. Sonny was the manager of both places located on Hanover Street. Part of the cocaine network included a tie-in to the Chinese organized crime whose headquarters was located in Boston's Chinatown. In a matter of a couple of weeks, Sonny had both places up and running—employing five to six people. Sonny was manager of five pizzerias, two located in the North End and three in nearby Mass General Hospital. It was not clear who the owners of those pizzerias were, but it didn't matter. For sure, it was not a mafioso, but probably a relative.

Managing a pizzeria is straightforward once the workers have learned the recipes. However, trouble was brewing on the horizon for Sonny. One sunny day in the summer, there was a big fire in the Chinese restaurant located next to his pizzeria. It was set off by electrical wires. The firehouse was just across the street and damage was minimal. On further investigation by the firemen, it was discovered that the electrical wires from the Chinese restaurant were connected to power lines feeding electricity to the pizzeria. The Chinese manager was tapping electricity from the pizzeria. Electrical bills as high as $2,000 or more per month were common. It was no laughing matter to Sonny. His reputation was on the line. He did not register a complaint to the electrical company or to the Chinese chef. He could not afford to ruffle any feathers in those days or bring attention to the police, especially when he was transporting drugs via pizza houses from state to state. Sonny was becoming more polished and sociable in dealing with situations like this. In the old days, he would have cut the chef's balls off. Now, Sonny saw this situation as an opportunity to hide drugs in the Chinese restaurant. After much wrangling, Sonny and the chef decided that life was more precious than valor and the dispute was settled within days. Sonny became full owner of the Chinese restaurant. So, it didn't matter that electricity was shared.

Sonny and Davide's enterprise and that of Whitey were like two ships crossing paths on the high seas, one never noticing the path of the other. One dealt mostly with cocaine trafficking and the other mostly with heroin. People went about town doing their everyday chores never hearing of Whitey, but Billy, the politician, was a man for all seasons. He was on TV most nights cavorting with celebrities and politicians.

Sonny and family really enjoyed living in the apartment complex on Copp Hill. The apartment straddled Shaft and Quarter streets, facing Copp Cemetery, otherwise known as the Copp's Hill Burying Ground. They were surrounded by Historical sites all around and quickly made friends with neighbors from all over the North End. Within the courtyard Sonny was neighbor to some of the capos including his good friend Lorenzo, Alex's father.

Copp Cemetery is one of the main historical attractions for tourists. A notable burial is Robert Newman's, who was one of two people to place lanterns in the Old North Church. That started Paul Revere's midnight ride to Concord and Lexington [10-1]. It was a nuisance for the neighborhood to have tourists come by and visit the cemetery at all hours, especially late at night, year round. In addition, there was much rowdiness there during festival times among local teenagers. If that was not bad enough, in order to spruce up the cemetery, the City of Boston's Parks and Planning planted trees in the cemetery to embellish the site for tourists, as the "Freedom Trail" bypassed the cemetery. The object, of course, was to invite more tourists to the city, but it meant tourists spilling over to the courtyard where Sonny lived, and more nuisance. Sonny wanted none of those newly planted trees in the cemetery as they screened the sun to his apartment and blocked his view of the ship, USS Constitution, in Charlestown. Of course, he worshipped the sun more than the trees or tourists frolicking around the cemetery. Although it was never investigated, rumors circulated that Sonny had the trees cut at the base. The city decided that it was useless to fight the local "Mayor" and stopped the program of re-planting the trees. In addition, Sonny was made responsible for locking up the gates to the cemetery late at night to prevent rowdy behavior by teenagers.

The cemetery sits on top of Copp's Hill Burying Ground that overlooks the bocce courts and an inlet of ocean water leading up to the Charles River. Charlestown and Bunker Hill can be seen clearly from the cemetery on the other side of the bay, opposite the Old North Church. Paul Revere took a boat ride from the North End to Charlestown before riding a horse to Concord to warn patriots, the Minute Men. The revolutionary battleship USS Constitution [10-2] is docked next to where Revere anchored his boat. This battleship was engaged in 40 naval battles and won them all, early in the 1800s. The ship was able to take advantage of its long-range cannons to ward off other ships. It has been an active ship in the Navy since 1812.

About 100 feet to the left of the USS Constitution is the place where Paul Revere docked his boat in his famous ride from Charlestown to Concord. Bunker Hill Monument is in the background.

Paul Revere was an English immigrant from the island of Guernsey in the English Channel, but also an American hero of the Revolutionary War. He risked his life to warn the "Minute Men" in Concord and Lexington about British troops' arrival there. That was the beginning of the American revolutionary War. He owned a silversmith shop and he detested paying taxes to the king of England. Most local businessmen in the North End today are not aware of who Paul Revere was and what he stood for. Their American dream is painted in a background of green colors. How ironical, businessmen of 250 years ago resisted paying taxes even at gunpoint under British rule, whereas today they have been cowed into paying pizzu. The practices of pizzu in the North End took on different forms and/or practices from traditional Mafia practices.

Sonny took tourists on guided tours around historical sites in the North End, starting from Copp Hill. Sometimes, he extended his tour to Revere's boat landing site in Charlestown. Indeed, he was quite knowledgeable about the sites. He was an avid reader of the American revolutionary war. However, there was another motive for Sonny to chaperone the tourists. He would also "guide" the tourists to the local deli, gelato store (Italian ice cream), cafes, pizzeria, fruits and vegetables store, etc. for them to get a taste of the local foods. This was a way to entice tourists to return. Yes, there were kickbacks from the local businessmen, but Sonny loved to bullshit around with tourists. He was the ideal person to introduce tourists to the North End. Besides, history of the American Revolutionary War and kibitzing with his friends were his favorite pastime. So, it came natural for him.

Most of the stores, including professional offices, were like social clubs. Locals frequented them to do some shopping and, more importantly, to gossip about shared concerns or simply to vent. Also, local customers and store owners often were related to or emigrated from the same towns in Italy. It is through these social contacts that another picture of pizzu emerged. Usually, stores and restaurants were family run, whereby all, except for one extra employee, were family members. The "extra" person did not possess special skills to warrant employment, as the owner had no choice but to hire that person, who was recommended by a local mafioso. As such, owners complained to friends shopping at their stores that they had no control over whom to hire. Obviously, these owners trusted customers enough to vent their frustrations and complaints. They were stating the obvious to anyone who entered the store. Any non-family member working in the store stuck out like a sore thumb. This practice was widespread, including in professional offices. A composite picture emerged as to what really transpired between mafiosi and the local owners. The pizzu payment by an owner was made in the form of employment. As such, no cash was exchanged between owners and the mafioso. Hence, no evidence of coercion or corruption.

It was no secret that all businessmen and professionals in the North End paid some form of pizzu. On one particular visit by a patient to a doctor's office specializing in allergies, he was lamenting vociferously to him about some unscrupulous characters who came into his office proposing business opportunities or investments. The doctor was a second generation Italian-American who received his immunology degree from Cornell University. The proposed investments had nothing to do with stocks or bonds or real estate, but with buying large amounts of illegal drugs for distribution. Obviously, the patient and the doctor trusted each other enough to talk openly. The doctor was complaining that he didn't have an option to say: "No, thank you". He represented one of many merchants and professionals who were coerced into contributing to a pot of money for the drug purchase. As usual, the Mafia invested no money of their own, but skimmed off the top of any profits to be made. Thus, the doctor and others took all the risks and their profit was, at best, marginal, relying on the Mafia for payment! The real issue was that the doctor had no choice in the matter. That type of transaction was not exactly a traditional pizzu payment, but very creative from the perspective of the Mafia. The profits far surpassed the traditional pizzu payments from businessmen or professionals.

Usually, ownership of a family business stayed in the family, when the owner retired or passed away. Sometimes owners, who had no heirs, relinquished their businesses or sold them to the so called "extra" employee upon retirement. The new owner, most likely, was related to a mobster who had set up the indirect pizzu payment in the first place. Once ownership was established, the business operated legally. However, legal papers were in the name of the new owner, not the mobster. Thus, it was difficult to determine to what extent this type of corruption went on, since it was difficult to trace the paperwork. For sure, there was some form of an underground economy.

Although there was much to complain about by local owners, there was also much to be thankful for. Business was thriving and some realized their

American aspirations by buying homes in the suburbs. Others stayed behind and upgraded their dilapidated housing. Real estate suddenly boomed, and it became a chic place to live. Initially, tourists came primarily to visit historical sites, but, after awhile, other attractions began to appeal to them, such as: cafe scenes, restaurants, festivals and delis. Residents blended in the background as part of the package. It was like visiting Italy without paying the price of getting there. As for the locals, they knew all along that housing was sub-par, but they liked to believe that they lived in the best district of Boston. Hence, they made peace with the poor housing, because it was worth the price. For one thing, their town was the safest district in Boston. One could walk the streets at any time of the day and night and not get mugged. Also, they lived in the midst of historical Boston, close to downtown with the shopping centers, theaters, health centers, the financial district, movies, and city and state governments, all within walking distance.

Of course, locals were aware of who's who in their town. They even participated in the irregularities taking place in the neighborhood. For example, items that were hot (stolen), fenced items were made available for sale to the locals in the cafes. Many exchanges were done with a nod and a wink without going through the cash register. This was something that they were familiar with in Italy, where it was well known that there was an underground economy, especially in Southern Italy. It is claimed that it represented 50% of the total economy in Italy. Most, if not all, business people in the North End were not affiliated with the Mafia. However, to stay in business, they turned a blind eye to the irregular way of doing business. It was based on "I scratch your back and you scratch mine". Locals were not investigators working for the police, but business people. Thus, there was no incentive to be a whistle blower. It would have been financially suicidal. However, police underground detectives often walked the streets of the North End and they could be spotted readily by the locals. No tourist or local wears a three piece suit in the middle of summer.

The North End is also known for importation of exotic foods from Italy and the rest of Europe. The Mafia has controlled the importation of such goods from Italy, especially from Sicily. The importation of food products from Sicily dated as far back as the late 1800s, when the Mafia controlled that flow of produce to the USA. The Mafia in Sicily favored certain distributors in the USA to sell their products, as "recommended" by them in the USA. The Mafia is not a global syndicate, but Sicilian factions will collaborate with American ones on joint business ventures. Thus, only a few major distributors on the East Coast may sell or distribute imported foods to stores. This meant that an establishment in the North End had better toe the line or pay pizzu with the local Mafia or else go belly up financially. This special connection to food distributors was not just limited to the North End. A nearby supermarket ran out of Romano cheese. On further inquiry about when the next shipment to the store would come, a clerk answered tersely, "When the Don in New Jersey decides to ship it."

Typically, the modus operandi of the North End business world and the locals was pretty much the same, day in and day out, irrespective what was happening elsewhere, including South Boston and Whitey. The world of organized crime was about to turn topsy-turvy with the emergence of Whitey in the early part of the 1980s. He became the sole leader of the Winter Hill Gang. Howie was indicted for fixing horse races at Suffolk Downs. Whitey got away scot-free, although he was equally involved with Howie Winter, [6-7]. Also, Whitey was interfering more and more with Mafia's trafficking of heroin, and expanding into business ventures in the North End. These moves were very apparent to any mafioso, including Sonny. Bookies from all over Boston were turning to Whitey more and more for loans. Turiddu noted that Whitey always came out smelling like a rose anytime there were investigations by the FBI of corruption or indictments into Irish gangs as well as into the Mafia. Indeed, this was a clever way by Whitey to eliminate internal and external competition to his empire by assisting the FBI to do the dirty work for him in eliminating the adversaries. Obviously, he didn't want to share power with anyone, period.

ELEVEN

The Last Emperor

In contrast to Turiddu, Whitey's connections with the politicians, FBI, judges and Boston police department were excellent. It didn't hurt his reputation in South Boston that he got caught trying to ship arms to the IRA (Irish Republican Army). Similarly, brother Billy Bulger was building a political power base never rivaled before among the inner circles of politics in Massachusetts, especially in Boston. No one, even national politicians, dared to challenge Billy politically. As a result, the establishment in Boston backed off from Whitey, when his heroin trafficking began to expand all over Boston, including South Boston and other districts. Whitey declared South Boston to be clean of drugs. Clearly, the establishment was wearing horse blinders, except, perhaps, for the local newspapers. The drug situation was getting out of hand, as Whitey's enterprise was expanding into turfs controlled by the Mafia and other Irish gangs. This called for a meeting between the Whitey-Winter Hill Gang and Turiddu's Mafia faction. This was so reminiscent of the meeting of the Gustin gang and the Mafia in 1931. However, Whitey made sure that this time there was not going to be a repeat performance of that infamous meeting.

Prior to the meeting at Chandler's nightclub where he joined forces with Howie Winter, mobs were not well organized even within their respective territories [6-7]. Bookies ran independent operations, drug dealers had their own networks, bank robbers were not accountable to any gang, etc. After that meeting, no other gang had immunity from police and the law, except for one group, the Winter Hill Gang. Whitey had this dream about bringing order to the independent bookies, etc., but he needed cooperation from Turiddu. There was still much interference between turfs. Whitey had something to offer the Mafia that they never had before—special connections with the establishment—police, politicians, judges, etc. However, the offer was strongly diluted with venom. The Bulger brothers hated the Mafia with a passion, just as much as Sen. Robert Kennedy did. Whitey, being a student of Machiavelli's credo: "Keep your friends close, but your enemies closer" adopted this approach with the Mafia at the meeting. This was time for payback for what the Mafia did to the Gustin Irish gang and Frank Wallace in 1931.

The pursuit of the Mafia by the FBI started with a bold executive directive in 1961 by Attorney General Robert F. Kennedy [5-6]. He ordered the FBI to investigate the Mafia nationally, although FBI director J. Edgar Hoover's main preoccupation at that time focused on the activities of the Communist party in the USA. He especially investigated actors, screenwriters, directors, musicians and entertainers who were blacklisted in the 1950s. Hoover just provided lip service after the Mafia's retreat in Apalachin, NY, in 1957 [2-1]. The "Cold War" in the 1950s dominated storylines in newspapers. The threat from Communist Soviet Union seemed to be so real that it became popular for people to build home-shelters to protect them from nuclear explosions. Reluctantly, Hoover started to investigate the Mafia and initiate a policy for infiltrating it.

Every big city in the USA budgeted more money for the FBI to investigate the Mafia, including the Boston Office. The FBI hired informers to infiltrate the Mafia. For example, Flemmi and Whitey were hired by the FBI to be informants in 1965 and 1975, respectively. Usually, a cheating gambler has an ace hidden up his sleeve, but Whitey had two aces; first ace, the FBI covered his ass no matter what. Second ace, he had political connections to the establishment. As an informant, he could plant any information to the FBI that served his purpose. Unbelievable, but true. Thus, his aim at the meeting was to cooperate with Turiddu, assuring him of political support and putting him at ease, but assisting the FBI's investigation of the Mafia with the purpose of serving indictments that, eventually, led to jail time for most of the capos. Machiavelli could not have planned it any better.

It was no secret that Turiddu and Whitey mistrusted each other. In reality, there were many infractions between Whitey's gang and the Mafia. Turiddu wanted very much to have his Sicilian "zips" expand into South Boston selling heroin, tapping into that large demand. Whitey had his eyes on the number rackets, vending machines and shylocking businesses in the North End. Somehow, Whitey was not aware of the thriving pizza-cocaine trafficking in Boston managed mostly by Alex and Sonny. For sure, Turiddu was not about to share the cocaine trafficking trade with Whitey in his backyard. Lucky for Sonny, he was not caught in the middle of a tug of war between two titans of organized crime. Davide did not enter the picture, since he ran a semi-autonomous operation in Medford. In short, both wanted to expand into each other's turf and collect protection money. Hence, they looked at each other not as potential collaborators, but as arch-enemies to be eliminated. It was the type of relationship in which one dared not turn his back on the other for fear of being surprised.

A meeting was arranged between the Mafia and the Winter Hill Gang in which the following were present: Howie Winter, Whitey and Raimondo's underbosses, Turiddu, and Tebaldo, a mafioso. Cleverly, Whitey gained the confidence of the Mafia at the meeting by offering them police protection, not FBI cover, and political connections carefully cultivated over the years in South Boston. For the first time in the history of the Mafia in Boston, a political connection to the establishment! Turiddu was more than ecstatic by this turn of events. He was quoted [5-9, 6-7] years later about the meeting. "Say what you want about Whitey, but he has got some pair of balls coming here alone, offering protection from the law." As a result, the Winter Hill Gang and the Mafia collected more protection money and had something they never had before—protection from the establishment. Wow! Yes, Turiddu fell for it, hook, line and sinker.

The comment by Turiddu oozed contempt and hatred for Whitey and the feeling was mutual. The Mafia got what they wanted: political connection and more protection money from independent bookies as well as from other independent drug dealers who operated within their turf, mostly the North End. Thus, all independent illegal operations ceased after that meeting. Political connections were like buying life insurance for the survival of the Mafia in Boston. The beauty of it was that they didn't have to pay a single penny for it. The only person who could have guaranteed political cover was perhaps Billy. If Joe "Schmuck" and Howie Winter entered that meeting alone, it would have been a repeat of what occurred in 1931. This was a courageous move by Whitey, especially when the Mullens almost killed him. However, that political protection was just an illusion as the intent never materialized. Whitey just bought time by lulling his arch-enemy into a stupor and taking his guard down. His intent was to rat on the Mafia to the FBI. The ultimate goal was to eliminate and incarcerate every mafioso to avenge the Gustin brothers.

National politicians came to Boston to kiss Billy's ass. Whitey was just a gopher who happened to be Billy's brother. At election times, he reminded people in South Boston of the IOUs owed to Billy. It was remarkable with all the investigations by the FBI, Boston police and State police that it never correlated Whitey's rise in the Irish gangs with Billy's rise in politics. According to Leonardo Da Vinci, there are three classes of people: those who see, those who see when they are shown and those who do not see. However, there is another class of people who choose not to see. The establishment in Boston chose not to see.

In the history of modern organized crime there has never been a case whereby a mobster like Whitey rose from obscurity to become so powerful in Boston. The fundamental question is the following: would Whitey have succeeded in New York City or any other big city without the support of the political system and the establishment? Absolutely not. As a teenager, everybody in the underworld knew of Whitey as a male prostitute and a drug addict. With that background and those credentials, it would have been difficult, if not impossible, for anyone else to rise up from a scumbag position to the most powerful gangster in Boston history. None of the powerful cadre of government officials would have given a second of their time to deal directly with someone like Whitey, unless someone more politically powerful overlooked their behavior toward him. As a young man, he smelled, looked and oozed trouble, given his past performances as a troublemaker. The only way that his past indiscretions could have been overlooked was if someone politically powerful "cooked" the books and cleaned the slate for him. The Air force was forced, by political pressure, to give him an honorable discharge in 1952, although he was jailed for going AWOL.

As much as it was an implausible situation, Whitey actually gained the confidence and trust of both the FBI and the Mafia at the same time. That, in itself, was a remarkable achievement. Since the FBI was protecting his back, Whitey started to eliminate his competition, Irish mobsters and mafiosi, indiscriminately. To begin with, he eliminated his closest ally, Howie Winter. Whitey had him indicted by the FBI for fixing horse races. Whitey was paranoid about anyone rising above him or, for that matter, for sharing power with anyone. Whitey and Flemmi were originally going to be included in the indictment with Howie Winter, but Zip, of the FBI office in Boston, was able to persuade prosecution to drop the charges against Whitey and Flemmi at the last minute. They were, instead, named as unindicted co-conspirators. The information he supplied to the FBI in subsequent years was responsible for the imprisonment of several of Whitey's associates whom he viewed as threats.

Whitey could not have been any closer to the Mafia. He assisted the FBI in eavesdropping on every conversation that the mafiosi were having in their "headquarters". For any closer contact with the Mafia, Whitey would have had to share the same bed with some mafiosi. Thus, Whitey made good on his plan to keep his enemies closer. Interestingly, a lot of associates of Whitey, as well as mafiosi, were indicted or sent to jail during a period of ten to fifteen years while Whitey and Flemmi were never indicted. It is remarkable that no one in the Irish gangs suspected that Whitey was a rat, in view of the fact that everybody else around him were indicted. Lucky Luciano once remarked about murders of mobsters: "If you want to know who did a murder or misdeed, just look around to see who is alive yapping about it." Whitey was the only one yapping, especially after all those indictments.

By the early 1980s, the Mafia in the North End was actively investigated by the FBI for racketeering, horse race fixing, shylocking, drug trafficking, murder, etc. Turiddu was indicted, convicted and sent to jail in 1983. That was the beginning of the end of many mafiosi in the North End. Paradoxically, neither Flemmi or Whitey were aware that the other was a rat. Whitey and Flemmi then took over the remnants of the Winter Hill Gang.

After the incarceration of Turiddu, Whitey was in a position to go after the big boss, Raimondo, who was based in Federal Hill, Providence, Rhode Island. The 1970 RICO Act was invoked by the FBI to indict Raimondo and his associates. Thus, Raimondo and associates in Providence and the North End were either in jail or in hiding. The Rico Act allowed the prosecution of a Mafia syndicate as a whole, rather than individually. The Rico Act was ratified by Congress for the expressed purpose of legally fighting Mafia syndicates as well as other corrupt organizations. The word RICO stands for Racketeer Influence and Corrupt Organization. Prior to 1970, a capo mafioso could order one of his soldiers, a mafioso, to commit a murder and get away with it, since the capo did not commit the crime personally. With the passage of the law, the capo and the syndicate, as a whole, could be indicted for a crime committed by one of the underlings. The penalty for a RICO offense was $25,000, 20 years in prison and forfeiture of all ill-gotten gains and interest in any business. Thus, there was no incentive for a capo to own anything of value for fear of losing it all to the government. It took ten years before the application of the law took effect, because law enforcement officers did not understand the full implications of the RICO Act.

Thus, by the end of the 1980s, much of the Mafia leadership in the North End, as well as in Providence, went through major shakeups. Turiddu, was in jail. Raimondo Sr. died a natural death, and his son, Giulio Raimondo Jr., replaced his father as Capo of the New England Mafia. He staged the induction of new Mafia members in a private house in Medford, MA, and it was recorded on a video camera. The scene was reported on the evening news of all major networks. The ritual of spilling blood with a needle had been a very sacred and a well kept secret of the Mafia for over 500 years. Mafiosi never forgave Jr. for the sloppy way he handled the secret ceremony. Mafiosi as far away as New York City, Palermo, and other big cities were calling for Jr. to step down from his position as Capo Mafioso. Thus, the center of gravity of the Mafia power over New England States shifted to Philadelphia, PA. The Capo from Philadelphia took over the "jurisdiction" of the New England states.

With Turiddu and Raimondo out of the way, Whitey dominated the landscape of crime in the city. Anything illicit was possible by Whitey and the establishment put on horse-blinders to cover up the crimes. Not only did it affect the type of illicit crimes to be condoned, but it also affected peoples' lives in all communities of Boston and nearby towns. In effect, he was the "emperor" of crime enterprise in Boston. In addition to Whitey's long list of crimes, he expanded his repertoire into other crimes including, allegedly, art theft of a museum and the sharing of a winning lottery ticket with a stranger. Every major crime in the city had to have his blessing.

The FBI blamed the Mafia for the theft of 11 paintings and two minor art objects, worth 500 million dollars, from the Isabella Stewart Gardner Museum in Boston, March 18, 1990. It was alleged that an aspiring young

Mafia associate, Bobby Donati, orchestrated the robbery. He belonged to the renegade Mafia faction and was a friend of Vinnie (Vincent Ferrara). In 1990, Ferrara was convicted to 22 years under the RICO Act. Bobby learned the trade of stealing art from museums at a young age from the best recognized art thief in the world, Myles Connor. Together, they had stolen five Andrew Wyeth paintings from a private home in Maine, when both were in their twenties and thirties, respectively. Donati concocted a plan to rescue his boss from the long jail sentence as he divulged the robbery to Vinnie in jail.

It had been alleged that Donati approached the FBI for a possible negotiation in which his Capo would be released from jail in exchange for information leading to the recovery of the paintings. Donati was exposed to the wrath of opposing factions and needed Ferrara's goodwill for protection. Whitey would have been the first one to know about the details of the negotiations, since there were moles, including Zip Connolly, in the FBI competing among themselves to inform Whitey about it. Unfortunately for Donati, Whitey must have discovered his identity. Soon, it became common knowledge in the underworld and, in 1991, the wannabe was decapitated. Clearly, there was no incentive for Ferrara to do away with Donati.

At that time, Whitey was yapping about it to the media claiming to be searching for Donati's killer. If indeed, Whitey was involved with the murder, what stopped him from keeping the paintings? At that particular time, it was too risky to sell the paintings, since the FBI was under pressure to get some leads on the case. The FBI and the whole art world was on maximum alert for those paintings. Keeping or selling them could only have jeopardized Whitey's empire.

So, where were the paintings? Here is a possible scenario. In 1990, there were about 40–50 attacks by the IRA on British troops in North Ireland. However, in 1992, there were 456 attacks by the IRA. Without additional armaments, it would not have been feasible to increase the number of attacks almost tenfold. The connection between IRA members and supporters like Whitey, who tried to smuggle guns to the IRA in 1984, was extremely close. According to Charley Hill, a retired art antiquities investigator for Scotland yard, Whitey gave the Isabella Stewart Gardner Museum paintings to the IRA and they are most likely in Ireland. However, there may be another intriguing possibility. The paintings are still in the USA. They are being used as collateral whereby rich Irish-Americans, supporting the IRA, would advance or loan money to buy arms in Europe.

Whitey then further consolidated his hold on the Irish gangs by making only himself "emperor" of one major Irish gang, the Winter Hill Gang. Flemmi was demoted to an underling. In summary, by the late 1980s, Whitey finally avenged the killings of the Gustin gang by the Mafia. He dispersed remaining mafiosi all over town and into suburbia. Not since Caligula, could anyone but Whitey get away with murder anytime and anyplace in Boston. To the locals of the North End, not much changed. They could still walk about late at night and not get mugged, unlike in the rest of Boston. Apparently, the muggers didn't get the word that there was a new order in town among crime gangs.

As long as mobsters (mafiosi or not) were indicted, promotions within the FBI Boston office kept coming and whenever an FBI agent retired, "uncle" Billy made sure an easy job awaited him at the State level. What a sweetheart deal! As far as the FBI was concerned, only the Mafia was the organized crime syndicate that had to be eradicated. Never mind that 95% of gangland murders in Boston were committed by gangs not associated with the Mafia. Whitey's gang was doing most of the killings! Flemmi, Martorano and Whitey, by themselves, committed more than fifty murders, depending on who was counting. That did not include members in their own gang who may have committed murders. For some obscure or warped thinking on the part of the FBI, it was OK for those three Winter Hill Gang members to commit murders as long as Whitey or Flemmi passed on information to the FBI about the Mafia. Whitey claimed that he passed little information to the FBI. Just enough? Again, who was reviewing it?

Martorano was not a rat and not aware that the other two were the ones. Whitey put Martorano out to pasture by having him indicted by the FBI for racketeering. He didn't want to share the leadership with Martorano. In order to avoid indictment, Martorano left for Boca Raton, Florida. Fortunately for Sonny and Davide, they survived the "inquisition" period by the FBI. Whitey and Flemmi often frequented restaurants in the North End, strutting down Main Street like proud peacocks as if they owned the street, daring anyone to challenge the new order. This was about the time, when Vito and Rie first saw them in the North End. However, it did not register as to who they were.

As Billy gained more political power in the State Senate, Whitey began to take over more and more of the illicit business from the Mafia by simply incriminating more of its members. He created four drug networks in South Boston competing directly with the same operations in the North End. He started the gambling rackets in college and professional football, took over the shylocking business from the Mafia, and was still active in contract killings of potential enemies who competed with him. Although the FBI had ample evidence of Whitey's participation in the killings, they never indicted him. If Gotti In NYC was the "teflon don" in those days, Whitey must have been the "platinum emperor".

It didn't take long for new businesses to appear in the North End, displacing old residents and shop owners. An Irish pub, a restaurant, a boutique dress store, a wine store, a hair salon and a toy store appeared for the first time in the North End. At that time, it marked the time when Vito visited the North End from his home in Newton. The impression then was that, finally, the area was catching up with the rest of the world in sprucing up the place with new stores. All around the North End, new condominiums were also being built, as real estate prices were skyrocketing, even in dilapidated apartments within the North End.

Whitey created the "perfect" discord among merchants in the North End as to whom to pay protection money, the Mafia or him. He did not dare collect protection money directly from local businessmen for that could lead only to a confrontation with Mafia Capos on the whole East Coast. Most of the distribution centers rested with the Mafia in New Jersey and they controlled distribution of foods to the North End as well as to the rest of USA. For the local mafiosi, the protection money was the only source of income, together with drug dealings in the suburbs, away from the watchful eye of Whitey. The loyalty of local businessmen rested with the remaining mafiosi, as they knew that sooner or later the nightmare was bound to be over.

Retaliation from the remaining mafiosi was swift and furious. A pipe bomb was exploded in the Irish pub at 4:00 am to deliver a warning. Whitey counter-attacked in broad daylight by shooting up the apartment complex, where Lorenzo, Sonny, other mafiosi and another family of police officers lived. This was nothing more, or nothing less, than brute intimidation from Whitey. They stormed the courtyard and the living quarters of known mafiosi and had a shootout. Luckily, within the courtyard, the apartments of police officers were located next to Lorenzo's apartment. The police officers were able to beat back the onslaught of visitors. It resulted in one dead and three seriously injured. The shooting made front page in the Boston Globe. Police investigation yielded nothing as to who was behind the shooting. In all the news reporting, Whitey's name was not mentioned once!

When friends asked Lorenzo at the bocce courts what happened, he replied: "What are you talking about?" He must have been drunk on omerta wine. He appeared to be nonchalant and dismissive, as if to say: "What's the big deal." In another encounter, it pitted the same family living in the courtyard against some young thugs, who dealt in drugs who were affiliated with Whitey. In a restaurant in Charlestown, a shootout took place, again, between these two groups resulting in three dead people and one slightly injured. These two groups, one representing the Winter Hill Gang and the other local mafiosi, were fighting over control of turf in selling heroin in the North End. Again, no mention in the local newspapers of Whitey's involvement. People walked around in numbness, not knowing what to expect next. Vito's family lived in Newton then and he was not aware of these dramatic changes in the neighborhood of the North End, even though he visited the North End often. Sonny, was in the middle of those encounters in the courtyard.

Sonny took notice of those scary events and the message came loud and clear. It was not safe to hang around the North End. He joined his brother in Medford helping Davide to run his pizzeria. However, he still lived with the family in the apartment complex on Quarter Street. Sonny's pizzerias in the North End and nearby were taken over temporarily by Alex. Sonny and Davide decided to stay low until better times. Lorenzo did not have that luxury and stayed put resuming his independent bookie activities. Remarkably, with all that turmoil, the locals went about town as if nothing happened, and the tourists were totally unaware of these skirmishes.

When Vito moved to Boston in early 1990s, the dust had settled. Turiddu was in jail. Whitey was king of the road anywhere in Boston. Everything to Vito, in the North End, appeared so magical and quaint and reminiscent of the old times in Italy. Former mafiosi would return on Sundays from the suburbs to socialize with their friends in cafes. That is where Vito and his wife met some of them and saw "Blondie", Whitey's associate, fencing stolen merchandise. It was such a surreal scene, but so incomprehensible then. The subtle changes of the landscape, such as the establishments of Irish businesses, were not noticed either. Remarkably, residents of the North End as well as surrounding communities went about their lives in as normal way as possible, like any other town in the USA. They simply refused to register in their minds what was going on. The locals just wanted to be left alone in their oasis, no different than times before all that shooting. It was not so much that they were oblivious to or complicit to all that turmoil around them, but there was not much they could do about it anyway. The police did not help in quelling anything.

Sonny made some appearances in the North End on Sundays congregating in front of cafes bullshitting around with other visiting mafiosi from suburbia. Vito may have noticed him, but did not associate Sonny with the name Guido Alvaro of Cervinara. Sonny was a flamboyant little fucker who ran around Hanover St. from one cafe to another planting his ass in front of cafes waiting for wannabes to adulate or court him. He greeted customers entering the cafes, as if he were a majordomo doing them a favor. Vito's first impression was, "What a fucking hypocrite. How dare he assume a name like Sonny, when his heavy accent reveals his origin." For whatever reason, Sonny kept an eye on the company that Vito and wife kept in the café. Most likely, he had an eye for beautiful women like Anna, Vito's wife. It was not clear whether Sonny was curious about a new resident in town or simply admiring Anna. Either way, Vito would like to have choked him.

Although Whitey claimed that he was not pushing drugs in South Boston, stories reported in newspapers revealed otherwise. In fact, Whitey extended his empire beyond South Boston into Roxbury, invading Martorano's turf. African-Americans controlled the drug scene in Roxbury, since the 1950s. They were affiliated with Martorano. His flight to Florida was concocted by Whitey to keep the Roxbury operation at a low level, not seriously competing with his other drug dealings in the rest of Boston. Whitey could pick and choose any mobster, connected or not connected to other gangs, to sell drugs, since he didn't have to be concerned with omerta. Drug dealings in suburbia were not controlled by Whitey so that Davide and Sonny fell from Whitey's radar screen.

The scenery at the Bocce courts soon changed. Young drug dealers from South Boston, Charlestown and North End would often show up in groups of ten to twenty to conduct their drug dealings in the open. They used the old timers as a background to shield themselves from police or potential federal investigators. The old timers who were regulars at the place were shocked to see this and to witness to what was going on. They all nodded over to Sonny or some other mafioso as if to ask: what the f..k is going on. The new order went beyond the Bocce courts.

Billy was fond of titles like "emperor". He accomplished what his idol, Cicero, could not accomplish all his life, and that was the following: Cicero, in ancient Rome, thought that Senators were better leaders of the Roman empire than dictators and generals and/or warriors on the field. Cicero died trying to reign in the military all his political life. In the end, Octavian had him killed as he could not afford to have him around alive and active. As a Senator, Billy succeeded beyond expectations. He controlled the "warriors" on the field via Whitey. Boston and the State were at his mercy and he wasn't shy about telling people as much. He flaunted his power and the only thing that he didn't do was to wear a Roman toga, when he walked on the streets of Boston. Everything in the State had to have his approval, even a janitorial job at the State Government. To the opposition, he gave them crumbs. For example, the hair stylist under the fake name, Jean-Claude Sassoon (Aniello), who was associated with the Mafia, needed to obtain Billy's approval for a job at the subway transportation department. It helped that his wife was Irish-American and her father, at one time, was a member of the Killeens, an Irish gang in South Boston. Most likely, Aniello's Mafia association as a bookie was not revealed to Billy.

Potential sottocapos (underbosses) went to jail before they assumed a leadership role. There was always some dirt in the past that was overlooked by the police. Thus, it was just a matter of time before the FBI would investigate the individual. Whitey was a source of information, since he kept tabs on both the Mafia and Irish gangs by virtue of having direct access to both camps. It was not until Whitey became a fugitive from the law in 1995 that mafiosi had some relief from FBI investigations. Residents were well aware, of what was happening. They were more upset with the local mobsters for bringing outsiders to their neighborhoods to rattle their cages. They just shrugged their shoulders and went on with their lives, as if nothing happened. However, they shed no tears or sympathy for the plight of the local mafiosi during the years of turmoil, because they understood very well that mafiosi were no angels. Capos rose to the top of popularity by the gun.

151

The cadavers discovered all over the city and outrageous behavior by Whitey were becoming increasingly noticeable to the public that even the establishment had to remove its horse blinders. From past behavior, it was bound to happen. As such, things began to unravel for Whitey, when the Boston Globe newspaper began to investigate the cozy relationship between him and some members of the FBI in the Boston office particularly with John J. Connolly (Zip), [6-7]. Within a couple of months after publication in the Boston Globe, Whitey hit the road. He disappeared from Boston and became a fugitive from the law. Billy Bulger was never investigated or mentioned in the media in the same sentence with Whitey, although Whitey could never have gained the power that he did without the assistance of the political establishment. No evidence has ever been produced to link Billy to Whitey's gangland murders and drug dealings, although they had a very close brotherly relationship and often consulted with each other.

The FBI placed Whitey on the Most-Wanted list in 1995. In June 2003, William (Billy) testified in front of the US Congress stating [11-1], "I do not know where my brother is. I do not know where he has been over the past eight years. I have not aided James Bulger in any way while he has been a fugitive." Billy said that the only contact with his brother during the fugitive years was a short telephone call in January 1995, shortly after Whitey was indicted. That was an interesting testimony in view of the fact that John "Jackie" Bulger, a retired Massachusetts court clerk magistrate and brother to Billy, was convicted in April 2003 for perjury in front of two grand juries regarding sworn statements he gave concerning contacts with his fugitive brother. The question that begs to be asked is, "How is it that Jackie was in contact with Whitey from 1995 to 2003, but not with Billy?" It was inconceivable for Billy not to know what Jackie knew about the whereabouts or news about Whitey, unless one of them lived on the moon. Yes, Billy was not lying to Congress, but he was talking with a forked tongue (a comment attributed to Chief Sitting Bull, the famous American Indian). After 16 years at large and 12 years on the FBI Ten Most Wanted Fugitives list, Whitey was apprehended in Santa Monica, California, on June 22, 2011. On October 30, the 89-year-old Bulger was beaten to death in the United States Penitentiary, Hazelton, West Virginia. Fotios "Freddy" Geas [11-2] was the primary suspect in orchestrating the killing of Whitey and he has not disputed his role.

TWELVE

Blindsided

At the peak of Whitey's empire, Sonny helped Davide operating the pizzeria in Medford, drawing as little attention as possible from Whitey. The only respite from work were infrequent visits to the bocce courts, cafes, and managing his softball team. The bocce courts were impervious to all that turmoil surrounding Boston during Whitey's heydays. As for the bocce players, they couldn't care less about Whitey for he didn't affect their lives. They were aware of him only because his pictures were plastered in newspapers and TV news media, when he became fugitive from the law. Prior to that, his name appeared sporadically in the gossips column of the newspapers. In general, no one in the North End or at the bocce courts gave a crap about gangs or the whereabouts of illustrious mobsters. It never entered or allowed in their minds the subject of Whitey Bulger.

In the period of time when Whitey was a fugitive from the law, many of his subordinates were apprehended and incarcerated. The FBI in Boston was re-organized. Agents who collaborated with Whitey were indicted for abetting Whitey's crime syndicate. In particular, Zip Connolly was indicted on charges of alerting Bulger and Flemmi to investigations, falsifying FBI reports and accepting bribes. Although Whitey left town, he left an epidemic of drugs throughout the area of South Boston, North End, Dorchester, etc. for which he was responsible for. Familiar faces were returning more and more to town. Sonny was showing his face often at cafes and at the bocce courts, especially on weekends. Yes, the town was coming alive again.

Vito was surprised to see Martorano again many years later at Haymarket. In passing, he asked Martorano, "Are you the one? "Yes, I am", Martorano replied smiling. No one else noticed him, although Haymarket was extremely crowded then. What made the encounter so unusual was that, at that time, Martorano was under the government witness protection program, since he served as government witness in the Zip Connolly trial [12-1]. Also, his demeanor appeared to be somewhat deceptive. He looked like a nice old man with a gentle face, curly reddish brown hair, a beautiful suit and a demeanor that would not harm a fly. Yet, he allegedly murdered more than 22 other mobsters. Today, just thinking about having to come face to face with him gives Vito the creeps.

Once Whitey disappeared from the Boston scene, some form of normalcy returned to the neighborhood. For one thing, Sonny returned to pizza making with Alex on Lancaster Street and he helped Alex open up one more pizzeria near the MGH. Also, with Whitey gone, Alex was one to be reckoned with, since he thrived even in bad times, during Whitey's reign. As for Davide and Sonny, they were ecstatic.

They no longer had to look over their shoulders. Carlos Marcello died in 1993. They had been worried that one day Carlos would be looking for them. Carlos eliminated all the people attending those meetings 30 years earlier. Thanks to Trafficante, they were able to avoid the clutches of Carlos. Vito Genovese, in New Jersey, was off their backs long ago, and Whitey was a bad memory. Contrary to popular movies, life in organized crime is full of surprises, fraught with dangers. There is no second chance. The brothers were not about to test their luck again and again in those troubling years.

As a teenager Carmela dated with her mother's consent but, without Sonny knowing about it. When it came to such things as Carmela's dating, Sonny believed in a very strict code of protocol. He was as stubborn and proud as a goat. He himself never adhered to those protocols. The stubborn part stayed with him for the rest of his life. The Italian heritage part of him left long ago, when he wholeheartedly adopted the American spirit. As a young man, he had dated many girls, and no one reminded him of any protocols. After Carmela graduated from Suffolk University, she was employed at Boston City Hall, and married her high school sweetheart, Ryan. For all those teen-age years, Sonny was unaware of their special relationship. However, once the family learned about it, Sonny was extremely happy, especially knowing that the groom was a Boston police officer.

Ryan met Carmela again at a reception for new hires at City Hall where Mayor Ray Flynn was the featured speaker. Carmela was hired as a community representative to the Mayor's office. She took all the complaints from the residents of the North End and East Boston and brought them directly to the Mayor. Most jobs were filled by people with special contacts and this was no exception. The old saying, "It is who you know, not what you know that matters", applied at Boston City Hall. In all fairness to Carmela, she was a people's person who represented the people extremely well and, therefore, was very qualified. However, one could be talented but, without special contacts, it would be difficult to land a job at Boston City Hall. In essence, these appointments are political in nature, particularly in Boston.

She knew most of her constituents by first name and enjoined in welcoming new immigrants to the neighborhood. After all, most of the people that she knew were former immigrants. She was the ideal person for the job and the Mayor soon realized that. She could anticipate problems before they were splashed on the local newspapers and that was exactly what Mayor Flynn needed. Someone to put out the fires before they started. In addition, this was a clever move by the Mayor in hiring Carmela. Normally, the people of the North End and East Boston were represented by two city councilors. By hiring Carmela, the councilors were short circuited. Thus, the mayor was in direct contact with the people, avoiding politicians! He wanted to hear the unvarnished truth from the people. Clearly, he trusted the people more than the politicians. The bottom line was that the Mayor saved campaign money and secured the people's votes without spending time and money campaigning in those districts.

Carmela's groom, Ryan O'Toole, was an Irish-American, who emigrated with his family from Ireland. For generations, the men in his family were employed in the police department. The wedding took place at one of the most expensive hotels in Boston. There were politicians, capos, lawyers, bocce players, policemen, friends from the North End and the groom's friends and members of his extended family from Dorchester. A live band entertained 300 guests, featuring Italian, Irish and hard rock music. The setting was like a Hollywood-staging, with singers and dancers. No expense was spared. The married couple moved into an apartment next to Sonny's but not in the same courtyard where other police officers and Mafia capos lived. This can only be described as an unusual combination of Italian-Irish smorgasbord, very prevalent in Boston. Carmela gave birth to Anthony and Ken soon after marriage.

Carmela's older brother, Sal, was something else. Trouble seemed to follow Sal. The poor kid tried to emulate his father, but fell short. He had that wild spirit of Sonny, but his energy was channeled toward mischievous things that tended to annoy people. Sonny was more a sociable person who loved to interact with people. Sal was no Sonny. For one thing, the times for great opportunities in contraband were closed and, therefore, new illicit businesses were limited. Nevertheless, it did not deter the kid. Newspapers reported a rash of arsons in the North End. Restaurants, bakeries, beauty salons, etc. were set on fire. Money collected from insurance companies paid to upgrade their establishments. Most buildings were dilapidated and in need of repairs, especially restaurants. However, the situation was getting out of hand, when fires were set in apartment complexes. Some of the apartments were not equipped with fire alarms. One tenant jumped out of a second-floor balcony, as smoke from the fire filled her bedroom. Fortunately, the fires did not reach higher floors yet at that time.

Restaurant owners turned to a group of young men led by Sal to set fire to their establishments. It was profitable all around and no one got hurt. Sal and friends from High School organized the scheme to generate enough money to purchase drugs. He was becoming an "earner" according to his own appraisal of the situation. Sonny was not aware of Sal's whereabouts, and, certainly, he was not about to supply Sal with drugs to stop this madness. However, the scheme was short-sighted for there were a limited number of establishments in need of such service. Sonny sensed that something did not add up, no job but plenty of money. They became further apart every day. Sonny tried to avoid even talking to Sal, when they met in the streets. The kid became withdrawn and reclusive and an embarrassment to the family. Jesse blamed Sonny for not reaching out to Sal and getting him out of this nightmarish trip with drugs. In short, the family was torn apart by Sal's behavior.

On the very last assignment, Sal set fire to the basement of a laundry store and the flames from the fire trapped him in the basement. In setting the fire, the wooden steps leading up to the laundry room on the ground floor caught fire at a fairly rapid rate before anything else in the basement. The fire spread from empty boxes to the wooden steps in a matter of seconds. It didn't take long before smoke filled the basement and there were no other escape routes. Sal died. When his body was discovered, he was clutching a picture of his papa. Sadness pervaded the family from Boston to Miami and put tremendous strain on the family. For one thing, Jesse blamed Sonny for Sal's drug addiction by making drugs too available to Sal. But that wasn't true. Sonny tried desperately to find the source of drugs sold to him. If anyone could find out, it would have been him. He never did. It was no mystery how Sal was able to conceal the source. Most likely, the source of drugs came from dealers in South Boston or even the North End. Sonny didn't have a ghost of a chance of finding out. That area of South Boston was out of bounds for him ever since he moved to Boston. He survived Genovese, Marcello, and Trafficante, but not the long reach of Whitey's on his only son.. He could not save his only son. Obviously, Sal loved his papa so much that he wanted to be like him. Jesse blamed Sonny for not being more adamant in steering Sal away from his type of life. By then, Jesse knew very well who Sonny's friends were, but had chosen a blind eye to it, but no more. The rupture between them was too great to overcome. Somewhere along the way the old flame was no longer bright enough to keep the two together and weather the storm. They separated and Jesse returned to her folks back in Miami.

No one on the bocce courts was aware of Sonny's family problems, as he carried on like always, kibitzing with people as usual. But people could sense that something was not right with the man. That special Sonny spark was missing. The first indication of changes in his mood and behavior was watching him play bocce. There was no more of that teasing, sniping and special kibitzing between him and the players. Bocce players leave their personalities, like fingerprints, on the courts in the way they play. The loss of Sal hit Sonny very hard as it was so sudden and unexpected. There were other changes that came to Sonny which again were unexpected. Events taking place in a very different world to Sonny's had dramatic and far reaching effects on his life that snapped him out of his doldrums.

Unbeknownst to anyone in the area, Suffolk University decided to implement the Title IX Law as it applied to athletics on campus, although there were no playing fields on their campus. The law, ratified by Congress in 1972, prohibited discrimination on the basis of sex at federally funded universities. This meant that any university receiving federal funds must make available the same number of athletic scholarships to both men and women students. Suffolk University is located within a stone's throw from Boston City Hall. After 20–25 years of the passing of the law, Suffolk initiated contacts with City Hall via Carmela, an alumna of the University, to secure the softball field at Puopolo Park, also utilized by Sonny's team.

When Carmela informed Sonny about Suffolk University's intentions, he blew a gasket. He declared that he was not about to share "his" softball field with a bunch of "sissies". Sonny coached the men's softball team representing the North End. There was a meeting among Sonny, Suffolk University's representatives and others from the Community Center, with Carmela chairing. After several hours of wrangling with each other, with no give on either side, Claire, the Suffolk softball coach for women, stood up and said: "Listen, you fucker, we are here to stay whether you like it or not. City Hall has already decided. It is the law of the land so get used to it." No one ever talked to him that way with that tone of defiance before, but he liked it. It was love at first quarrel on both sides.

After the meeting, the men's softball field near the bocce courts was shared with the women's softball teams from Emerson College, Suffolk University and other small women's colleges. The men used the field during the week and the women over the weekends. Sonny was a gracious host, when the Suffolk team showed up. He would line up the field with white chalk, make available the softball bases and other equipment from his shed. He was not required to do all that field work. The college only had a permit from City Hall to play at the field and it didn't include janitorial field preparation. The girls brought their own softball gears and equipment. He just happened to like Claire, the Suffolk coach, who was a strikingly beautiful woman.

As a result of the happy confrontation, he spent more time umpiring Suffolk University women's softball games next to the bocce courts. Obviously, it was a way to get together with Claire and, also, help her out with the game. He had coached for more than 20 years and was the life of the party socializing with beer parties after the games with the women players, just like old times in Miami Beach. Bocce and men softball players scratched their heads wondering what the hell he was up to. It was like watching Fellini's movie "Eight and a Half" live for all to see after the games. Sonny's secret did not last very long. It was the gossip of town. Initially, Sonny umpired at home plate in the games on Sunday afternoons. Eventually, he "graduated" to assistant coach of the women's team with no pay or recognition from the University. After a couple of years of traveling around to softball fields at various New England universities, the two moved in together sharing their apartments.

Soon enough Sonny became the team's mascot and "co-coach" of the women softball team. He was personable with the girls and would advise them about anything they wished to talk about. However, Sonny had eyes only for Claire. A relationship soon developed between the two. The girls would take their "mascot" along in the bus to away games in the Boston area as well. He was dubbed the lucky charm. Sonny was in seventh heaven, when Claire told him that the team practiced at Miami-Dade college near Miami for the spring training season, and that he was welcome to come along. Usually, spring training started in mid-March. Miami-Dade college was close enough to Fort Myers for Sonny to take trips there, which happened to be the Red Sox training camp in spring training. Being a Red Sox fan, he looked forward to previewing Red Sox players. Again, the role of Sonny would be the team's adviser or co-coach. Suffolk University did not pay him or recognize his new title, but, no matter, Sonny got a free ride to familiar territory. He needed a break from the cold weather in Boston anyway.

Everything was honky-donkey with Sonny until he had a freak accident. He was hit in the eye by a foul ball, as he was umpiring behind home plate in a women's softball game. Often, these injuries heal by themselves given time. However, his sight got progressively worse. It forced Sonny to get medical attention for which he procrastinated over a long time. In this case, the injury blurred his vision so much so that a surgeon recommended surgery. If that wasn't bad enough, the other eye was diagnosed with advanced-stage of glaucoma. The man was going blind. He had no health insurance or enough cash to take care of his eyes. There are no health benefits and retirement plans when associated with the Mafia. For once in his life, "He rowed up the .... creek without a paddle!"

He came to the realization that whatever he was doing for a living was not going to cure his condition. The only thing that he could afford was medicine prescribed by a pharmacist to delay the inevitable. The pharmacist gave him some financial relief, as he knew Sonny from the days they both shepherded in the mountains of Italy. The pharmacist emigrated from Benevento, near

Cervinara. It seemed that most locals went to this pharmacist for medical advice and medicine, but the pharmacist had no medical license. The pharmacy was owned by two brothers. One of whom was a licensed pharmacist and the other was not. The locals did not discriminate as to which brother gave them medical advice. Medicine was not what Sonny needed in the long run; he needed surgery. He just fooled himself into delaying it.

This was the worst of times for Sonny. In life, a man can put up with the ups and downs but not the death of his only son. Things could not get any worse, when the doctor's prognosis was that sooner or later Sonny needed major surgery on both eyes, better sooner than later. Also, he was color blind. On the bocce courts, players had to tell him the color of the bocce balls. Bocce balls come in two different colors assigned to each adversary, respectively. His only choice was to become a real wage earner and, for the first time in his life, pay taxes to the city, state and federal government. As a limousine driver, he bucked the odds that he would be in a disastrous car wreck yet to come, two collisions in two months. At this rate he would have wrecked all the limousines in the company within three months and endanger himself. Finally, his friend, Maurizio, employed him as a waiter in his restaurant and Sonny was a natural at it. He had the gab and the personality to enjoy the job. Most importantly, he enrolled in the Social Security system.

Everyone in town rallied around Sonny and wanted to help him. He soaked up all that attention and blossomed like a flower, despite his many personal problems. A woman by the name of Filomena, married to a friend of Sonny, was on a mission to help him get Medicare insurance. She was not the only one coming out to console Sonny. It seemed that the whole town cared about his welfare, because he represented, in spirit, who they were, enjoying the American dream.

Filomena's husband was a mafioso sent to jail for a contract killing that he never committed. Sonny knew all about the circumstances under which the husband was arrested, although the FBI in Boston flubbed in this case. FBI agent Paul Rico framed four men for murder imprisoning them [12-1]. In addition, two other mafiosi were also falsely accused on the same contract killing. They were later acquitted, when new evidence was discovered in the FBI files in the Boston office. Rico possessed the critical evidence but never disclosed it to the courts. The evidence was finally disclosed at Zip Connolly's trial in which he was accused of abetting a murder by Whitey.

The three falsely accused men sued the government for $100 million dollars for false accusation and incarceration and won the case, but it didn't stop Filomena from continuing to work for the social Security Office.

She introduced herself to Sonny as a Social Security worker in the Boston Office and impressed upon him that, for the first time in his life, he had to work for a living and be a regular wage earner accumulating points in the Social Security system. As such, he could qualify for health insurance to have his eyes cared for medically instead by quacks at the pharmacy. She would be able to inform him of his status on requirements for benefits or speed up the process. Sonny took the challenge head on, thanks to the moral support of the locals and business people willing to hire him. His vision did not improve, but the extrapolation of losing his sight soon was real. It was a race between when he would get insurance coverage from Social Security versus when he would lose sight.

With all that attention and loving, life was beautiful once again for Sonny. His good friend and restaurant owner, Maurizio, besides hiring him as a waiter, also sponsored Sonny at all bocce tournaments. Thus, he had two sponsors, Alex and Maurizio, and possibly more. Local restaurant owners were kind to him. He never paid for a meal in the North End. In the mornings, for example, he would have breakfast at Luca's restaurant. He and the owner were once co-owners of a race horse. They enjoyed each other's company so much that they performed a comedy skit for the benefit of customers. After serving breakfast, Luca would approach Sonny's table asking if that was all. Sonny replied, "Put it on my bill", dismissing Luca with the wave of his hand implying "get lost", a typical Italian gesture. Luca retorted sharply and loudly, "What f....g bill?", coming out of the kitchen with a long butcher knife. Sonny would get up from the table and embrace Luca and say, "How did I do this time?", in a hushed voice. They kept throwing invectives at each other, as Sonny walked out of the restaurant. Some customers were in total shock, as if they were about to witness a murder. Both Luca and Sonny craved for that reaction from customers. Later, they would compare notes about this or that customer, true clowns. They fooled Vito the first time, but never again.

In a very short time, Sonny went from sitting pretty on top of the world to the bottom of the pits with no means to raise himself to a normal life. In best of times, he was respected by his peers as he was an "earner" in the Mafia for many years. A lot of wannabes aspired to being an earner like him and to be "made" by the Mafia. Wannabes admired and followed him around the North End. Every Sunday, Sonny behaved like a majordomo at a local cafe, although he didn't own the cafe. He would sit in front of the cafe basking in the sun much like a lizard and greet the customers. As always, he offered to pay for the espresso for people that he liked. All he had to do was wink to the cafe owner and declare to his guest, "it's on the house". At first it was awkward for a stranger to accept, but after a while, it was "why fight city hall", Sonny.

About this time, Turiddu and other mafiosi were released from jail, because of bad health or because they had served their time. Most of them were getting up in age, in their seventies and eighties. They were incarcerated in the 1980s with assistance from the informer, Whitey. Sonny was pushing seventy. Alex was thriving and welcomed Sonny with open arms from his exile in Medford. For one thing, Alex was a mafioso to be reckoned with, as he was vying to become the next Capo in the North End. He was no longer that High School kid that Sonny hired to keep him off the streets. He was an adult who knew his way around in the Mafia world. Turiddu was sickly and looking to retire. Like Turiddu, Sonny could not be bothered with internal strife among mafiosi vying to be the next capos.

Most elder mafiosi, including Sonny, had no desire to resume their former roles in the Mafia. They thanked their lucky stars that they were alive, and that they had survived to old age. What they needed most was a retirement plan and health insurance, especially Sonny who needed eye surgery. The Mafia does not provide health insurance. If anything, the Mafia steals from insurance companies, like union funds for retirement. Sonny, of course, was identified with Alex for a long time. He didn't need a hole in the head or to swim with the fishes to be caught in the middle of an internal struggle among mafiosi. Sonny and Davide survived Genovese, Marcello and Whitey. The odds were against him to survive another internal war among the various factions. Also, Sonny was tired of looking over his shoulder. Thus, it was a no brainer for Sonny to relinquish his hold on the pizzeria business to his protege, Alex. After all, Alex managed very well in the absence of Sonny and survived the FBI inquisition and Whitey's meddling. It was time to hang it up, but he could still "pinch hit" here and there to set up new eateries shops. In short, Sonny just faded away slowly but surely.

The worst of times were just about to begin for Sonny. He was too old and uneducated to start a new career and he needed a lot of money to cover his medical expenses. It was traumatic to realize that his life was changing faster than he wanted it to. For one thing, he could no longer be an active "earner" in the Mafia, but was an excellent person for mentoring young people on how to open a new eating establishment like a pizzeria, restaurant, deli, etc. Once the word got around that Sonny was no longer running the pizzeria, the cadre of wannabes abandoned him and congregated around a new star mafioso, Alex. Usually, these changeovers result in bad endings, but not between Sonny and Alex. However, besides the steady waiter job, he moonlighted at other odd jobs. On those jobs, he paid no taxes. He was not exactly poor, since, in his heydays, he had accumulated a small fortune to be able to afford finer things in life. But, he had also spent a lot of it foolishly. Although paying taxes pained him, it was a necessary evil.

In the meantime, Sonny detached himself more and more from the Mafia. In such a situation, the Mafia may "lean" on a former member for favors or advice about routine things, but he is no longer in the inner circle of the "family", or "Cosa Nostra". It is like putting away old china dishes never to be used again. However, the oath of "omerta" is for a lifetime. He or she cannot divulge information about other mafiosi. Sharing information with anyone else was tantamount to compromising their secrecy, omerta, and that would be the last thing a former mafioso would want to do. It puts everyone in danger. In short, Sonny was a has-been.

In some sense, one gained freedom from the Mafia, if one survived to old age. Thus, one left one secret cult society to join another society of civilized people. Other changes included trading in his beloved Mercedes Benz for a Vespa motor scooter. Sonny's eyes prevented him from driving a car at night, but he didn't mind driving around town in the streets and even on the sidewalks with his Vespa in daylight, endangering pedestrians. After a while, the scooter and he were inseparable to the point that he sometimes drove it into public toiletry at the Bocce courts. People quickly moved to get away from the scooter as they knew that he was blind as a bat. Sonny loved his Vespa so much so that he sometimes stored it in his studio apartment for fear that someone might steal it. He had enough financial resources to be able to rent a studio apartment in the North End. This was a financial move for both himself and his daughter. Carmela moved into his large apartment so that her family no longer paid rent. However, she took over rental payments of Sonny's studio which was considerably less than what she paid before. So, it was a win-win situation for both Carmela and Sonny.

Sonny behaved as if he was on top of the world once again. He simplified his life devoting most of his energy on the waiter job. Most importantly, people in town loved him. He was determined to fight like hell to take care of his eyes, since he had so much support. The Community Center at the North End honored him by naming a bocce tournament in his name. He organized the tournament so that an experienced bocce player (often referred to as the captain) was paired with a novice. The pairing was done randomly as the names were picked from a lottery system (out of a hat). However, Sonny could not help but show favoritism. He managed every year to pair Vito with his novice son. Sonny just drew the two names out of his pocket without anyone noticing it, rather than from a pool of names. The other event that he organized was a talent show with children and teenagers performing on stage. The event used to be called "North End against drugs", NEAD. How f…g ironical that he promoted the festivities with such a catch-phrase, when, at one time, he was king of cocaine trafficking. Obviously, he went through some sort of conversion along the way. Both of his grandsons, Ken and Anthony, performed in the first-year's singing contest. Thereafter, Anthony bowed out of the talent show.

Ken and Anthony were as different as night and day. Whereas Anthony was mischievous, Ken was timid and polite. He referred to people as Sir or Madam. Anthony was anti-social. Every greeting from adults was greeted with a snarl, much like an angry dog, as if to say, "Get away from me". He had no time for small talk with anybody, even with Sonny, except with his teenage pals who were up to no f…g good. Whereas Anthony hated school, Ken was bookish. In today's world, he would be called a nerd, but he loved most of all to sing, especially songs made popular by Frank Sinatra. He was a good student and took singing lessons with the hope of following in Sinatra's footsteps. His teacher was a former "big band" leader of the 1930–40s, and very familiar with Sinatra's style of singing. The teacher and Sinatra attended the same High School in Hoboken, N.J. and left town about the same time as aspiring entertainers, one as a trumpeter and the other as a singer. He was very familiar with the music of that time and with singers like Frank Sinatra, Ella Fitzgerald, and others like them.

At Christmas time, Ken's music teacher put together a small band to play music from that era and Ken sang one or two songs made famous by Sinatra. Often, Ken entered singing contests at festivals organized by grandfather Sonny. Sonny had plans to pave the way for Ken with his contacts at the casinos in Las Vegas. Ken improved to the point where he would sing at weddings for pay. As is often the case in sibling relationships, the two brothers fought for attention from their parents. Whenever Anthony was short-changed in affection, Ken paid a price for that; he got beaten up by Anthony. Soon enough a schism developed in the family whereby the two had to be physically separated. Naturally, Sonny was worried about Anthony as he knew, as the sky was blue and the ocean was deep, what road lay ahead for his beloved grandson. He dreaded Anthony's friends as they were a bad influence, but he was powerless to do anything about it. He knew those kids from birth and they were trouble the minute they took their first steps. However, Sonny didn't realize that Anthony was the bad influence, not the other kids. For the first time in his life, he could not control events that affected his destiny or, especially, that of his grandsons. Desperation was oozing out of him in everything he tried to do on behalf of Anthony. He was a broken man, because he loved his grandsons immensely. From Sonny's perspective, it was not clear whether Anthony was mischievous just to get attention from him, or that Anthony was up to no f...g good. Love has a way of rationalizing the worst in a person.

THIRTEEN

Golden Age of Bocce

Vito and Anna were no strangers to the bocce courts, the restaurants and the cafes scenery ever since they rented in Newton. They were attracted not so much by the restaurants food, but by the local immigrants and the different Italian dialects spoken by players at the bocce courts. From their dialects, Vito could tell where they came from in Italy. Even so, he still did not pick up on Guido or Sonny's presence at the courts. Sonny tended to clam up every time tourists or strangers showed up at the bocce courts. Instead of being like tourists, Vito and Anna decided to move to the North End and partake in local activities, like bocce and social clubs. They purchased a condominium on Commercial St., the main street, about five blocks from the Bocce courts in early 1990s.

In their first two months, traffic was unbearable, especially with the highway artery in place then. In order to avoid traffic, Vito sometimes took the orange or the green subway line to the University and was there no later than 9:30 am. He enjoyed reporting that late. At NRL, he reported to work at 7:30 am, and it took him a couple of hours to get his internal "motor" going. Now, he taught one course for the day and attended to his graduate students in the laboratory to go over the latest experimental results generated by them and to plan for future experiments. Lunch was the social hour where he would meet with other faculty members to discuss everything and anything. There was always someone who liked to pontificate and hog the conversation, which turned everyone else off and made them leave lunch early.

At other times, he drove to school and, by mid-afternoon, returned home. Often, he would stop by the bocce courts and kibitz with the players in Neapolitan dialect. Vito purposely spoke in his native dialect just to tease two players, Onofrio and Lorenzo, as they took pains to speak proper Italian-Florentine dialect, although they were from the Abruzzo province in Italy. No one there speaks Florentine-Italian but their own dialect. What a bunch of ball busters! By then, he was known to others at the bocce courts as Vito. It was clear to him that the players there were very talented and, perhaps, had been playing bocce for many, and many years. What made it so pleasant to be there was the players' cordial manners, very unassuming personalities and acceptance of others. It was this combination of personalities and talent that gave rise to a special period of time, when it was relaxing just to be there playing bocce. It was the beginning of the "golden age" of bocce in the North End.

Nevertheless, there was reluctance on their part to engage Vito in a more relaxed atmosphere. The exchanges were formal and respectful, totally opposite of their personalities. Generally, they were suspicious of anyone, especially a visitor who spoke in a Neapolitan dialect and who was also fluent in English. It confused them. Speaking in Florentine-Italian was their way of keeping the conversation formal, and strangers at a distance. Vito's stubbornness in speaking only in his Neapolitan dialect, stubbornness of a goat, only infuriated them more, which he took delight in doing. In truth, they loved to hear the dialect and they did their very best to provoke Vito into speaking it even more. Of course, it was all done in good humor.

His stubbornness resulted from his last visit to Florence, Italy, when he ordered a meal at a restaurant. The waiter refused to take an order unless Vito spoke in proper Italian, because the waiter claimed that he did not understand a single word in the Neapolitan dialect. Thereafter, Vito vowed that he would order only in the Neapolitan dialect at an Italian restaurant. His attitude was that if you want my money, then, meet me halfway. He was not going to be told to speak proper Italian anymore at any place, period. Interestingly, the dialect is dying, even in Naples today. Modern communications, like television, are homogenizing the Italian language throughout Italy. Vito reminded Onofrio and Lorenzo that he spoke the language that his mother taught him, and he was not about to learn a new language. They got a chuckle out of that.

Lorenzo loved the game of Bocce. So much so that he would compose poetry while playing just to distract opponents. The rest of the players couldn't stand a word of his poetry, especially Iaccarino and Sonny. Iaccarino was basically illiterate and shouted at Lorenzo, "Va fa Napule va." The literal translation is, "go to Naples", but the real intent was "go f..k yourself". That only inspired Lorenzo to compose more poetry. It was a way of prolonging the distraction to both Lorenzo and Sonny from their game. On the courts they were fierce competitors. Anything was fair game. For them, the game was beyond the mechanics. It was all mental. After the game, they behaved like lost brothers, kibitzing, joking, amusing and enjoying the summer ocean breeze. Lorenzo would shout, "When will you learn to speak with proper Italian grammar." Iaccarino, who emigrated from Naples, could only talk in the original Neapolitan dialect which is as far away from pure Italian as one can get. "Imbecile, Neapolitan dialect is not even a language. Come to my house and I will teach you Italian," Lorenzo followed up. They just enjoyed throwing "darts" at each other and watch their reaction. All the bantering back and forth was indeed entertaining to the tourists who flocked to the bocce courts curious as to what all the bantering was about, although they did not understand a word of it, except for a few Italian tourists. Other tourists were desperate to find out what was happening, witnessing a murder?

Uberto shouted to tourists watching this spectacle, "Please don't toss peanuts, just bring us wine." However, there was never a lack of food or wine at the courts. Johnny, the owner of the pastry shop, Ciccio's boss, made sure that pastries, wine and food were available to the players. All that bribing didn't do Johnny any good as he rarely won at bocce. When it came to winning or losing a game, nobody took prisoners. They all went for the jugular.

Uberto was born in Reggio Calabria, same town as Gianni Versace, the clothing designer. Both apprenticed as teenagers in Gianni's mother dress shop. Usually, apprenticeship is reserved for family members, but Uberto was talented and the family made an exception for him. Besides, the two were good friends. However, their careers took different paths. Uberto left Reggio Calabria at the age of twenty for Paris, where he apprenticed again at one of the Paris fashion houses, while Gianni stayed with the family business and moved on to fashion houses in Italy. Uberto emigrated to New York City where he worked in the garment industry. There, he was moonlighting, making suits for mafiosi like John Gotti. In Boston, he opened his own tailor shop and continued making expensive suits for mafiosi. His reputation for making the finest suits traveled far and in between to people who could afford them. It was unavoidable that Uberto developed a special clientele of mafiosi and soon entered into joint businesses, like importing expensive suits from Italian fashion houses. He was involved in the "laundering" of money to South America and expanded into the restaurant business in the North End.

His restaurant featured typical Calabrese food, as he was also a good chef. His specialty was vodka-spaghetti in fresh tomatoes. However, the main purpose of the restaurant was to cover its drug distribution. Ironically, his best customers represented law and order in the City of Boston. Mayor Ray Flynn and Police Commissioner Francis M. Roache often frequented Uberto's restaurant, especially during festival times. As the two sat down to order lunch, Uberto would plop on the table a bottle of Carlo Rossi red wine, the gallon size. By the time the food was served and eaten, they drank all of it. They walked straight as an arrow out of the restaurant without paying, with just a smile and a pat on the back on the way out. It was impossible to engage in illicit business without special connections to politicians and policemen. That was and is rule 101 in the Mafia's way of operating. However, to be fair to Mayor Flynn, he was not aware of Uberto's illicit businesses.

Even though there was bad blood between Mayor Flynn and Billy Bulger, Flynn was elected Mayor three times during the heydays of Billy in the Senate. The bad political relationship between the two was due to the fact that Whitey shot the Commissioner's brother, Dennis "Buddy" Roache, in a bar in South Boston. Buddy was paralyzed for the rest of his life. He was a member of the Mullens Irish gang. It didn't help matters, when Flynn appointed Roache over Zip Connolly for the job of Commissioner. Most likely, Billy tried to leverage a political IOU to persuade the Mayor to choose Zip. Apparently, loyalty won out over the IOU, since Roache and Flynn were childhood friends.

The Mayor and Uberto were good friends from way back. Their friendship started from a dire situation for Uberto at his restaurant. Every time it rained, his basement, where he kept food and wines, flooded. Uberto called everybody at City Hall to no avail, since the water drainage was the result of road erosion outside the restaurant. The cobblestone road was built in pre-revolutionary war times and slanted to one side, toward the restaurant. The water drained directly into the restaurant's back door and down to the basement. He requested the county Office of Public Works to at least level the road so that the rain water could drain down to Commercial Street, a main road. As luck would have it, Mayor Flynn walked into Uberto's restaurant for lunch one day. City Hall was only two blocks from the North End, and most employees moseyed down there for lunch, including the Mayor.

The two of them got along splendidly. As soon as the Mayor entered the restaurant with police commissioner Roache, Uberto declared, "Don't bother with the menu. I will cook a lunch for you two." He made a dish of gnocchi in white vodka sauce with a side dish of Italian sausages with red peppers, typical Calabrese farm dishes. He then brought a bottle of Carlo Rossi red wine, claiming that it was his last bottle due to the flooding of the basement. The two visitors finished the whole bottle and looked for more. Uberto was in total shock as he rarely saw anyone finish drinking that much wine and stay sober. That was Uberto's opportunity to show the Mayor the damage in the basement. Within two months, the cobblestone road was leveled and a narrow sidewalk was added to prevent water seepage into the basement. Each Friday, the two visitors returned to Uberto's restaurant and left it up to Uberto as to what to cook for lunch, but Carlo Rossi wine was always a must. Often, the two solicited Uberto's opinion about internal politics of City Hall. The Mayor was most relaxed in the company of Uberto and others at the bocce courts after lunch.

By the mid 1990's, Uberto was married and raising three children in sub-urbia. His pride and joy was his son, Uberto Jr. (Ubertino), who attended the University of Massachusetts, enrolled in pre-med. Ubertino worked part time at the local hospital as a nurse and sometimes he brought a nurse's uniform to his papa. Uberto wore that uniform to the bocce courts and shouted at the top of his lungs, "I have a dream." The response from other players was just as loud, "Yes, but we are going to give you a nightmare." However, Uberto meant something else. His dream was that his son would someday become a medical doctor.

He loved to pretend that he was a medical doctor wearing the hospital's blue garment and jokingly referred to himself as Dr. Bendover. Of course, tourists would take him seriously and some confided to him all that was ailing them. Uberto would jot it all down on a piece of paper with a stern and apprehensive look and say, "I see." Bocce players were shocked to see that none of the tourists could see through that bullshit, but could not help but get a chuckle out of it.

The Bocce courts were built by the Police department of Boston in the 1950's. The person who oversaw the construction was Onofrio. Most afternoons he could be seen maintaining the courts. This required watering, sweeping and rolling a steel drum to level the courts. The city provided Onofrio with a shed in which the bocce balls, brooms, drum roll, and other accessories to maintain the courts were stored. Initially, only Onofrio had the key to the shed. Then, five keys were issued and, after many years, Onofrio grudgingly relinquished the keys to others. He was in charge and City Hall recognized him as the person to go to in regard to the courts. He was born in the Abruzzo Province, and his helper was Iaccarino. The two of them were formidable bocce players and challenged everyone on the courts. It was impossible to have a game without constant chattering from the two of them. They knew all the tricks of the game and were willing to share their secrets to pretty lady tourist. If the lady was pretty enough, lessons on bocce were given free by Onofrio. All the players were amused by that courtesy extended by Onofrio. He was a total ham for pretty ladies. He introduced himself to the ladies as the "lost" great grandchild of Garibaldi from Uruguay, where Garibaldi started a revolution, as well as in Italy later. What a f…g bullshit artist.

When Vito first appeared at the courts in the early 1990s, they were in disrepair. Onofrio handed a list to Vito noting things that had to be done to repair the courts. The dialogue between Onofrio and the Parks and Planning department was non-existent due to language problems. First of all, it was difficult, or near to impossible, to find out who was in charge at Parks and Planning of the courts and softball fields. Onofrio provided Vito the name of the person who had conversations with him in the past. It was like talking to the wall in conversing with the Parks' people. They always kept passing the buck to someone else. The end result was that nothing ever got done at the courts. After many calls and attempts to contact a representative, a meeting with the Parks and Planning employee was scheduled for a Saturday morning, since Vito was busy at the University during the week.

There were too many requests listed by Onofrio. So, Vito cut the list down to the essentials: dirt on the courts needed to be replenished, and there was insufficient lighting at night. The employee immediately accepted the suggestions. Onofrio had the balls to request a bigger shed to house the

Typical crowd at the bocce courts.

big metal roller, wooden benches for tourists to sit on, planting of new trees to beautify the courts and a metal table anchored near the courts to play cards on. Vito was flabbergasted. "Where in the fuck did that come from?" It was not on the list! He thought that somebody must be pulling a lot of strings or bribes in the right place. But then again, Vito was naïve as to the ways of City Hall. Vito wondered who in the hell invited this Sonny? That was the last time that the park employees showed their faces at the courts. At this point, Vito was confused about what role this Sonny was playing. He seemed to hover over both Onofrio and Iaccarino like a mother hen. Was he the son of one of them? Vito couldn't tell from Sonny's dialect. He always spoke English in the presence of Vito. Onofrio was Abruzzese and Iaccarino Neapolitan and their dialects were very distinct. Was he there to bribe the Park and Planning people with a meal at his pizzeria. Yes, Vito was dumbfounded by Sonny's appearances and disappearances at the bocce courts.

Fortunately for the bocce players, Mayor Ray Flynn sometimes came in the afternoon basking in the sun, lying atop a bench built of granite stones. All the players there wondered why he was not at City Hall working like the rest of those "bums". As Onofrio approached him, Mayor Flynn got up and put his arm around Onofrio like he was family. He asked Onofrio, if the courts needed anything. He turned to Sonny and asked him the same question. Fortunately, Sonny had a list ready-only because Vito tried for one year to get Parks and Planning to do something about repairs and additions to the courts. The list was kept in the shed just for such an occasion. Sonny handed the list to the Mayor expecting nothing to be done, because the Mayor appeared to be drunk anytime he came to the courts after eating at Uberto's restaurant.

Within one month, a water fountain, bathroom facility, a new set of lights, new dirt for the courts, new trees all around the courts, new shed, four wooden benches and a card table and chairs were added to the courts. Wow! Onofrio thanked Uberto profusely and instructed him to bring the Mayor to the courts more often. Surprisingly, personnel from Parks and Planning showed up to inspect the works about a week later. Also, they let it be known that next time anything needed to be done around the courts to call them directly instead of contacting the Mayor. Furthermore, they instructed Onofrio to inform the Mayor's office that the work was completed and inspected by them. What a bunch of con artists, Onofrio thought to himself, "Why call them for anything, when the Mayor usually came by weekly. These fuckers only respond to a whip". Although Onofrio was sociable and a people-person, he was naïve about the subtlety of politics. The request of calling the Mayor's office was just a way for them to get political brownie points with the Mayor. He was totally taken aback with all that politeness and courtesy from a bunch of people who couldn't care less, for one year, to even show their faces at the bocce courts.

The budget for parks' maintenance in Boston was approximately ten million dollars in the 1990s. Most of that money was spent in the South Boston, Charlestown, Dorchester, etc. in Irish neighborhoods, although the North End had always supported a democratic Irish or Italian candidate for mayor. For that matter, any Democratic candidate was supported in the North End. For the first time in more than ten years about $30,000 was spent on Puopolo park. Vito tried to explain to Onofrio that as long as the people of the North End voted automatically for any Democratic candidate, the North End will always end up getting the short end of the stick, and it may be their cock. Onofrio understood the latter part of the conversation and agreed. Politicians took his vote for grant. Hence, there was no need to spend any money on the courts. He told Onofrio that he had to learn to vote for the person and not the party. Furthermore, because of tourists, the North End generated 5–10 times more taxes than South Boston and, yet, the North End received one hundred times less money than South Boston from Parks and Planning's budgets. Yes, the North End had been especially f..d over even during the administration of an Italian-American Mayor, Mandolino. It took an Irish-American Mayor to repair the bocce courts!

The first one to benefit from the renovations of the bocce courts was the same person who approved the requests for improvements, Mayor Flynn. He would doze off now under the shades of the trees on a beautiful sunny afternoon after leaving his favorite restaurant in the North End. Again, Uberto would relay to Sonny and others, "I don't know where in the fuck he puts all that wine. He drank one gallon of Carlo Rossi wine at lunch and walks out in a straight line." "Did he pay for the wine?" "Are you kidding," Onofrio retorted. Mayor Mandolino, who was a descendant of Italian immigrants, was more Irish than Ray; he would only spent his vacations in Ireland. He didn't do a thing for the bocce courts. However, when there was a tournament with photo opportunities at tournaments, Mandolino would toss one ball, have his picture taken with the riffs-raffs and leave. It worked as he was elected Mayor many times. He received both the Irish and Italian votes and that was enough to win elections. To insure victory, he would bribe the African-American vote with grants for parks in their neighborhood. The North End got curaz (polish word for stu cazzo).

Vito tried to warn the riffs-raffs that Mandolino had little regard for their needs and that they were being used to no avail. In all the years that he was Mayor, he never appeared at a Town Hall meeting in the community center for questioning or to ask the people a simple question, "What can I do for you to improve your life?" His attitude toward the North End was one of indifference which is the worst feeling a person can have toward another human being. There was much to complain about. The streets were dirty and there was a manifestation of rats all over town. Tourists did not pick up garbage in the streets that they left. Garbage was dispersed all over the streets and garbage pickups were random and usually in the middle of the night. There must have been at least a thousand requests to have garbage pickups at sane hours during daytime, when people worked. Many requests went unheeded.

North End Trash Problems Continue

Garbage galore in the North End.

The Mayor's attitude toward the locals was best expressed in an incident involving Sonny. The Mayor came to visit the Bocce courts and bought a tee shirt commemorating the NEAD (North End Against Drugs) program. As usual, he was in a hurry to get out of there as quickly as possible (after a picture opportunity) and in pulling money out of his pocket, a $20 bill fell out of his pocket. Both Sonny and the Mayor saw the bill on the ground. The fucker was so much in a hurry to get out, he didn't bother to pick it up. Sonny picked it up and ran after him waving the bill. The Mayor turned to Sonny and said, "Keep it." Sonny rolled the bill in his hands and threw it in the back seat of the car and said: "Next time shove the money where there is no daylight so that you won't drop it." He treated the locals as criminals or as a piece of shit, worrying about whether or not it might tarnish his reputation. It was not clear whose reputation: the Mayor's or the limo driver's. A simple thank you would have sufficed.

Sometimes in the mornings, Iaccarino and Onofrio would gather at the bocce courts just to shoot the breeze. Those two were inseparable and their lives centered around the bocce courts. On the days when tournaments were held, they would get the courts ready by noon. This meant sweeping the courts with a large broom to collect leaves and stray small pebbles. This was followed with spraying water on the courts. Then they would bring out from the shed an enormous steel drum roller to press and level the courts. The drum roller was hollow, but still it was an enormous task for these two seventy-year olds. The size of the drum roller was four feet by five feet. If one could "touch" passion, it would have been on those courts. After the roller use, water was sprayed again over the courts to prevent dirt from flying off with gusts of winds. They knew very well that once they took the roller out of the shed, Sonny would come running to them to help out. They enjoyed his company.

There was enough traffic passing by the courts on Commercial Street that sooner or later someone would warn Sonny that the old men were at it again, pushing that monster. Often Sonny would show up berating and lambasting these two old men for undertaking such an arduous job. The two would welcome Sonny as the "prodigal" son that they never had and Sonny felt kinship to both of them. He treated Iaccarino like the father he never had. All that shouting and berating was just a reflection of his love of them. He was a conflicted guy who, on one hand, loathed all the old timers who did not assimilate very well with the American culture. He liked to believe that he was as American as apple pie and ice cream. On the other hand, he was very tender to their feelings and hardships. Sonny may have been one of the most powerful and influential mafioso in the North End, but, yet, he was as soft as a pussy cat to the two old men. Both loved to have Sonny around and watch him finishing up the job while chit-chatting with him. All that berating was forgotten and forgiven.

Bocce players loved to help out and were willing to do the menial work on the courts. They all pitched in to help Onofrio maintain the courts. He was getting up in age and those metal drums were heavy for anyone to push up and down the steps. However, he invariably refused help from anyone. It was a matter of pride to him. The players all thought that he was out of his mind to refuse help. Players loved to watch Vito work around the courts and would tease him about it. Comments like, "Where in the hell did you learn to sweep like that", were hurled at him. It could have been anyone saying that, perhaps even Guido or Sonny. Then, Iaccarino would yank the broom out of Vito's hands and seriously show him how to sweep. He put so much heart and soul into it that people were crying from laughing. Yes, it was sheer theatrical, but it was fun.

Onofrio and Iaccarino knew the North End better than anyone else. They were a source of information and they had no qualms about sharing it with anyone. For whatever reason, they trusted Vito, although Vito never revealed what he was doing for a living. Besides, they never asked. There was an unwritten rule at the bocce courts that no one asked anyone else what he or she did for a living. This rule did not apply to tourists. Onofrio got frisky with tourists, asking them rather personal questions. He would ask for their names, why the visit to the North End, what they were doing for a living, where they came from, and on and on. Sometimes, Onofrio offered a glass of water or wine to a tourist, especially to a pretty woman. Remarkably, when tourists returned to the bocce courts years later, they would remember Onofrio for his kindness, generosity and warm-heartedness. Most times, they returned with a bottle of wine or a gift. By far, Onofrio and Iaccarino were the best players in the Boston area. One thing that Onofrio did not share with Vito was his bag of tricks in playing the game. He looked upon Vito with suspicion as a future competitor. Onofrio noticed that Vito was paying too much attention to his style of playing. He guarded his secrets as if his life depended on it. He was right. Vito schemed to one day depose him as the champ.

Iaccarino was a Neapolitan through and through. He never changed his mannerism and persona: suspicious, superstitious, and proud. Sometimes, he sat on a bench staring at the ocean, lost in thought and no one dared to disturb him. If one did, he would just smile and ignore that person, being very docile. He retired as a vegetables manager at a local supermarket and supplemented his salary by working at the Farmer's Market, Haymarket, on Fridays and Saturdays. About 50% of the fruits were rotten, 25% barely edible and the rest were of high quality. The price and quality were negotiable. Iaccarino was the best negotiator that Vito ever encountered, and cool as a cucumber. He gave the impression that he didn't give a fuck whether one bought or not. He was truly at peace with himself, never pretending to be anyone or anything. For a Neapolitan, he was quite big, about six feet two inches and 250 pounds. Even speaking to him in Neapolitan dialect didn't soften Iaccarino for the easy touch. However, all that changed, when Vito made appearances at the courts. He was one of them and was accepted.

Thereafter, Iaccarino would pick the best quality of fruits for Vito at ridiculously low prices. Furthermore, he would advise Vito as to whom to stay away from in the market. The man was fiercely loyal and brutally honest. After work at Haymarket, he would gather the best fruits of the day and share them at the bocce courts. The man was all heart.

It was amusing to Vito when invited by students at the University to play a game called bocce on campus during lunch breaks. He didn't have the heart to tell them that the name of the game was correct, but the rest of the setting was not. The ground was grassy, uneven and rough. It was more suited for the French game of Boule. The students were enthusiastic and in a blissful mood to play the game. Vito mused to himself, "Why spoil the fun." So, he simply begged off by saying, "It is a very strange game to me. I haven't played this type of game in a very long time." In a way, he was telling the truth and, at the same time, he was lying between his teeth. Besides, when on campus, Vito was dedicated to academic matters, period! However, he did not fool everybody there. Some students had seen him at the North End bocce courts. They gave Vito a "pass".

The bocce courts were surrounded by two softball fields for men and women. The men's softball teams were drawn from local talent and included mafiosi, policemen, lawyers, doctors, bankers, butchers, waiters, financiers, and laborers. By and large, they had been friends for many years, growing up together and enjoyed each other's company on summer evenings by the ocean in Puopolo Park. In the summer evenings, bocce games drew big crowds of interesting personalities, tourists and aficionados of the game. Bocce players came mostly from the North End. However, old friends from the suburbs often drifted back to the city during weekends and would gather in the evening hours on the bocce courts to play, and reminisce about old times. The comradeship among the players was truly heartwarming. Tourists often came by and watched the games. Some knew the rules and others were just curious about it; locals would explain the rules to them. Quite often, sports celebrities and politicians from the State Capitol would show up. Most bocce players had no clue as to who they were. Politicians' aims were to capture or influence voters, and sports celebrities came to unwind or relax.

Sonny was an excellent coach/manager of the men's softball team and loved the job of managing the team as he was basically a showman. Spectators enjoyed watching his games just for that reason. He was a clown, but their clown. There was not a single ounce of mean spirit in his blood. He chatted with the audience during games and reminded them to stay out of his business, although he often instigated the conversations. It was a ruse just to distract opponent players. Regardless of the outcome, a beer party followed the game wherein all were invited, including spectators.

With the coming of summer, Sonny had his hands full with his own softball team and bocce tournaments. North Enders came out in full force to celebrate the Fourth of July. Boston City Hall sponsored a picnic at the Puopolo Park encompassing the bocce courts and the softball fields. Watermelons, hotdogs, hamburgers, corn on the cob, apple pies, and drinks were free to all, including tourists. A stage for children's entertainment, softball and bocce tournaments were organized for that day. Besides being a place for games, people socialized and enjoyed the festivities all around the park with their friends. The master of ceremonies was Sonny. As usual, the Mayor showed up to toss the first bocce ball of the tournament, making sure to have his picture taken with Sonny, Onofrio and the Bocce players. The Mayor was as phony as a three-dollar bill; he had no interest in spending time with the riff-raff of the bocce courts. It may have tarnished his reputation, although he rose from being a limo driver for Mayor White to become Mayor himself. The appearance may have cost him some votes, if he stayed there too long. As always, he left soon after tossing the ball and was photographed with other politicians and bocce players. What else! That was his only appearance in the North End for the year.

On average, there were about 40–50 players playing on three bocce courts. At most, twenty-four players took up each of the three courts. The competition was keen as some of these participants had played the game for fifty years or more, and, most had played since they were 6 or 7 years old. The players were very skilled and may possibly have been the best players in New England. Vito and his wife, Rie, loved the atmosphere, and the sheer intensity of competition among players. Vito surmised that some of these players were not what they appeared to be. In particular, there were some shady characters that one dared not ask too many questions or even dare take a glance at. Most of them avoided picture taking by tourists, whereas Onofrio must have appeared in a "million" (slight exaggeration) pictures taken by tourists. In one instance, one player ripped the camera out of a tourist's hand, who had taken his picture without permission, and took out the roll of film. The players were there to compete in the game that they loved and not necessarily to pose for pictures, supposedly. In that particular case, the motive may have been somewhat suspicious, since Onofrio identified him as a mafioso from the North End.

In the winter, the bocce competition moved inside the skating rink arena where there were two Bocce courts. This was a state facility maintained by state employees overseeing youth hockey programs. Thanks to Onofrio, this frenzy for the game lasted all year round, in contrast to other communities in the USA, which only had summer playing. Enthusiasm for the game, as embodied in the North End, really never existed in Italy. Perhaps, the nostalgia of remembering the times as a child and the comradeship with other children may have re-kindled the interest in the game in the USA.

Most of the bocce players from suburbia were former residents of the North End coming back to the courts for nostalgic reasons and also to reacquaint themselves with old friends. By and large, they were as good players as the locals. They assumed that, since Vito fraternized with the locals, that he was one of "them". They loved to engage Vito about things that occurred well before Vito arrived on the scene. As such, they took the liberty in disclosing a lot of their past experiences which, in some cases were somewhat awkward, since it was difficult to relate to those times in the past. They would ask Vito, for example, if so and so was still swimming with the fish. If that was a joke, Vito conveniently forgot to laugh. Vito wasn't there in the past and didn't want to be there either. Sonny put a stop to this type of chattering by informing them that Vito was "not one of us".

On one sunny summer day, it was beautiful just to be alive enjoying the sun and the breeze. Out of nowhere, a group of students from Fairmont University plopped themselves down around the Bocce courts, as Onofrio was holding court for the tourists. Vito noticed the appearance of the students. Before he could say anything, they rushed over to greet him. Onofrio noticed and said, "I didn't know you were that popular with students." Vito replied that they were boy scouts from PA where he was from. Vito was not about to tell him what he was talking about with the students, no more than other players divulging anything personal. He wanted to keep it that way. Onofrio was an old fox. He knew damn well what happened. He was a nosy prick.

Regular bocce players at the courts.

The game of bocce pits two players assigned with eight ceramic bocce balls of about four inches in diameter [13-1]. Four of them have one color and the others in another and are assigned to two players. Typically, one color is a shade of red and the other green. The "pallino", colored white, is a small ball of about two inches in diameter. The game is initiated by one player (player A) tossing the pallino to a spot on the court. A typical court is about 75'x10'. The surface is flat and smooth consisting of pressed clay dirt similar to a clay tennis court surface. Player A tosses the first of the four balls as close to the pallino as possible. The object of the opponent (player B) is to get closer to the pallino. If player B is not closer, then he or she must repeat tossing bocce balls until he or she gets closer. However, if player B is closer to the pallino, player A must toss however many times until he or she is closer. At any given stage of the game, a player may demand a measurement to see who is closest to the pallino. The measurement in itself invites arguments among players. At the end, when all the balls have been tossed, a point is awarded for each ball closest to the pallino. The maximum points awarded in one round is four, the minimum one point. Whoever reaches 12 points wins.

There are two components to the game: the mechanical and the mental parts. It takes about a year to learn to toss the ball, regulate the speed and the angle of departure from the hand – mechanical part. The mental part has to do with sizing up an opponent exposing the weakness and strength of an opponent, and, most importantly, how to get to the adversary mentally. That is a lifetime endeavor to fine tune the mental part. As in any game, personality traits mark the style of play. A lot can be deciphered of a person's personality from the way the person plays the game. Some are fidgety, others just don't give a fuck one way or the other and then there are the ones who always play mind games.

The bocce courts were designated as courts 1, 2 and 3. The best players played on court 1. Everybody aspired to play on court 1. However, it was no mystery who wore the scars of battles in court 1. It was an honor and recognition to be invited to play in court 1. The aspirants played in court 2 and there were many. Court 3 was reserved for the "scamorse", which translates to smoked mozzarella cheese, beginners or the ones flipping bocce balls in the air. As such, the bocce ball digs holes in the court which is a no, no. Onofrio loved to give bocce lessons to tourists. He was just a flirt socializing with the women. Also, politicians were steered to play on court 3. Onofrio, again, was the point of contact with politicians. In short, Onofrio was the master of ceremonies, the circus ringmaster. He was the glue who bound everybody together at to bocce courts. "Why in the fuck are you doing all of this?" Sonny asked. "We want to spread the word about bocce to everybody", was the answer. He had a dream that someday it was going to be the most popular game in the USA and be part of the Summer Olympic Games. What a dreamer! One had to have respect for such a person. What a beautiful nut case!

On the bocce courts Sonny loved to win and cheated only against old timers. For him, it was like a grudge match against them. It was love and hate relationship between him and the elders, much like the relationship between a rebellious son and father. The old timers reminded him of where he came from and the value system that he was raised with. In a strange way, the old timers represented the father figure that he never had. He hated the fact that the old timers never made peace with the American ways. Sonny would comment to anyone there: "These fuckers don't even know who the Red Sox are."

Vito loved to be a spectator during some of the grudge matches between Iaccarino and Sonny. It was like being at the bull ring arena for the main event. Nobody volunteered to inform Vito about this fellow (Sonny), not even Onofrio. Sonny was a cheater, but Iaccarino couldn't care less. He was going to beat him anyway. Nothing bothered him. Sonny could stand on his head and Iaccarino would not react to it. It was truly a grudge match between these two. Sonny would hurl all kinds of insults and profanities at Iaccarino during the game to unsettle him, but Iaccarino just shrugged it off and returned kisses with puckered lips. That was the only time Iaccarino concentrated so hard on anything. Most of the time, he was aloof about things around him, much like an ape. However, Iaccarino was as good as Onofrio, but more modest. To the spectators it was utterly hilarious and entertaining.

In bocce, there is a constant measurement of distance between two bocce balls and the pallino in order to determine which ball is closest to the pallino. Invariably during the measurements, Sonny would take an extra ball in his pocket without Iaccarino noticing. The extra bocce ball laid furthest from the pallino hidden from Iaccarino's sight. He could have played with two or more extra bocce balls, and it would have made no difference on the outcome. This meant that Sonny played with five bocce balls instead of the regular four. All the while, the spectators would break into a raucous laughter with shock and amazement. Sonny loved the attention from the audience. Iaccarino showed no mercy, as he trounced Sonny often. Then, he would smirk and gently walk over to Sonny to shake hands. That just infuriated Sonny no end, but, within one minute, they drifted toward the benches on the side, and started to play scopa, a card game. They would chit-chat about anything else and forget that they had even played a game. So, all that bullshit and sniping during the game was just theatrics and showmanship for the consumption of visitors. Both loved an audience to show off their art of theatrics. Deep inside, Iaccarino loved an audience, just like the Neapolitan clown Pulcinella of yesteryears.

Usually, the match started out with the two of them staring at each other and with a simple nod of the head from either one of them, like a matador greeting the bull. In this case, the bull was Iaccarino and Sonny the matador ready for the "slaying". Sonny started the barrage by being obnoxious to Iaccarino. It was like watching a live argument between a father and a rebelling teenager. He even changed his name to Sonny so that his name, he thought, would rhyme with apple pie and ice cream. The name could not be more American. Simply put, Vito thought that Sonny was a hypocrite and

This is very serious business—the measurement.

unnecessarily obnoxious toward the older generation. "What a fucking joke," Vito muttered to himself. Sonny continuously berated Iaccarino for not being with it, the language, mannerism, etc. He looked at Iaccarino as someone from the Stone Age who never changed his ways. Players would smirk, laugh, and take sides in support of one or the other. Most of them supported Sonny. Vito sided with Iaccarino, but he kept it to himself. He had the feeling that this is one guy not to mess with. Vito noticed something familiar about that trick of picking the extra ball, but he could not place it from where.

It was difficult to decipher what Sonny did for a living or where he emigrated from. Vito had a pretty good idea where most players emigrated from based on their dialects but had no clue about Sonny. For whatever reason, he kept his distance from Vito and the exchange between them was short and in English only. One thing for sure, he clearly demanded presence and respect and walked around as if he owned the place. He was always surrounded by burly young men. Vito asked Onofrio what gives with this Sonny. Onofrio nodded his head and walked away as if to say: "I didn't see anything." Sonny's mannerism appeared familiar to Vito but he could not place him anywhere in the past. Also, Vito recognized a trait in

Sonny's personality in the way he played. On every toss, he would spit on his thumb and wipe it off on his pants, a nervous tic.

Finally, it dawned on Vito; on one particular afternoon, Vito stopped by the Bocce courts and, as usual, Sonny was there waiting for Iaccarino. Iaccarino was nowhere to be found. So, by default, Sonny and Vito engaged in a friendly game. Vito noticed the way Sonny held the bocce ball, putting a back spin to it. In his mind, only one person did that and that was Guido from the days of Monte Avella. No doubt in his mind that he was playing Guido and not this impostor Sonny. He blurted out, "Just like old times, eh Guido." "Vituccio bello, forget about the old times. Next time the cops are going to nail your ass and throw the book at you." Vituccio is the diminutive of Vito and Sonny wanted to impress on Vito that he was the big man in town. Sonny was referring to an incident when a police cruiser chased Vito's car into the condominium where he lived.

Apparently, Sonny knew a lot about Vito from some source. According to Sonny, he was aware of Vito the instant he stepped into one of the cafes in the North End. It was not clear if it was facial recognition or the way Vito sipped his espresso or his dialect that tipped Sonny in recognizing Vito. Yet, he never let Vito know of his identity. Perhaps, he didn't want to get Vito in trouble by exposing him to the wannabes, surrounding Sonny in the cafe. After all, that information is not public. Psychologically, he was not about to introduce himself as a made-man. That was not an accomplishment to be proud of. Sonny decided to let it go with the flow.

Thus, after more than 50 years the two of them, Guido and Vito, would meet again. Vito approached Sonny as if he were going to choke him, demanding: "Where is the money that you owe me." Apparently, Guido owed Vito ten lira (equivalent to twenty-five cents) after a bocce game, when they were kids. It was a moment in their lives reminiscent of when they were little boys. He then shouted at Vito like old times: "I paid your f..g ten lira many times over every time you came to the cafe." Other players, Onofrio and Iaccarino were perplexed and curious as to what was taking place. They shrugged their shoulders and walked away, wondering what that was all about. Sonny simply explained, "Nu sim de Cervinara e Avella", we are both from Cervinara and Avella. "So what", replied Onofrio. Finally, Sonny could not contain himself, shouting, "fatti i cazzi tuoi", mind your own f..g business.

Apparently, Vito was driving on Fulton street approaching the intersection of Fleet and Commercial streets. The traffic on Commercial street was backed up all the way back to the Aquarium (a mile from the intersection) waiting for the traffic light to change. It would have taken at least half an hour to break into the line of cars on Commercial St. In a bold move, NYC taxi drivers' style, Vito drove in front of the leading car timing his move onto Commercial St. just as the light turned green. The only problem was that the leading car happened to be a police cruiser. Vito went ahead straight to the garage of his condominium to park his car. The cruiser, with siren full blast and flashing lights, gave chase. As the police officer stepped out of the cruiser, he shouted, "You got to be shitting me, man." Upon further examination of car registration papers, the officer recognized Vito as one of the elders playing at the bocce courts. He then shouted again, "Get out of here before I change my mind." This officer played on Sonny's softball team and reported the incident to Sonny. Yes, even the cop liked that move by Vito.

By now, Sonny knew everything about Vito that there was to know. It was his business to do so in the North End. Henceforth, Vito was not allowed to pay for his espresso at the cafe after church. Sonny picked up the tab with a wink and a nod to the owner. Sonny sat together with wannabes in front of the café facing the street soaking the sun and greeting newcomers. His disposition was jovial and gregarious and welcoming to residents. Sometimes, he went inside the café to chit chat with Vito and Anna. Henceforth, their friendship never missed a beat from the past. Sonny impressed Vito with his "long arm" reach of people in the North End. He knew everybody by first name.

At this point, Vito had a dilemma; should he re-kindle his friendship with Sonny as in the old days in Avella or simply stay away from socializing with people at the bocce courts in general. It was no secret who to stay away from. Onofrio had a pretty good idea who's who in the North End or who was connected with the Mafia. Once Onofrio learned the true identity of Vito and trusted him, he took him under his wing. He warned Vito who to stay away from. He would say, "That one is bad news." In regard to Sonny, he added, "Sonny barks a lot, but doesn't bite."

Clearly, Sonny felt that it was not important to tell Vito what he was doing for a living. In short, he didn't put up any pre-conditions for renewing their friendship. Besides, who in the hell was Vito to demand anything?

A similar situation arose, when Vito first arrived in Aliquippa, PA. His grandfather, Stefano, was lying in bed dying from the dreaded "black lung" disease which was common to many people working in the steel mill. The grandfather asked Vito's mother to call his brother, Antonio. He wanted to see him for the last time. Apparently, they didn't see eye to eye on many things or hadn't talked to each other for more than sixty years. They had a fallout ever since Stefano discovered that Antonio was a mafioso in Detroit. Thus, it was more important for Stefano to make peace with Antonio than to hold a grudge.

At that time, Vito didn't think it was worth making a fuss over. One of his heroes in Avella as a child was Giuliano, a Sicilian mafioso, who was treated by the national newspapers and radio broadcasts as a modern day "Robin Hood". Obviously, Vito was rather naive about the Mafia then. He surmised that it was not his f...g business to judge other people for what they do for a living. He decided to let it go and enjoy what's there, including his childhood friend, Guido. To him, it was always Guido, not that phony name Sonny.

In a classroom at school, Vito recognized one student whom he had seen working at a local store in the North End. The store specialized in the sale of coffee beans from all over the world. Vito had seen him grow up in the North End, when he was selling Italian ices at a street corner. After class, Vito invited him to his office and asked him, if he was from the North End. The student replied, "You know me. I work at Polari store." Vito was concerned about the student's performance in class and suggested, "If you need any help with the course work, come to my lab anytime between 10:00 am and 5:00 pm. If I am not there stay put and wait." That was an order, not an option! Vito took on the parlance of North Enders which the student understood very well. Normally, office hours were specified at a given time and only for one hour.

It didn't take long for the word to be spread in the North End as to Vito's identity. They knew that already due to Guido's big mouth. Besides, they couldn't care less where Vito worked. It didn't ease up the bocce players from busting their balls in trying to beat him. Besides, judges, lawyers, professors, surgeons, etc. walked around the North End incognito. So, no special attention was given or taken. Vito finally had arrived in his element, thanks to Guido as well. Most importantly, the bocce players looked on

Vito as one of their own, a scum bag. He had returned home. Vito's brother remarked on one of his visits to Boston, "You feel comfortable here. You haven't changed at all, since the days you were up in those mountains." "That is true, but I am an American first." Vito replied.

Although most locals were becoming familiar with Vito's family, former residents from the suburbs still treated Vito as an outsider and with suspicion. One suburbanite asked outright, "What do you do for a living and where are you from?" "Sono un Barbiere di Qualita." "I am a barber of high quality." Two locals who were trailing along with Vito looked at each other dumbfounded and were amused by Vito's reply. In unison, they started singing, "Figaro qua, Figaro la, tutti mi vogliono ......". The aria from the opera, The Barber of Seville. The suburbanite was perplexed and confused, because he was not aware of the opera and questioned why the singing. Vito explained the opera part, but not about what he was doing for a living or where he was from. He felt, if people wanted to sing, why not.

Often, Vito went to scientific conferences in Europe and/or in USA and on academic sabbaticals. Onofrio and Iaccarino knew that if Vito was missing for a week or so, he was on travel. They cornered him, when he got back with a lot of questions about his travels. Their curiosity had no bounds. To begin with, they would ask: "Where have you been you so and so?" Vito would take the time to tell them all the details of the trips, but not about science. The two of them sat down like school children listening to every word Vito had to say about those places he visited. They loved the feeling of being there with Vito, although it was only in their minds. Their concentration level was so high that even an exploding bomb next to them would not have been noticed. They needed that distraction from bocce and the North End. After all, they were homebodies who never traveled beyond home. It was the only way they could travel abroad, with their minds wondering and asking a lot of questions about the food, the people, the city and its history, museums, the buildings, monuments and the excursion trips that Anna took with other wives. Sometimes, they wanted to hear more from Anna's perspective than Vito's. Of course, Anna loved to indulge them with their questions. For whatever reason, they preferred Anna's panoramic descriptions of places where she visited with other wives.

The one conference trip that blew their minds was where Vito and Anna visited the Pueblo Indians up in the mountains of New Mexico during a break from the conference. In particular, they liked the Indian dance which Vito partook with the Pueblo Indians. They insisted on Vito showing them how the Indians danced. They absolutely wanted to see Vito dance like an American Indian in the middle of the courts. Then, they joined Vito in dancing along. Of course, they kept f…g up, but, most importantly, they truly enjoyed trying and the laughing. All of a sudden, Sonny and Lorenzo jumped onto the courts and danced along. It was unbelievably hilarious and surreal, five to six Italian immigrants emulating American Indians dancing and humming. They asked about the color of the feathers and pants that they were wearing, what kind of food, what do they do for a living, rhythm of the music beat, on and on to the point of exhaustion. They were mostly interested in the ceramic art work of American Indians as explained by Anna.

They were amazed that there were still American Indians in reservations. They kept asking whether or not the Pueblo Indians were "real" Indians and not actors. The same question was asked at least 100 times. Apparently, they didn't believe that American Indians still existed anywhere else in the USA, but only in movies. Obviously, there was a big gap between their understanding of American cultures and their background. They had no idea how diversified this country was. Given a choice between listening to Vito talking about those trips and playing bocce with Vito, Onofrio preferred the former. Onofrio was getting leery about playing Vito one on one, mano e mano. The competition was getting stiffer by the day from Vito, and he was not about to divulge any secrets, especially before tournaments.

On one sunny afternoon at the bocce courts, Onofrio came over to a bench and sat next to Vito slipping him a piece of paper. He was recounting on the note the episode when he was on guard duty at a roadblock on Via Tiburtina, the morning of September 9, 1943. He described a caravan of 7–8 cars stopped at the roadblock, where, in one car, the King of Italy, Victor Emanuel III, sat in the back seat with his wife. Vito had been forever asking Onofrio to relate to him about his experience in WW II. Onofrio was stationed in Rome during World War II at Fort Bravetta. His face was glowing with pride telling Vito all about the incident. Vito could tell that it took Onofrio a long time to write that two-page note. His handwriting was so meticulously neat with perfect Italian grammar which can be difficult for someone of only third grade education. Someone had helped him put it together, most likely Lorenzo the poet. The two of them talked often about the events of WW II.

Vito brought updated news about Rome to Onofrio and Iaccarino. Onofrio was very interested in Fort Bravetta. When Vito visited Fort Bravetta, it was a museum area in memory of all those partisans (insurgents against Nazis) shot by the Nazis and was no longer an active military base. Names of the victims were inscribed on the monuments. Another museum of those times was the residence of Mussolini, Villa Torlonia, on Via Nomentana, where Onofrio served guard duty also. Now, it is full of drug addicts and homeless people. Onofrio was taken back, more like shocked, when Vito told him that he stood on the balcony facing Piazza Venezia, where Mussolini gave those harangued speeches. Onofrio asked: "How did you get in?" "You have taught me how to be like the Romans when in Rome. Also, you advised me how to grease palms in Rome.", replied Vito. Onofrio was proud as a peacock. Vito could tell that Iaccarino was getting restless. He bluntly blurted out, "Why go to Rome, when you could go to our beautiful Naples, you are a f…g traitor." Obviously, this North and South mind set will never go away, as long as there are people like Iaccarino around. Conversations like that went on forever. Each day different inquisitive questions came up from both of them. They behaved like students in a class. If only University students behaved like that in class, we would have the greatest school system in the world.

On one particular sabbatical leave, Vito visited the physics department at the University of Rome. Usually, when in Rome, Vito loved to stroll in the old Jewish section of Trastevere on Sunday afternoons, researching mementos of WW II during the German occupation of Rome. Also, he enjoyed a unique dish of "Carciofola Ebrea" (Jewish artichoke) prepared only at that location, Via D'Ottavia. As he was walking on Via Lungaretta near the Tiber river, he thought that he saw a glimpse of the former Mayor of Boston, Ray Flynn, sitting at a dining table spread out in the street. At that time, Mayor Flynn was Ambassador to Vatican City or the Holy See. He was appointed by President Clinton. It was a beautiful Sunday afternoon full of sunshine and Mayor Flynn, beaming from ear to ear with a glass of Frascati wine, invited Vito and wife to join his party. He recognized Vito from his interludes at the bocce courts.

The first thing that the Mayor inquired about was the latest news of the whereabouts of Whitey. Vito reported that rumors were floating in the Boston

Globe newspaper that Whitey was hiding in Vatican City and, in turn, Vito asked the Mayor if, perhaps, he might have seen him. The Mayor was taken back, and there was a moment of silence followed by a burst of laughter by both of them. It was just a joke. In a very serious tone, the Mayor related that if he had seen him, he would have chocked that SOB and thrown him to join other emperors in the Tiber River. "Another emperor who belongs in that river is Billy", the Mayor said, talking to no one in particular. Years later that was exactly what happened to Whitey, chocked at the hands of a jail cell mate.

The 1990s and thereafter represented the "Golden Age" of Bocce in the North End. Anyone who was a "who's who" in bocce drifted to the North End, because that was where the best players congregated. They left behind a legacy; only a few have remained. It was an honor to be part of that era.

FOURTEEN

Like a Roasted Peanut

The North End became the Mecca for bocce, as it attracted very good players from all over New England. For one thing, the award money and the food were good. Typically, as much as $50,000.00 was raised at tournaments for college scholarships and players' award prizes. There were 8–10 bocce tournaments a year. Half of them were for the benefit of beginners and the other half for experienced players. The Community Center sponsored two tournaments for the medical staff and employees of the infirmary service, under the auspices of MGH. No ringers were allowed. Coaching was allowed by the older players. This allowed them to partake in the elaborate picnics set up by the Community Center. Boston City Hall sponsored tournaments for handicap children. Each month, Sonny and Uberto were involved in teaching these children about the game and organized their play. It was a labor of love for both of them and the reward was seeing those children smile and have a good time. Each year this tournament grew bigger and bigger as handicapped children from suburbia were invited to the tournament as well as locals. Sonny and Uberto were like saints for they never ran out of patience with these beautiful children. In later years, the program expanded to include also slow learners and autistic children. As this tournament grew in size, other bocce players happily came to the rescue and helped Sonny and Uberto.

As always, Sonny loved to have his grandson, Ken, perform at these events and was going to do everything in his power to promote him to be the next Sinatra. He loved to say: I have a dream for Ken. Anytime Ken sang on stage,

Tournament in which beginners and experienced
players were admixed to compete.

Sonny stopped everything on the bocce courts so that he could listen to him
sing and cajoled others to do the same. Ken exuded confidence and was a
good singer. Players didn't mind taking a break from the tournament. All
the while, Sonny was the master of ceremonies introducing the performers.
However, the other grandchild, Anthony, was altogether another story. Just
like his uncle Sal, he had a knack for getting himself in trouble. He was
knifed by a boy from Charlestown in the yearly scuffles between North End
and Charlestown teenagers. Sonny was determined to keep an eye on this
grandchild. He was not letting Anthony out of his sight and have a repeat
of what happened to his son, Sal.

In the first year of the bocce tournament for beginners, Sonny was hell
bent in wanting to win the tournament at all costs, since it was named after
him. He was teamed with a novice from out of town, supposedly a tourist.
As it turned out, the tourist was no novice but a "ringer" from New Haven,
Connecticut. A ringer is one who pretends to be a novice, when in fact he
or she is a damn good player. He also happened to be Sonny's cousin. There
were 32 teams to begin with, but, in the end, it pitted Sonny's and Vito's

team. However, Vito's teammates were truly novices, Jens and a stranger. The stranger was a tourist from Toledo, Ohio, who happened to be at the picnic munching on food. Vito invited him to be on the team, as he had a soft heart for Toledo. He needed a lot of instructions on how to play the game and Jens helped coach the novice. He looked lost and pleaded with Jens as to what to do on every toss of the bocce ball. During the game, both Sonny and Vito kept an eye on each other making sure that one did not cheat to gain an advantage over the other. It was like a cat and mouse game of matching wits with each other since they knew each other's tendencies. However, it didn't stop Sonny from distracting the visitor from Toledo by singing loud Beatles songs and engaging him in useless conversation. Vito would retort by saying, "Va fa Napule" (go to Naples). That was a polite way of saying, "Go f..k yourself and leave my man alone." Sonny's team was leading by the score of 10–1. Twelve points were needed to win. Sonny was happy as a pig waddling in mud, shouting at the top of his lungs Martin Luther King's famous line, "I have a dream". In the end, Vito's team made a strong comeback to defeat Sonny's team 12–10.

After kicking dirt on the ground, in the manner of Billy Martin, the Yankees baseball manager, and fussing about Vito's cheating to the referees, Sonny came over to Vito with open arms to embrace him and said: "Of all the people here, I am very happy you won. Just like old times, hey." Together they formed a team to take on major Bocce tournaments of professionals any place in New England. This meant that they needed sponsors to enter such tournaments. It cost a minimum of $200 per player to enter. The team of Sonny and Vito would certainly be in a position to seriously challenge the team of Onofrio and Iaccarino for the first time. At the very least Onofrio and Iaccarino would be put on notice that the two Avellino players were ready to dethrone them. Promptly, Sonny assured Vito that he would take care of the sponsors from the North End, Alex and/or Maurizio. After all, he was the social king of the North End and would have no problem doing so.

On average there were 3–4 major (professional) Bocce tournaments per year in the North End. On June 3rd, the Italian consulate of Boston sponsored a tournament celebrating Italian Republic Day. It was open to anyone. However, beginners didn't have a ghost of a chance in winning a game. Bocce teams from New Hampshire to Connecticut came to the North End to compete. The winning purse was $5,000 for first place and competition was fierce among a hundred or more contestants. Each team was composed of four players; Sonny, Vito and two other local players made up one team. The main competition came from the "old guards", Iaccarino, Onofrio and two others. The jockeying for the make-up of the teams was unbearable.

Players practiced before the tournament to impress would-be teammates. Sonny lived for this moment and loved the atmosphere of the festivities surrounding the courts. Politicians, such as city councilors, mayoral candidates, congressional candidates, gubernatorial and senatorial candidates came by to munch on hotdogs or hamburgers and push the envelope for financial support or a vote. Local restaurant owners would bribe players to come to their places to eat for free, if they won. A hotdog and hamburger cook out was temporarily set up by Luca's restaurant near the courts with non-alcoholic drinks and watermelons. Music was blaring from a nearby stage with children full of enthusiasm displaying their singing talent on stage. Police directed traffic away from double parked cars. Spectators outnumbered the players tenfold cheering their players or trying to distract or taunt opponents. It was simply a madhouse, but Sonny and Vito lived for that moment, since they were born.

Onofrio and Iaccarino, combined, had been playing bocce for at least one hundred years. Iaccarino would watch Vito and Sonny play from a distance, scouting the two of them, as well as opponents from other teams. A week to two prior to a tournament, players would jockey for teammates. Basically, they would scout each other to see who had the "hot" hand. Usually, Abruzzi players would form a team from their region and others did the same. Players from the suburbs formed their own team. Although politicians came often to the tournaments, nobody dared invite a politician to play on their team. Putting it diplomatically, they were simply inexperienced players. Politicians usually had their pictures taken and left right after. Sometimes, they stayed a bit longer by tossing one bocce ball and leave. In short, they were a nuisance and a pain in the ass.

Each player was financially sponsored by a local business, since there was a team's fee of $1,000 to enter the tournament. The winning team won a monetary prize of up to $5,000 and a golden trophy handed out by the Italian Consul of Boston. The trophy most often ended up in the lobby of a restaurant or in the window of local business' store that had sponsored the winning team. One pizzeria owner plastered large pictures of bocce players covering all the walls in the establishment. In addition to all these perks for the winners, the restaurant owner invited them to a lavish dinner. The results of the tournament and photos of the winners, politicians, and sponsors were published in the local newspapers. The stakes were high and tension in the air was so high among players that one could cut it with a knife. Jean-Claude Sassoon (Aniello) was so nervous and hyper that he could have flown away easily, if his wife didn't tie him down to the bench. The verbal sniping among players and spectators reached such high intensity that the director of the tournament had to blow a whistle a number of times to quiet things down. The Italian Consul General, the Mayor, City Council members and State Representatives returned five to six hours later to hand out trophies for another photo opportunity. All of them were as phony as a three-dollar bill.

Typically, 80–90 teams consisting of four players, competed in a round-robin elimination. Hamburgers, hotdogs, watermelon, Italian pastries, sausages, French fries, onion rings, salad, on and on were offered. By the time people finished eating, they felt more like taking a siesta, which some did lying down on the benches for a brief rest before returning to the tournament. Remarkably, most tourists and/or spectators stayed around until the end. The biggest problem for the old timers was that if the competition did not eliminate them, dehydration did. Some appeared delirious and hot sitting on a bench and their shirts drenched in perspiration. Sonny was very good at keeping an eye on Onofrio, Iaccarino and other older players seeing to it that they stayed hydrated.

The competition was so keen, players often requested measurements of the positions of the bocce balls relative to the pallino. It was truly a marathon contest. Like a marathon race, it was important to pace oneself in terms of liquid and food intake. In the middle of a game at one of the Bocce tournaments, Sonny's nemesis, Onofrio, came over to him and whispered: "I don't feel good. I am about to pass out." Sonny asked: "Where are you now?" He began to douse him with a water hose. Sonny thought to himself: "He must be cracking like a roasted peanut under the pressure of competition and heat." No, it was mostly dehydration. Although Sonny and Onofrio were foes at tournaments, Sonny admired Onofrio for being a fierce competitor despite his age. In addition, he was the glue that had kept players together to maintain the courts all those years in Boston. He was recognized as the de facto boss of the bocce courts. More importantly, Onofrio was honest and not corrupt as in bribing the referees.

It was pure pandemonium in the end. The winners embraced everyone in sight at the finish, including the Consul General, protocol or no protocol. It was more a feeling of having survived the marathon rather than beating the competition. Sonny and Vito's team won the tournament three times. In twenty-five years the two of them won at least one major tournament each year. Sonny's team was sponsored by Alex who, in turn, prepared a sumptuous dinner for the winners and their wives or girlfriends at his restaurant. It was a five-course meal including two appetizers, grilled filet mignon and dressing, champagne, red wine, dessert wines, etc. The opulence was overwhelming. However, the display of the trophy in the lobby and newspapers covering the tournament and the dinner event with the Consul General gave free ads for the restaurant.

Winners of the beginners/experienced players tournament.

Another tournament which drew more competition and money for the winners was sponsored by the financial district of Boston: Merrill Lynch, Smith & Barney, Morgan and Stanley, etc. In the first tournament, stockbrokers were mixed with the professional players, but that was like mixing orange with apples. It was very distracting for professional players to teach a novice about the game, when there was so much money riding on every toss of the ball. Later on, the stockbrokers ran a separate tournament while professionals coached them from the sidelines.

Besides the financial district, business stores sponsored these tournaments. Vito's small business consulting company (EMA, Inc.) sponsored his team once. He kept the trophy. Food at the tournament was catered by a well-known and expensive caterer and served by waiters wearing tuxedos. Each sponsor paid $5,000 entry fee to the organizers of the tournament. There were 32 teams entering the tournament representing teams throughout New England. Sonny and Vito obliterated the opposition including Onofrio and Iaccarino's team. They dethroned the champions, but Onofrio was a true gentleman and gracious. He knew sooner or later that it bound to happen.

At the ceremony, $2,000 in cash per player and trophies were awarded to both Sonny and Vito and the other two teammates. Sonny motioned to one of his wannabes and ordered him to drive Vito to his apartment, about five blocks away, since it was late at night. Sonny warned Vito, "You never know." At this point, Vito froze and had a chill running up and down his spine. Sonny certainly demanded respect and authority. It reminded Vito of Tony Massimo at the Cafe in Aliquippa, where his word struck fear in people's hearts. By that time, Vito knew Sonny's true identity. Sonny was not the same person Vito once knew in Cervinara. He was not about to challenge Sonny's authority. Vito further thought to himself: "Why are so many people kissing his ass and showing so much respect, even though he cheats like crazy in bocce?" The conclusion was inescapable. "That son of a bitch is connected to the Mafia." This confirmed why Sonny always walked around the North End with bodyguards night and day.

In the winter months, only one major tournament was scheduled indoors. Italian restaurants in the North End and the Suburbs sponsored the event displaying foods from restaurants during the tournament, referred to as "The taste of the North End tournament". A team consisted of one restaurant owner and two professionals. The players reward was a $100 coupon to a local restaurant. The old timers boycotted this tournament for they didn't particularly care for the so-called Italian cuisine of the North End anyway. They preferred their own original peasant food. Besides, they cooked better than the restaurants and demanded cash awards instead. A compromise was reached whereby some cash went to the winners, $500. So, players like Iaccarino put aside their reluctance and participated wholeheartedly. The rest of the money went to high school seniors at banquets. The award ceremony was a sham, because all of the recipients were related to the banquet organizers.

Besides the Boston area, Bocce tournaments took place all over the New England states. As a student in New Haven, Conn., Vito and Anna, would often drive to the little Italian community for Italian pastries and/or restaurants. On one hot summer day, they noticed a lot of commotion with people yelling and cheering in a nearby park. When they arrived there, people were playing bocce at fairly high level of competence and waging bets on every toss of the bocce ball. Right there and then, he realized that that bocce was indeed alive and kicking in the USA, but only in Italian-American neighborhoods. It was just a matter of looking at the right venue or district in a town to locate a bocce court. When he moved to Boston, he sensed that there had to be a Bocce court in the North End.

None of the politicians ever entered a tournament, except for one person. The Governor of Massachusetts Paul Cellucci and his father, Argeo, visited the bocce courts at Puopolo Park often. They had a bocce court in their backyard in Hudson, MA, and Argeo was preparing there for the big times in tournaments in the North End. He was as giggly as a child just at the thought of entering a tournament of professionals. Although he was eighty years old, he liked to be called Junior (Jr.). Players admired his spirit. He needed a lot of practice to improve his mechanical skills which is a prelude to the mental game. Simply put, it was not his game. His talents lay someplace else. Everybody at the bocce courts tried to avoid him so that Jr. would not be placed on their team. However, since he was the father of the Governor, it was difficult to avoid him. However, Jr. decided to play on Sonny's team. That was the only time Sonny and Vito did not finish in the top three finalists. Unbeknown to Vito, it was Onofrio, being a farmer at heart, who planted the seed in Jr.'s head to play with Sonny's team. That was the turning point, when Onofrio saw Sonny as a future competitor in tournaments. Both Onofrio and Iaccarino won that tournament. Sonny and Vito drew a line in the sand, "You fuckers, that is the last time you two are going to fuck me over at tournaments." Sonny yelled at Onofrio and Iaccarino. Both of them smirked and, with puckered lips, laughed, "Quanto si bello." "How beautiful you look."

Jr. had an infectious spirit that permeated all around him, especially with bocce players. His beautiful personality and trying very hard to succeed at bocce was very inspirational to others who were regulars on the courts. His enthusiasm was admirable. It was hard to tell him that bocce was not his game. After all, he was the Governor's father. Who was going to tell him that? So, both Sonny and Vito were stuck with him for the summer tournaments and gave the appearance of being enthused about the pairing. Needless to say, the team got trounced not once but many times. Even the Governor came over to give his father instructions and moral support during the tournaments and practice sessions. Sometimes, the Governor came incognito and unexpectedly to the bocce courts from the State Capitol, about a mile away, just to let Jr. know that he was there to encourage and support him. That was something very special about the Governor going beyond the call of duty as a son. Obviously, Governor Cellucci didn't come with a full entourage of limousines and police escorts, since it was a private matter between father and son. Clearly, it was a special relationship and love between them that was so beautiful to watch. Most tourists and others there did not recognize him, and the few that did understood the situation and minded their own business. Sonny and Vito were envious of the Governor, not because of the immense power he represented, but because he had a father that the two of them never had. So, they busted their rear ends to improve Jr.'s game for the tournaments.

The winning prize at these tournaments was rather minimal, one hundred dollars per player plus restaurant coupons. However, the prize money did not really motivate the players. Winning was not it either. The game of bocce is about matching wits with your adversary. To come on top of many good and clever players with tremendous talent was indeed very satisfying. Losing was never a consolation, especially being outmaneuvered in putting a team together. Usually, Vito and Sonny always paired together but, the other two members, were enticed and cajoled by other teams. Vito and Sonny saw Onofrio and Iaccarino smirking and smiling during these tournaments. After all, it was Onofrio who assigned Jr. to Sonny's team. The feeling between Sonny and Vito was mutual. They would have liked to fondly wrung Onofrio's neck, jokingly of course. Sonny and Vito cornered Onofrio and told him, in no uncertain terms, that Iaccarino and Onofrio take on Jr. Otherwise, they would abstain from any other tournaments

Jr. at one of the practice sessions with two advisers about bocce.

until Jr. found someone else to play with. However, Sonny did not have the heart (balls) to break up the pairings with Jr. Basically, he and Vito were soft hearted.

Onofrio, being as an astute one, convinced Jr. that an indoor bocce court was desperately needed in the skating rink building which belonged to the State. The idea was, of course, for Jr. to go there in the winter time tournaments. Wow, bocce all year round as well as all the social gatherings taking place indoors. That was Onofrio's dream. The Governor and Jr. adopted the project as their own and in a matter of one year it was completed. This Governor truly must have believed and listened to the will of the people, since Onofrio spent a lot of time explaining to him about required specifications of a bocce court. The indoor facility housed two bocce courts located next to the skating rink with an ocean front view. Initially, Onofrio tried to persuade the mayor, but Mr. Flynn could not do anything about it. The skating rink fell under the jurisdiction of the State. It took a while for Onofrio to understand the distinction. Once he understood that, he knew whom to persuade and Jr. was the one. High power politicians like

Romney, Cellucci, DiMasi, Finneran, etc. often convened in the indoor bocce courts to hold private bocce parties. Sonny, Onofrio and Uberto were there to assist them in bocce playing.

Soon after the opening of the indoor bocce courts, Jr. became seriously sick. The Governor invited Sonny and Uberto to play bocce with Jr. at his home. He was frail, but his spirits were sky high. It was deeply moving and inspiring for both of them to spend the time with him. Here, this man had a date with Saint Peter and yet was oblivious to it. Going on as if he was about to conquer the world of bocce. What a man! What a dreamer! Saint Peter planned for a front door entrance to a bocce tournament in Heaven for people like him. Jr. gave a beautiful parting gift to bocce players that they will never forget. He was responsible for building the indoor bocce courts.

Commemoration of the indoor bocce courts attended by then Governor Mitt Romney and former Governor Paul Cellucci (Jr.'s son) standing.

For seven months (April to November), the outside courts were available to anyone. Parks and Planning maintained the courts and Onofrio was in charge of their daily use. In the cold months, the players hibernated like bears inside the skating rink. The manager of the rink was in charge of the bocce courts, not Onofrio. This meant that locals could play bocce all year around. Since the state was in control of the courts, they were able to schedule events where only politicians, or other VIPs, had access to the indoor courts. Typically, three VIP events were scheduled in the winter. The rest of the time, it was open to the locals. In the fall, Vito was most active in academic matters and he rarely had time to play bocce. Besides, he was nowhere near Boston; he spent the winter months on Academic leave at the University of Miami, FLA. The Physics department made office space available to him and he participated in research with students and faculties there.

In Florida bocce courts are very popular and are located throughout the state, not necessarily in Italian communities. Big time tournaments are scheduled in Naples and many other cities in Florida each year in spring. Giorgio and Orfeo, part time residents of Naples, FL, and Melrose, MA, were avid bocce players in the North End and Naples. They were forever extolling the bocce scene in Naples to both Sonny and Vito. Vito had no problem getting to Florida as he was also a part time resident of Miami, but not so easy for Sonny, who was stuck in Boston in the winter. Giorgio was a radio host for Italian language programs in which news in US and Italy was reported in Italian. The radio programs included special broadcasts of soccer games and political events. Orfeo retired from a construction company in Weymouth, MA, south of Boston. They paired together in tournaments. On a bocce court, Giorgio was a nervous wreck who drove everybody nuts, especially Sonny. He would hold the bocce ball as if aiming a bow and arrow, a very unusual stand. His teammate, Orfeo, would whisper in Sonny's ear and say: "Look at him play. He will find a way to f..k it up". However, Giorgio was well informed about tournament schedules in Naples and shared that information with Sonny. He could not very well drive all the way to Miami, from Boston just for a tournament that did not cover his expenses. However, the lure of big-time money at bocce tournaments was overwhelming.

It didn't take long before Sonny contacted Vito in Miami and Giorgio in Naples arranging to enter a tournament in Naples. The entry fee was steep, $250 per player, but Sonny had already secured a sponsor in Boston, Alex, to pay for the fees. No one wanted to sponsor Giorgio as he had gained a reputation of fucking up sooner or later. However, he was kind in hosting

Sonny and Vito in his house for the duration of the tournament. Vito drove from Miami to Naples, and Sonny came with Claire by bus in the spring, since the women's softball team was training in Miami-Dade Community College. There were about two thousand people at the tournament, and two hundred players. About $50,000 or more was collected at registration. It was single elimination and Vito and Sonny paired as a team.

Vito did not like the crowd there. It was like a mob scene. The largest contingent of people came from the New Jersey-New York City area and they were loud and boisterous. The owner of Francesco Restaurant in Morrisville, New Jersey, sponsored six teams. Vito could tell that they were not going to take any daunting from anyone. Some of them talked, looked and smelled like wise-guys from New Jersey, according to Sonny. Vito was familiar with their accent, from when he was a student at Toledo University. At that time, there was a huge contingent of students from New Jersey that had a peculiar accent easily identifiable even by him, although he himself had a heavy Italian accent. As usual, Sonny began yapping away at some of them to distract them. One burly and menacing type came over to Vito and said: "Tell your friend to keep his mouth shut or we will permanently shut it." From his tone and appearance, he meant business. While he was talking to Vito, his boss kept staring and smiling at Sonny. Vito went over to Sonny to convey the situation. He told him: "Do you want to get out of here alive, then shut the f..k up." Sonny was taken aback by the tone of Vito's voice. Like old times, he knew, when Vito meant business. For the rest of the tournament Sonny behaved like an altar boy. By the end of the day, Sonny and Vito qualified for the quarter final round of sixteen teams. This meant that they were into the money round. The two of them left with $1000 each. Needless to say, they never returned to that tournament. The next day they were eliminated from competition. However, Giorgio and Orfeo were still in it, although talent wise they were below average. Giorgio had decided to register with Orfeo at the last minute out of their own pocket money. They had a great advantage in that they played on those courts many times before and were familiar with the roll of the bocce balls on the courts. Sonny stayed around to give them moral support.

Nevertheless, Sonny and Vito won prize money which was not bad for one day's work. As they started to go their separate ways home, the owner of Francesco's restaurant, came over to congratulate and embrace Sonny and re-new their old friendship, like two loving brothers. Apparently, they knew each other when Davide was managing a pizzeria in Sturmville, NJ. All that bravura or mouthing off during the matches was just posturing and getting at each other nerves. Thus, Sonny knew all along that bullshit talk coming from Francesco's people was just that. Sonny acquiesced to Vito's request only to make him happy and relaxed. Vito was not about to find out what that was all about. He left for Miami. He had had enough of that bullshit.

FIFTEEN

An Oasis in The City

The "golden" age of bocce lasted from the early 1990s to about 2015, coinciding with the rise and fall of Whitey. This is not to say that at other times the bocce courts were not as active, but they definitely not as popular. On appearance alone, the locals were well aware of the changes taking place in the North End because of Whitey, but, at the bocce courts, Whitey might as well be living elsewhere. Consciously or subconsciously, the subject of Whitey was never an item of conversation among the players, although they were well aware of him. Nevertheless, shady characters, ten to twenty strong, showed up a number of times at the bocce courts brazenly trying to sell drugs to anyone in sight, including tourists. Players just froze in their pants and remained calm, if that was possible. They were an ugly looking bunch, unshaven, dirty and simply mean looking. It got so bad that these punks were toying around with pistols for everyone to see, only to intimidate everyone. Drug addicts occupied toilets for hours denying the older bocce players access to them, forcing them to urinate in the park across the street. Obviously, they represented the new wave of drug pushers launched by Whitey all over Boston. Somehow, bocce players just simply ignored them or shut down their brains for fear of registering them in their thoughts. They just kept busy without paying attention to their whereabouts. It was not clear whether it was fear or a case of mind over matter. They liked to believe that it was just a bad dream or a mirage in the oasis. The bocce courts were becoming more of a social club where locals could gather to unburden themselves of the trudges of the day. Also, tourists and interesting personages would return to the bocce courts and re-acquaint themselves with players and just unwind. Sweet thoughts did come back for good, when Whitey was captured by the FBI. Lucky for Sonny, he had an outlet this period that allowed him to relax and be himself, hiding from his mounting family and health worries, in an oasis in the middle of the city.

Tourist buses would stop by and watch the spectacle put on by the players. Sonny and Uberto, sometimes, would shout in unison at tourists: "Peanuts, please.", as if they were in the setting of a zoo. At other times they would be very quiet like little kids and talk about their families here and there (Italy) and offer helpful suggestions or sympathy. Their favorite time was playing cards under a shady tree, hiding from the hot afternoon sun, drinking homemade wine. They were in a stupor as though they were in a completely different world. Nothing bothered them even though there was heavy traffic and noise from the street and tourists all around asking silly questions like: "Where is the Mafia headquarters?" or "Where is the best restaurant?". The temptation was to tell them where to go, but they bit their tongues. They were oblivious to the outside world. A grenade could have dropped and they would not have budged an inch. They loved to wear handkerchiefs over their heads to shield themselves, much like in the old days in Italy. The summer ocean breeze was like a velvety feeling, caressing the players. It was a magical moment.

By the turn of the century, Sonny was working full time as a waiter. He had difficulties maneuvering the Vespa around people due to his poor vision. He learned to gently bump into a tree or a bench before tying it up. In short, he was becoming a pain in the ass to all. Whenever he didn't care about the tenor of a conversation between bocce players, he would say "frigetz" ("forget about it") and take off on his Vespa. That was an expression often used in the movie "Goodfellas". However, the old timers had no clue as to what he was talking about. Anytime he would say that to the old timers, he would wink at Vito and smirk. It was a love/hate relationship between Sonny and the old timers anytime he was tired of the bullshit talk from the elders. He no longer had the patience to listen and provide them the needed sympathy or support for their everyday complaints. Everybody noticed that irritation oozing out of him. Players didn't want to get caught in the whirlwind of his irritation.

As always, Onofrio was a dreamer. He liked to think big ideas. He would come to Sonny and Vito often and say: "Why did the Winter Olympic Committee approve of that stupid game of curling whereby a metal piece of shit on the ice is guided by a broom. Why don't they consider our beautiful game of bocce where human skills are at play." Sonny and Vito stared at each other and sighed, "Bo", meaning in Italian, "Where did that come from?", or what "planet is he living on?" The old man knew what he was talking about. Unbeknownst to all but himself, the Massachusetts Bocce Association petitioned the Summer Olympic Committee to consider bocce as part of the Summer Olympic events. The decision is still pending. However, it didn't stop Onofrio from forming a team for the Olympics. He invited both Sonny and Vito to join him and Iaccarino to be on the team to compete for the qualifying rounds. What a dreamer! Like many old men, he wanted to leave a legacy behind, especially in bocce. In another idea of his, he suggested to Sonny that the little marble monument depicting a sunken Navy ship, commemorating WW II by the Coast Guard nearby, at the bocce courts should be replaced by a small bust of someone associated with bocce, since the area of the park is mostly about bocce. Sonny surmised what Onofrio was up to and asked: "Should the bust have a hand tucked in the chest like Napoleon?" They all got a laugh out of that.

Onofrio had retired from working at a supermarket as a butcher. Whereas Onofrio had the talent for the gab, Iaccarino was quiet, unassuming and thoughtful. After emigrating from a town near Naples, Italy, Iaccarino worked at the same supermarket as a fruit and vegetable manager and, on weekends, part-time at the Haymarket. Coming from a town very near Naples, he was well aware of the Camorra (Neapolitan Mafia) way of doing business. He kept his nose clean and steered away from the lure of easy money, although his pension barely covered his house expenses and rent. The same applied to Onofrio's financial situation. They basically stayed within their means and shied away from any wise-guys except for Sonny, since he was treated as their son.

Tourists loved to see a happy and lively atmosphere among players, especially when Onofrio was clowning around with them. Onofrio was at heart an entertainer who craved the tourists' cheers and attention. Often, he would stop the game and take time to explain to tourists what the game was about. The players stared at each other and wondered, "What the f..k! Which woman is he looking at now." They loved to hear Uberto shouting many a times: "I have a dream". He had no idea that those famous words were once shouted at civil right events by Martin Luther King. He was once reminded about King, but he just shrugged his shoulders implying ignorance. How ironical, basically, King's and Uberto's dreams were about the same thing, a better life for the under-privileged people including his children.

In contrast to Onofrio, Iaccarino appeared to be anti-social. In Italy, he was a farmer, part of the poor class, often labeled as the "peasant class", according to Levi's description [1-7], author of the book: *Christ Stopped at Eboli*. He owned a small parcel of land which he shared with his brother's family. They barely carved out a living. That class of people was disenfranchised by the central government in Rome. It fostered mistrust and indifference not only with other peasants but especially with the local authorities, such as tax collectors. They were viewed by the peasants as agents of the central government interfering with their lives. This created an atmosphere of suspicion and superstition among all the classes. Peasants looked upon any stranger with suspicion, especially the Carabinieri (police). Not surprisingly, Iaccarino was reticent about striking friendship with anyone new at the bocce courts. He was distrustful of politicians and, in general, anyone he was not familiar with.

Basically, he was a prisoner of his up-bringing. In America, it was hard to let go of the old mind set. Also, he was more isolated, as he spoke very little English or proper Italian. However, once he befriended someone, his loyalty knew no bounds. He tended to "look over" new acquaintances, much like an ape looks over viewers, staring through the thick glass panels at the zoo. Vito knew that Iaccarino had looked him over, when he first appeared at the bocce courts. It was not until Vito beat Iaccarino in a couple of games that he opened up and started to talk non-stop. That was the beginning of a wonderful friendship accentuated with both talking together in the Neapolitan dialect that they were comfortable with. Together they would tease the rest of the players with their proverbs spoken in their dialect. Sicilian and Neapolitan proverbs are like riddles and may be described as flirtations of the mind whose true meaning can be elusive. To others, it was exasperating to understand them. Underneath that withdrawn look, the man had a sharp mind full of wisdom and tremendous perception of human nature.

Iaccarino was as big as a mountain with a heart just as big, easy going and jovial. Every time Iaccarino would smile or wink at Sonny or Vito, that was the cue for another joke or riddle. Although he had little education, he was very observant and insightful about anything that interested him. Sonny tried for a long time to snap Iaccarino's frame of mind from those miserable days in Naples, but to no avail. However, when it came to proverbs, Sonny loved to hear them, especially spoken by Iaccarino. It reminded him of those days spent on the mountains chatting with the older shepherds. Vito on one side and Sonny on the other side of Iaccarino, sitting tightly on a bench, listening to every proverb spoken by him. It just drove the poet, Lorenzo, nuts seeing the two of them cozy up to Jaccarino and pay so much attention to those proverbs. To Lorenzo, proverbs represented the worst literary examples of the Italian language.

Shopping at Haymarket

The first time Vito met Iaccarino was at the Haymarket, where he went shopping every Saturday morning. Negotiating with Iaccarino was very frustrating for him. Iaccarino was the vendor who did not allow Vito to touch any fruit or vegetable. To an Italian, it is sacrilegious not to be able to do so. Only Iaccarino could fondle them. It upset Vito and he swore at him in a Neapolitan dialect with the hope that he would not understand. He understood it, and replied in kind. Both were startled with the realization that, most likely, they came from neighboring towns close to Naples.

Thereafter, Iaccarino would put aside fresh fruits for Vito. Otherwise, he would say, "Frigetz (forget about it)", implying that there was nothing to be had. He loved to use that expression just to impress Vito and others that he was as hip as Sonny. Indeed, shopping at Haymarket was a hit or miss proposition. His favorite time of the day was after the Haymarket closed for the day and he would be sharing a bag of figs or watermelons with the "boys" at the oasis. He was poor but shared everything he had. Besides food, he shared his wisdom and knowledge and old-time proverbs. Besides proverbs, Sonny loved to chat with him just about anything that Iaccarino wanted to talk about. However, on the playing court, they were arch-enemies. For the locals, it was entertaining to watch them bickering the whole time about nothing important, just to annoy each other. They were just having fun.

The poet, Lorenzo, entertained the tourists with his poetry at the courts. He would quote from Ovid in Latin and Plato in Greek. No one understood a word he was saying, but that didn't matter. To add insult to injury, to the crowd at large, he would translate the quotations in pure Italian and in English. It was sheer agony for the bystanders and especially for the players. Most people were aware of Ovid and Plato, but not of their works! The urge of the players was to throw anything, except bocce balls at him to keep him quiet. Lorenzo was a Carabiniere of Finance (custom police officer) in Sulmona, Italy, before he emigrated to Boston. He was raised on a farm with two older brothers, but farming was not his call. His aptitude was in schooling and the family enrolled him in private Catholic schools. He was at the top of the class in the Lyceum school excelling in Greek and Latin classics.

One evening Onofrio upstaged Lorenzo in quoting a Latin phrase. He was poking fun at Lorenzo. He stood on a picnic table and declared to all at the bocce courts that he wanted to paraphrase our honored friend Ciccio (Cicero) from Arpino in Latin. The famous Roman Senator, philosopher and statesman was born 106 BC in Arpinum (Arpino) which is about 25 miles from either Sulmona or Avella. To Lorenzo, it was sacrilegious to refer to his Roman hero Cicero as Ciccio. The name Ciccio is a slang word for Francesco. Sometimes, it implies a bumbler. According to Lorenzo, Onofrio got the name and the derogatory slang wrong and two wrongs don't make it right. Vito thought to himself, "At least he got the math right". It was disrespectful, according to Lorenzo. Onofrio was not about to be derailed and blurted out: "Cogito ergo sum un strunzo", meaning: "I think, therefore, I am an asshole." The sentence was a mixture of Latin and Italian slang. Lorenzo blew a gasket. "First of all, Cicero never said that, Descartes said it differently. You have no f…g business insulting our beloved Cicero. Besides, neither one of them used the derogatory word strunzo (asshole)". At this point, it was outright hilarious to everyone there and they couldn't contain their laughter. It didn't stop Lorenzo from being what he was, a poet, and it didn't stop Lorenzo from quoting Cicero in Latin. No one knew what he said. If anything, it encouraged him to defend the honor of those Roman and Greek writers more.

Corvo was a typical old time mafioso from Sicily, a man of few words. He was no longer active in the Mafia. However, omerta was instilled in him from youth. His family was chased out of Sicily in the late 1940s by a Mafia faction in Sicily that did not favor the return of "Lucky" Luciano to Sicily. His family's faction favored the return. As it is well known, Lucky settled in Naples, Italy, and died there in 1962. The US Justice Department deported him as an undesirable alien. Lucky's enterprises included casinos in Havana, Las Vegas, etc. Corvo's family emigrated to Havana, Cuba, to work in a casino. The casino business took him to places like Miami, Havana, Los Angeles, Las Vegas, etc. rubbing shoulders with the "muck-muck" of the Mafia hierarchy. It was not until after the turmoil of the 1950s in the Mafia in the Northeast that his family finally moved to the North End, Boston. When he was no longer active in the Mafia, the only income supporting his family was rental property that he owned. Few mafiosi lived long enough to die of natural causes. Unfortunately, he died when he rolled down the steps of the basement. He was drunk and had lived up to his name, Corvo (the name of his favorite Sicilian wine).

He outlived all of his contemporaries of the Havana days. He loved his stogies, Sicilian cigars. He would chew on them until there was nothing left. Vito asked him why he came to Boston. "I had no choice. They were going to kill me. They already killed most of my family." He never explained to Vito what he meant by "they". Vito didn't want to follow up on that, because he knew that Corvo would be irritated with him for asking what he considered to be a stupid question. All conversations with Corvo were like deciphering a cryptic code. He scraped for a living here and there. He built a special contraption to harvest apples from an apple tree every year near the bocce court. A lot of the vendors at Haymarket would be lenient with his negotiation demands. However, Corvo really did not negotiate, and he was allowed to touch the fruits. He just told them what he wanted and expected to get it at the lowest price.

Corvo was tight lipped about his past, being drunk on omerta. However, in one awkward moment for Vito, he once reminisced about the old times. He may have been drunk. He recalled the times when he was having lunch at Wolfie's on Twentieth St. in Miami Beach with Meyer Lansky. Meyer Lansky was a "colleague" of Lucky Luciano and responsible for the killing of Joe Masseria in NYC. Again, it was too cryptic for Vito to make sense out of his recollections. Vito did not pursue the conversation anymore for fear of antagonizing him. Besides, it was none of his business.

Corvo loved to blow smoke in people's eyes during bocce games, just to be a nuisance to the other players. Then, he had the balls to ask, with a smile from ear to ear, if the smoke bothered them. There is a Hebrew word for that behavior, chutzpah. Corvo was a provocateur galore and, the worst part, he just enjoyed being obnoxious. Being in Boston and declaring himself a Yankee fan did not sit well with Sonny. Sonny was a die-hard Boston Red Sox fan from the day he stepped onto the USA. However, Corvo had only one purpose in mind and that was to needle Sonny and upset his game. Corvo loved to say: "I don't know much about the game of baseball, but the better team won, the Yankees". That infuriated Sonny, and he retorted, "For sure, you don't know much about baseball!" Unfortunately, for Sonny, the Yankees won most of the playoff games against the Red Sox in those days. Corvo loved to throw imaginary darts at players with his truisms and Sicilian riddles and stand back, observing their reactions. He was a pain in the ass and an instigator who was not shy about confronting people directly at the bocce courts. Most players just ignored him, except for Sonny. Exchanges between the two were terse and loud. To Sonny, Corvo was the hated Yankee in person.

Other old timers were transients who came to the courts for nostalgic reasons and to kindle past relationships. Of these 10–20 transients, one stood out. His name was Bruno, from Medford. He loved to sing Neapolitan songs in the middle of the courts while playing bocce, after just one glass of wine. Fortunately for him, he was a decent singer and, therefore, tolerated by others. Then again, old timers loved to hum along with Bruno. It didn't take long before others joined in to harmonize. Of course, tourists loved it. The performance was top class and the price was just right, free. In short, the old timers were rather eccentric, romantic and proud of it all. Obviously, they got along very well. Players like Onofrio were annoyed by the singing. Soon enough, Bruno was relegated to Serie B (court 2) at the bocce courts. Serie A was the top soccer level in Italy and B the lower level. This meant that serious players refused to play bocce with Bruno for fear of his taking time out to sing. He could sing in court 2, but not in court 1.

The middle aged group assimilated much better with the American ways and culture. Often, they served as the translators of the American system or politics to the older players like Iaccarino, especially. Sonny, Uberto and Vito represented the new breed of Italian-Americans who were equally at ease with the old ways as well as with the new trends in America. Uberto was an interesting character from Calabria. His creative spirit took him to different business experiences: tailoring, cooking, hair styling, and interior decorating. He loved bocce as much as Sonny, Vito, and the old timers and He was the clown of the courts, craving any attention from the tourists. However, there was also a serious side to him. Although he took detours in life, he wanted very much for his three children to hit the road pursuing books and not to take detours. All three of his children finished their college studies and one became a medical doctor.

There was a disconnect between the yuppies and the old timers. Even when exchanges between them were translated, they simply did not comprehend or relate to what they were talking about. One young man, Chuck, who was a stage hand at the Metropolitan Opera House in NYC, and his friends visited punctually every weekend. He was mentored by Onofrio to play the game and Onofrio took special pride in this pupil. Another one mentored by Onofrio was Victor who eventually became more skillful and creative than Onofrio. He adapted his skills to the styles of other elders as well. He was a gifted player, when he was sober. The use of drugs limited his potential to become a great player at a relatively young age. Both Chuck and Victor were second generation Italian-Americans living with their parents in the Boston area.

The other two yuppies were born in Italy. In particular, Eric, a computer jock, needed no mentoring as he learned to play the game in his hometown of Sulmona. Jacopo, the Sicilian, turned out to be a great strategist of the game. The young foursome were a handful to contend with in tournaments. The elders were very respectful of their skills, so much so that they, in turn, learned from these young ones. Sometimes, they organized a picnic for all to join them, including tourists. There were others of the same age who drifted in and out of the bocce scene and had little interest in socializing with old timers or partaking in the game of bocce. They were from a different generation whose interest had little overlap with the players there. Even the ones who were regulars on weekends had no common interest with the old timers. The hope of the elders was that these young men may not carry the torch of bocce then, but, perhaps, in the future.

There were other young groups, but most of them were transients who lived in the neighborhood from six to twelve months either attending universities or in training for new jobs in the financial district. Other younger yuppies were left alone to "stew" in their own style of playing, as they preferred to come and go to the courts to socialize with their own group. The bocce courts provided the perfect setting for picnics: picnic table, benches, the courts, ocean view, and even a playground.

University students who lived in the North End made up the rest of the young group. However, they did not mingle much with the regular bocce players. They brought their own bocce balls to the courts. The relationship between the young students and the locals was very cordial and friendly. Often, the young people invited the old timers to their parties or picnics and shared beers with them. As always, Onofrio availed himself with a helping hand to teach them about the game, all the while keeping an eye on the beautiful gals. He just couldn't help himself. As regards to the young generation of Italian-Americans in the North End, they had no interest whatsoever in bocce.

By the turn of the 21st century about 60% or more of the original immigrants moved to suburbia from the North End. Most restaurant owners also resided in the suburbs. For a lot of them it was a step up in their standard of living—better housing, cleaner streets and shopping malls. However, Bocce aficionados kept coming back to the bocce courts to engage in serious playing of the game which they fondly remembered from childhood. They came at any time but mostly in the evening after work, and on weekends. After finishing his mail delivery rounds, the mailman rested on a bench at the courts and engaged in a round of bocce. It was like an oasis stop before going home. An oasis does not discriminate as to who may enter it. There were bums and some homeless people drifting in and out of the courts seeking shelter or panhandling tourists and the players. The only thing that the old timers could offer them was sympathy.

Often, celebrities came to the courts incognito and unescorted. The list included politicians, Las Vegas entertainers, famous musicians, singers, NFL players, NBA players, etc. In early fall, Boston increases its population by roughly 25% due to students enrolling at local universities. Vito didn't particularly like to see visitors from Fairmont University as he didn't feel like taking the time to explain the subtleties of the game. Invariably, he would steer them to Onofrio, who enjoyed doing that. He wanted to remain distant from academic affairs at the courts and just relax among his friends.

Most international tourists came from Europe and, surprisingly, from South Africa. Usually, these tourists were following the Freedom Trail which passes by the bocce courts. Often, they stopped by to ask for directions, because they had lost sight of the Trail. In Boston, there are many trails for tourists to follow. Quite often, they weren't sure which trail they were following. Onofrio loved to say to these lost souls: "Don't worry, even Paul Revere got lost on the way to Concord. He also followed the wrong trail." The irony of the comment was that Onofrio didn't know where Concord was located. He never left Boston, since he arrived here. Of course, during Revere's time there were no marked trails to anywhere. He always chit-chatted with them and re-assured them by pointing out the trail to follow, usually in the wrong direction. Bunker Hill was the favorite destination, which could easily be seen from the courts.

Tourists from Northern Europe usually did not know much about bocce, but Italian tourists felt right at home around the Bocce courts, especially the older ones. The young ones were amused that their generation did not take up the game of bocce as much as the ones in the North End. Obviously, things have changed in Italy since the War. Italian tourists were usually business people with the means to travel all over the world as well as in the USA. They were from a well-to-do class of people. Frankly, there was class consciousness and some animosity between the riff-raffs of the North End and these upper-class Italian tourists.

Although the old timers thanked their lucky stars to be living in America, they were relatively poor compared with those Italian tourists. They simply did not like each other. This was nothing new. This estrangement goes way back to medieval times, when peasants were subjected to a central government that didn't care whether they were dead or alive. To add insult to injury, the middle class exploited the peasants unmercifully. The animosity was oozing out of their body language and the manner of speaking between these two classes of people. This was a typical clash of the "have and have not". However, initially, the tenor of these conversations was kept in a civilized manner. There was loathing between Onofrio and these Italian tourists. They represented the elitists, an arrogant and fairly well-to-do class of people in northern Italy. Northerners have always looked down on southerners as leaches who depended on government handouts. Onofrio represented the old peasant stock of southern Italy with limited education but street smarts. The conversation between them was strained and was one of avoiding clash of the classes. So, they talked in generalities, such as: where to eat in the North End, and what is the political news from Italy. However, when the conversation turned to politics in southern Italy, the discussion erupted like Mount Vesuvius. There was no agreement on anything. The tourists blamed the "lazy" south for the economic mess and crime in Italy. Onofrio countered by saying that the north does not pay their fair share of taxes and they are no different. It all ended up on a sour note which was unavoidable. These arguments are as old as time itself, leaving a bad taste in their mouths after arguing about things that they could not control.

Other visitors included the whole cast from the TV production, "The SOPRANOS". The visit was sponsored by a local restaurant. The photo-session included the restaurant owner and the cast. None of the bocce regulars participated in those photo sessions. The owner had never sponsored anyone at Bocce tournaments. Entertainers from Las Vegas stopped by often after performing at the festivals in the North End, such as Rudy Vallee and others.

An unusual visit was from Mohammed Atta and two of his colleagues who hijacked planes in the infamous 9/11 attacks. They arrived on a Sunday afternoon looking relaxed and mingling easily with other tourists. They played bocce and Vito noticed their behavior as that of little boys, giddy and having fun playing a new game. After the 9/11 incident, it occurred to Vito that these "boys" were no angels, but murderers. It is difficult to fathom how it is possible to justify that horrific day in a human psyche. How could these murderers have been so jolly knowing what they were about to do? Innocent tourists playing bocce that day could easily have been victims on that fateful day. Truly incomprehensible.

Besides politicians, officers of the law came by. The retiring party of FBI agent M. Paul Rico took place at the Bocce courts. His fame to success was that he hired Flemmi as an informant for the FBI. The food was catered by Uberto's restaurant. The usual bocce crowd was also invited. Agent Rico was accompanied by a very young woman. Uberto and Sonny knew that it was a sham all along as they provided the escort service to cover the fact that Rico was allegedly [6-7] a homosexual. They were partners in the ownership of the escort service. Rico retired and joined Whitey's operation. Before retirement, Whitey bribed Rico to be an inside mole in the FBI office in Boston. At the peak of Whitey's power, Rico was instrumental in providing critical information about a potential nemesis of Whitey resulting in a murder.

On most nights, locals came for entertainment, watching a good bocce game, and socializing with others. Among the locals, there were wise-guys who came only to gamble on the games. The locals cheered for their favorite player to win. They tried to distract opposing players. However, the kidding stopped as soon as betting on the players started. It was serious business for there was heavy gambling on the sidelines among the wise-guys. Players heard comments from the spectator's gallery like, "I got a G-note riding on you SOB on this toss." That took the fun out of the game for the players. Most of the players never saw a C-note ($100 Bill), let alone a G-note (grand, $1,000). It just boggled their minds.

Sometimes, it was a surreal scene at the courts, when Boston police officers relaxed sitting on benches near the courts across from the wise-guys. The players knew very well by name all the wise-guys and police officers. These two groups even acknowledged their presence. In fact, some families consisted of police officers and wise-guys, such as the family living in the courtyard next to Carmela. The players tried to ignore the betting, but it was useless. The shouting and yelling from the wise-guys grew louder and louder so that it could not be easily ignored by the players. The stakes were high in terms of money exchanged and that made it exciting for all. However, money exchanged only between the wise-guys. Players were not tipped.

As the North End was becoming a chic place to live, yuppies and well-to-do people started to move into newly built condominium complexes. This group of people never really socialized much with the old timers of the bocce courts or the regulars. Some showed very little respect or courtesy toward the regulars. Their attitude was, "Hey, you, peasant, give us the bocce balls from the shed." There was no dialogue between the two groups, just do what I tell you and be happy. Onofrio or Iaccarino provided new arrivals with bocce balls and walked away to join their friends playing cards or bocce games. The newcomers were steered toward court 3, Serie C, lower than B, not realizing that they had just been put down. Onofrio may have been a peasant, but was too proud to be subservient to arrogant assholes like that with little respect and courtesy. He would have been happy to teach them the game. He had no choice but to give them the bocce balls. They were playing on public grounds. The regulars were somewhat amused by this type of arrogance. It did not sit well with Vito or Sonny nor, especially, Onofrio. They just bit their tongues. In fairness to other newcomers, they often invited the old timers to come over and critic their games. That went a long way in easing some of the tension between the newcomers and the old timers, but the bullshitting was strictly reserved among the established cadre of bocce players, the regulars.

When the locals came to relax at the courts, they had their favorite players and would try to get involved by engaging them in conversation. Sunday was special. Each group would have a picnic where food and wine were brought to the courts. Uberto often brought pasta dishes from his restaurant. Lorenzo secured the home-made wine from the locals. It was a festive atmosphere that all enjoyed. Even the police joined in the festivities by allowing double-parking by the courts where visitors parked their cars. It was near to impossible to secure parking in the streets of the North End unless police assisted. Whatever illicit business some of them were engaged in was checked at the street.

One local resident who often came to take in the ocean breeze with the old timers was "Maresciallo" (Field Marshal) Brese. The name was an abbreviation of the word Calabrese which implied a person from the "boot" of Italy. No one knew his real name. Brese was an interesting character from Calabria. He was no more than one hundred pounds in wet clothes and yet he had worked in the construction industry for fifty years. Sonny would hum a song from Calabria and Brese would end up singing the rest. It never failed to induce him to sing, just like a canary. That was one way of stopping him from sniping at players. At every construction site in the North End, no matter how small or big, he showed up and behaved like an inspector, giving instructions to the laborers on site. At the Bocce courts, people teased him by taunting him with, "Maresciallo, what is the report on such and such construction site?" With all the candor of an inspector Brese discussed, point by point, the shortcomings of the construction and people would marvel at his clarity and technical expertise. However, he was a biased man. His favorite bocce player was Onofrio and he would cheer for him like a little child. In his eyes, Onofrio could do no wrong in bocce. This meant that playing against Onofrio was taking on two adversaries, Onofrio and Brese. It was bad enough to take on a pro like Onofrio, but to have Brese on your back sniping was too much to contend with.

Alfonzo (Al), who was of the same mold as Brese, showed favoritism toward Sonny at the bocce courts. They were both from the town of Cervinara. He was a happy-go-lucky type of guy and nothing bothered him. It was a mutual admiration society between the two. The minute he showed up, he would be yapping at everybody incessantly. He had a kidney condition that required a replacement of one of his kidneys. Nevertheless, he would show up at the bocce courts with a dialysis machine. Whenever the Boston Globe would do a photo-op or an interview at the bocce courts, the players made sure that his picture was taken and that he was interviewed. The hope was that a kidney donor would come forward by featuring him in the newspapers. Sad to say, no donor ever showed up and he died.

In earlier days, Sonny helped Al in getting an allotted space to sell fruit and vegetables at Haymarket in order to supplement his income. Al had a low paying job as a clerk at a supermarket and supported a family of five, wife, one boy and twin daughters. Usually, the allotted spaces were handed down within a family for generations and the rent was minimal. However, the allotment of spaces was tightly controlled mysteriously by the vendors. Sonny prevailed upon a vendor, Gino, in Alex's pizzeria to share his allotted space with Al. Besides, who was going to argue with Alex who was mentored by Sonny. Alfonzo and Gino worked it out so that their goods complemented each other. For example, Al sold New England produce, whereas Gino dealt mostly with produce from California and South America. This arrangement did not have much of an effect on Gino's clientele, since that was what he sold before joining with Al. In fact, it drew more customers to his goods and vice versa.

The two families got along very well. In fact, one of the twins, Angelina, became engaged to Gino's son, Renato, and they eventually married. However, not everything was rosy. The landscape at Haymarket changed slowly but surely with the appearance of thugs that were once associated with Whitey. Usually, the produce at Haymarket was stored Friday nights on location with canvasses covering the goods. The place soon became infested with drug dealers, addicts, muggers, prostitutes and trespassers who took liberties in raiding the produce under the canvas. It was a nightmare to witness the turn of events at Haymarket. Some vendors put their goods in refrigerated trucks, but this only reduced the margin of profit. Those vendors eventually quit the business and were replaced by new vendors who were affiliated with Whitey at one time. This was a recipe for disaster yet to come. Now, not only was there chaos at night, but also at day break when customers would trek to Haymarket.

The feeling around town was that sooner or later, something was bound to happen at Haymarket and something not very pleasant. It did. In one memorable night, as both Alfonzo and Renato guarded their produce, an outburst of gunshots erupted all over the area when they were half asleep. To this day no one knows why it happened and who initiated it. The police investigated, but no suspects and no motive were found. Renato was hit with a bullet that lodged near his heart and Alfonzo was shot in one of his kidneys. Renato is still walking around with that bullet as it was deemed too dangerous to remove. As for Alfonzo the damaged kidney was removed and a search was initiated for another kidney. Remarkably, he was such a bubbly person after that accident and nothing bothered him.

One interesting character who didn't particularly like Onofrio's being the padrone (boss) at the bocce courts was a person by the name of Chuck. His real name was Scarpone, Big Shoe. He never played the game of bocce, but it didn't prevent him from mouthing off about the game itself to the players. No player paid attention to him, since it was clear that he didn't know much about the game. He was about the same age as Onofrio. It did not matter what Onofrio did or said, he sarcastically criticized the padrone. Not once did Onofrio try to defend himself. Sonny came over to Vito to warn him to stay out of it. Obviously, Chuck was envious of Onofrio, because he was well liked by all and respected for the way he was managing the courts. After all, Chuck thought of himself as a man of honor and demanded respect. Apparently, Scarpone was a cab driver in Miami before Sonny arrived in Florida. According to Sonny, he was the carrier who transported money to Meyer Lansky, as depicted in the movie Godfather III. At this point, Vito understood Sonny's warning. Big Shoe thought that he should be in charge of the bocce courts, because he could do a better job in procuring sponsors' money. Soon after that spat, Chuck died. Perhaps, all that diatribe was the result of his suffering from a terminal disease, more reason for Sonny to shy away from engaging or confronting Scarpone.

No words can adequately describe Aniello, the hair stylist, who had assumed the professional name, Jean-Claude Sassoon. Vito and Anna had met him earlier at a cafe. He must have been wired differently at birth. He was a bundle of nervous energy on or off the courts. On the courts, it was outright painful to watch him play. On every toss of the bocce ball, his body would go through all sorts of contortions, twists and turns with the hope of guiding the ball in his mind, as if it were possible. At tournaments he was sky high and so nervous that he developed a tic. When Donato and Aniello got together on the same bocce court, it was hilarious. One would be yapping incessantly and the other bickering about the yapping, like a duet. They didn't like each other, but for some strange reason they played as a team. Everybody at the courts dropped everything to watch the "show". His wife needed "nails" to tie him down to a bench to prevent him from flying off. Nobody knew what world he lived in. He was a part-time bookie who had run the numbers racket until the mid-1980s. With Whitey's emergence in the underworld and the state lottery appearing on the scene for the first time in Boston, he was "unemployed". Aniello's stylist job was just a part-time one, not enough to support a family until he was employed by the subway system.

On weekends, he worked as a women hair stylist on Charles St. and walked around the salon like a female model to give the appearance of being "chic". However, his Italian accent betrayed his French name. Then again, to the customers, it made no difference, Italian or French dialects. At the bocce courts, he would advertise his salon to female tourists. Some took the bait and, remarkably, they all had the same look, a sheared-sheep look. It didn't take much for the players to unsettle him and they loved to tease him. He was entertaining and it was relaxing to watch his many faces and appearances and bullshit stories. He was the court jester.

Vito and Anna often took a walk after dinner to spend some time in the evening hours at the bocce courts. For him, it was a welcome distraction from applying for government grants for research money, the intensity of research, and teaching. Besides, he and Anna felt at ease being in the players' company. He liked being accepted by them as one of their own bullshit artists. He understood them more than they realized, but, most of the time, he kept his opinions to himself. He didn't want to appear a nerd out of sync with them and mar any relationship or acquaintance. It really didn't matter, because the word was out, due to Sonny's big mouth, that Vito was a former shepherd and did not have any pretense about himself or others.

Anna socialized with the wives of other bocce players. They formed a women's-only bocce club in which they competed in bocce tournaments among each other. She was also a member of Donne 2000 Club, a women's club. They participated in the planning of banquets sponsored by each society raising money for festivals. The Saint Anthony Society sponsored a banquet in the fall for the sole purpose of raising money for Saint Anthony festival at the end of summer. Other societies planned similar banquets in the fall as well. This made for a close-knit community in the North End, where everybody knew everybody else's business.

SIXTEEN

No Virgins This Time

In the summer evenings, Iaccarino rarely spent time at home. He lived in a hot studio apartment where everything was crammed into one room. Any respite from the summer heat was welcome. At the bocce courts, he had entertainment all around the park, friends, food, and an ocean breeze to cool down. However, mother nature has a way catching up with good and bad times. People like Iaccarino and Onofrio were getting old and frail. On one memorable evening, Iaccarino was savoring a doughnut while leaning on a light pole to watch a women's softball game. When he opened his eyes, he found himself on the ground looking up at women staring down at him. He was at the bottom of the steps and women softball players were surrounding him. He must have thought that he was in heaven, like Muslim martyrs, except these women were no virgins, or women symbolized in Fellini's movie, "8 1/2". He had had a stroke. Sonny, who was on the other side of the bocce courts managing a men's softball game, heard the news and sprang into action. News like that traveled faster than the speed of light among this tightly-knit community of people. He took charge and quickly seized the moment by asking one police officer playing on his team to drive him and Iaccarino to the emergency room at MGH. Iaccarino was too big and too woozy to put him on his Vespa. They got there in less than five minutes, going through every red light in downtown Boston. It helped to have a police officer driving and flashing a blue light atop his car.

A nurse performed a rudimentary examination and placed him on a temporary bed in the hallway near the Emergency Room. Sonny and his police friend waited, waited and waited. It was difficult to say how long, but Sonny went berserk. He went directly to the intern's office bypassing the nursing station with nurses chasing him to block his path. Somehow, Sonny evaded them and made it to the office. The intern was on the phone, probably talking with his girlfriend or boyfriend. Sonny stared at him and blurted out to the startled intern: "Unless you examine my father within five minutes, I will shove a baseball bat up your ass. I will save you the time to call the police. There is a police officer right outside your office." Strange as it may seem, all that infighting and insults at bocce courts between Sonny and Iaccarino, was just a way of expressing care for each other. The police officer entered the office to calm down the situation and told the intern that he could remove Sonny from his office. He asked the doctor if he was willing to file a report and make a statement about the threat and added that Mr. Alvaro always keeps his promises. However, his body language belied his remarks, suggesting otherwise. Within a short time, Iaccarino was examined by the intern and assigned a room for overnight observation.

Iaccarino's dream in color. Painting of Camille
Corot, Musee d'Orsay, Paris, 1850.

Sonny stayed in a waiting room overnight waiting patiently for any news about Iaccarino's condition. After being informed that Iaccarrino had suffered a mild heart attack, he looked for the intern and thanked him profusely, inviting him to the North End to have dinner at the restaurant where he worked. Exhausted and sleepy, Sonny walked home relieved, still dressed in a baseball uniform and shoes with cleats. He felt good about the incident with the intern and laughed to himself about it on the way home, promising himself to clean up his act. For a shepherd, that was an impossible promise to keep. Anyway, the bluff worked, only because of his cop friend. No way, was he going to harm the intern. Iaccarino did get better and, eventually, left the North End to live with his brother's family in the suburbs. He never returned to the bocce courts. For whatever reason, not clear to the bocce players, his brother forbade Iaccarino from returning to the courts. The brother claimed that his friends at the bocce courts were a bad influence on him. What a f..g joke. Iaccarino was no saint. He was one of the main cogs, if not the leader of the riff-raffs.

Somehow, Sonny was destined to become the saving "angel" of the courts. On another sad occasion one elder player, Gennaro, keeled over while tossing a bocce ball. Lucky for him, Sonny saw the whole incident, as he was standing on the third base line managing his team, a distance of only thirty feet. He rushed over giving mouth-to-mouth resuscitation. Sonny was getting desperate as he didn't know what he was doing until a medical intern appeared out of nowhere, pushed Sonny away from Gennaro and applying mouth to mouth resuscitation. Gennaro vomited right into the intern's face. Again, Sonny asked the same policeman to drive him and Gennaro to the emergency room. This time, Gennaro waited only a couple of minutes before the intern examined him and assigned him a room.

The intern advised Gennaro to lose a lot of weight. He weighed 250 pounds over a frame of five feet and four inches. Thereafter, his family put him on a strict diet and forbade him to enter anymore bocce tournaments, where food was served ad-infinitum. His family kept an eye on him at on the courts even when there were no tournaments, just as a precaution. After a while, Gennaro lost interest in the game that he once loved. It was too much of a hassle with the family about food and bocce. For him, bocce, food and wine were one and the same. He loved the whole package.

How the intern appeared at the bocce court was a mystery. Perhaps, he was sent from heaven as a result of Sonny praying for the first time in his life while kneeling over Gennaro. Being helpless in that situation evoked some sort of transformation on his part. Anyway, no one ever saw the intern before or after that incident. No one saw the intern drive away in a car or bicycle, but they saw him walking away after the incident. In fact, Sonny went to search for that intern at MGH to thank him with a dinner at the restaurant, but was unable to find him. He searched at all other hospitals in Boston to no avail.

There was no let up on the misfortunes of the older players. For a time, Onofrio had complained to anyone who could stand to hear him talk, even to tourists, about his tooth ache. One tourist, who happened to be a dentist, examined his teeth and recommended that he go to a dentist or to a hospital immediately. He ignored the advice. Soon after, his skin started to turn yellowish color and his jaw was swollen. He was developing jaundice. Finally, Sonny told Onofrio: "OK, that's enough; you have no options. Get your ass on that Vespa of mine. We are going to the emergency room." This was amazing that Sonny, half blind, drove Onofrio, at dusk, to the emergency room at MGH. The nurses were all smiles and friendly at seeing him and made way for his entrance. By then, he was recognized by the nurses as the saving angel, which Sonny detested. He wanted to come off as the brute one, but they knew that he was as harmless as a pussycat. As such, he was able to get attention from the intern immediately. How could the intern forget Sonny, who was very tough and soft hearted at the same time. The same intern of past encounters explained to Sonny that Onofrio had developed jaundice due to a blood infection. Sonny provided daily reports on Onofrio's condition to the bocce players. But his body language and the tone of his talk gave away the "real" condition of Onofrio. It was getting progressively worse. A month later he died, never leaving the hospital. That was the beginning of the end of the "Golden Age" of bocce in the North End. Yes, he deserved a statue of himself next to the bocce courts.

By that time, Sonny was enjoying the limelight. The stories of his excursions to the emergency room were gossiped all over town. Everybody wanted to know who this good Samaritan was. People went out of their way, crossing streets in heavy traffic just to shake his hand and say hello. He was the local hero, but he was too self-conscious to accept all the accolades. Besides, it spoiled his image as a rough and tough fellow. Everybody else in town knew otherwise. All one had to do was to pat him on the back a little to rev up his motor and get a smile out of him. He was a rather complex fellow. On one hand he loved to be a ham on the bocce courts courting the locals, but to strangers he was a very private person, in fact, almost anti-social. Perhaps, there was still some of that peasant attitude in him derived from the mountains, to trust no one. If he wasn't at the bocce courts, he hid in cafes incognito. After all, in a matter of six months, he had lost his "adopted parents", Iaccarino and Onofrio. This pattern was becoming more noticeable as he got older. As his pals were dying left and right, he became more withdrawn and reclusive. For whatever reason, only clear to himself, he wanted some distance from people, mentally and physically. Perhaps, he was in mourning or just wanted to be left alone, in deep solitude, as if up on the mountains of Cervinara during a violent storm.

Another storm was brewing elsewhere. At that time the Diocese of Boston, under the tutelage of Cardinal Sean Patrick O'Malley, declared that some churches in the North End were earmarked for closure due to financial difficulties in raising enough donation money to upgrade the church. For one thing, Sacred Heart Catholic church needed a new roof. Ever since the stories of the Church scandals about pedophile priests [16-1] broke out in the Boston Globe, as well as in other major USA cities, Catholic church attendance was considerably down. As such, Sunday collections diminished enough to warrant closures of some Catholic churches. The rumor in town was that the Diocese of Boston was going to convert some churches into condominiums, since condominium prices had sky-rocketed in the North End. Supposedly, the Diocese was empowered to sell the church properties, since they owned them. In particular, Sacred Heart Church was scheduled to be closed in six months. Only Saint Leonard and Saint Stephen Catholic churches were slated to remain open, but at reduced services.

Residents walked around town like zombies with no purpose in their walk. Exasperation was beginning to set in people's minds. They felt that the Silesian order of priests in the church had let them down. It was a helpless feeling in that no one in the church hierarchy was willing to listen to their plight. In an effort to placate people's feelings, the priests of Sacred Heart organized a get-together of residents and former residents, mostly to vent their frustrations over losing their beloved Church. The reality of the situation was that the Silesian priests had no leverage whatsoever on the Diocese of Boston, since they were about to be transferred elsewhere. The only time that the church heard anything from the Diocese was in regard to the bad news! Many residents had been baptized, married and received first communion at Sacred Heart. Residents at the meeting related how important the Church was to them, even though some no longer lived in town. Although some lived in suburbia, members of their family had received religious sacraments over the years from the Church. Both of Sonny's children were baptized there. At the meeting, a former resident proposed to repair the roof at free labor costs. Soon enough, the "flavor" of the meeting began to change from complaining about the closing, and more about proposing ideas on how to counter the Diocese's arguments for closing it down.

Sacred Heart parishioners crowded into the North End church on May 6 to fight its closure by the Boston Archdiocese. Among them was Daniel L. Passacantilli (center, with hand on face), planning to be wed in the same church as his parents, 34 years ago.

Closure threat looms over parishioners' lvies

Meeting of the parishioners at Sacred Heart
Church displaying more than concern.

A restaurateur volunteered to pay for materiel costs. In effect, the maintenance costs that the Diocese blamed for closing was a moot point. No matter, the Diocese was determined to close the Church regardless of any arguments presented. It was time of desperation and the residents were looking for a miracle or another Paul Revere to come to their rescue. But where and who? All were intimidated by the Diocese, including the priests. The parishioners were afraid to antagonize the Diocese in resisting the decision, since they had to learn to get along with the Diocese after the dust settled.

Sacred Heart Church, North End

There was no budging from the Diocese. The parishioners were devoid of feelings, because they were running out of time. The only feeling was one of desperation. Out of nowhere, at one of these weekly meetings, Sonny, with a piece of paper in his hand rushed to the podium. The locals' reaction was one of, "We don't need a f..g clown at this time". In an eloquent speech, Sonny presented a brief historical background of both churches, Sacred Heart and Saint Leonard. He explained that Sacred Heart [16-2] was built well before Saint Leonard by Methodist church members as a chapel for seamen in 1833. Saint Leonard was built with church donations from Italian immigrants in 1900. Hence, Saint Leonard Church was owned outright by the Diocese, since donations collected by the Diocese went into maintenance, building and salaries. However, Sacred Heart Church was bought from the Methodist parishioners by Italian immigrants from Sciacca, Sicily, who had converted the building into a Catholic church. Since the Sicilian immigrants held the deed to the property, they owned it outright. In essence, Sonny explained that the Diocese did not own Sacred Heart, and, in fact, the Diocese owed back rent since 1900. He didn't call for a revolution, but close to it. Another Paul Revere? Far from it. Then, in a broad smile as wide as the Charles River, he said, "I am holding the original deed on the property." He added, "We are not about to donate the deed to the Diocese".

For the first time in a long time, the Church was filled to full capacity at that meeting. Not a sound was heard from anyone after that declaration. There was total silence for a minute or two, all stunned by the announcement. The reaction was, "Did I hear that right?" Once the announcement registered loud and clear to everyone, a loud sigh of relief could be heard throughout the church and a loud applause erupted spontaneously. An "Angel" came by and saved the parishioners from jumping into the ocean. Yet, not a single person approached the messenger thanking him for the message. The people there didn't care who was holding that piece of paper. Sonny excused the ingratitude by the locals as a sign that they were exhausted from worrying about their Church. They wanted to believe in a miracle, not the man. Sonny could have waived a piece of toilet paper and they would have believed him. They didn't bother asking him where he got hold of the deed and how. No one cared. They just wanted to believe in the good news. They didn't care for proof or to see the document. The deed had been held with a person at the Sicilian Religious Society, since 1900.

After much wrangling, the Diocese reached a compromise. Sacred Heart would remain open, but only on Mondays, Wednesdays, Fridays and Sundays from 9:00 to 10:00 am. The Silesian order of priests at Sacred Heart was dispatched to NYC and no longer allowed to serve Mass in the North

End, including Fr. Cucu. The Franciscan Order of priests (monks) from Saint Leonard Church would take over the religious activities and serve Mass at Sacred Heart. Since the Diocese did not own the properties, they would not be responsible for the maintenance of Sacred Heart Church. It was a hard pill to swallow, but at least the residents could hold on to their past memories, thanks to Sonny.

It had not been easy for Sonny to obtain the deed. Sacred Heart Church was often referred to as "our Church" among members of the Sciacca Religious Society for good reason. They owned the Church. Some members attended church on Sunday and, after Mass, they congregated in their private club at the Church's basement watching Italian soccer games or having an espresso. They had been instrumental in recruiting Father Cucu. Father Cucu was comfortable in their company and often joined them in the basement. The release of the deed to Sonny, only for the purpose of presentation at the church, had to be approved by Williams (real name Gusmano), and, as it turned out, he was a good friend and golf partner of Sonny, Lorenzo and Father Cucu. Williams emigrated from Sciacca and was a former President of the Society. From his retirement home in Florida, he barked out orders to release the deed temporarily to Sonny. Once again, Sonny moved a mountain for the good of the community, but received no thanks. He didn't need a pat in the back this time. He just enjoyed the happy smiles of the parishioners and that was good enough for him. He was alive again and kicking. He had a calling and delivered.

Psychologically, he had been down in the dumps before the meetings. He needed something to lift his spirits. He was the type of person who could not stand to be down for too long. He knew, from being on the mountains, that every violent storm was followed by glorious weather. He rationalized that his luck was bound to change. His friends were dying left and right and others left the area for good. Things could not get any worse, when the Diocese planned to close Sacred heart Church. The town went on a downward spin. He thought that this couldn't continue. So, he looked for that spark to lift himself up as well as the spirit of others in town—but where. He was well aware that the Sciacca Religious Society held the deed to the Church. The problem was how to extract it from its members. The deed was protected as securely as Fort Knox by the Society. He reasoned that he himself could never secure the deed directly even for one minute, but his dear Sicilian friend Williams would be able to. He worked feverishly to secure the deed on a temporary basis.

Whatever magic Onofrio brought to the bocce courts in the past in order to meld together all those people with diverse personalities and backgrounds, he took it with him to heaven. A lot of the regulars at the courts were either leaving for suburbia and did nor return or had passed away. Onofrio had the only key to the shed where the bocce balls and maintenance equipment were stored. Ten more keys and a new lock were issued after his death. Everybody wanted to be the padrone of the courts, but no one cared to clean or maintain them. City Hall was not about to get involved with the bickering among players. The Community Center took possession of the keys. Hence, it was a local matter to be settled among themselves. The up-and-coming new generation of players, Chuck, Victor, Eric and others, had simply lost interest and rarely showed up at the courts. They outright refused to put in the work to maintain the courts. For one thing, they had jobs, and did not have the time.

As a result, the courts soon were taken over by newcomers who had little knowledge of the game. After a succession of a number of padroni of the courts including Jack and Jill, Uberto assumed the mantle of running the bocce courts. It was just a shadow of what it was before. Again, he did not have the time to run a restaurant and maintain the courts at the same time. It required someone, who was retired, dedicated, sociable, loved the game and was willing to give his time to teach novices. There had not been many of those kinds of people around, except for Onofrio. It became a weekend activity for Uberto.

With Onofrio and Iaccarino gone from the courts, the electricity left the place. Yes, there were still tournaments and new people showing up, but there was not the same enthusiasm for the game and the people surrounding it. Vito was spending more time at the university, but still spending some time at the bocce courts whenever the old guards showed up for the tournaments. Sonny and Uberto were the holdovers from the past, and responsible for maintaining the courts for a short time. In addition, Uberto and Sonny organized a special bocce competition for handicapped and autistic children once a month. In some sense, going blind was a blessing in disguise. It brought him back to what gave him peace of mind or that special spirit, from when he was isolated up on the mountains. Perhaps, God chose Sonny to be the messenger of goodwill. He found a purpose in life and that was to make a difference to people who needed it the most. He asked nothing in return and was rewarded just knowing that it made people smile. He loved people and that explains much of his behavior. They put their hearts and souls into that project at no cost to the city.

By and large, the courts became rundown. Dirt had not been replenished for more than two years. In the past, Onofrio would have prevailed upon Parks and Planning to do that every year at the beginning of the summer. Vito was fortunate to have straddled two worlds for as long as he did, but no more. The world of his childhood was saying goodbye to him slowly but surely. His presence at the courts was too painful; it reminded him too much of Iaccarino, Onofrio, and others and especially of their loyalty to their friends. It was time to move on. His numbness to that world grew each day. The old guard was replaced more and more each day by new faces and retirement. Still, he was grateful and proud to have known these beautiful people for they had enriched people's life from every corner of the world.

After about a year, Uberto relinquished the job of the padrone and whatever little time he had in running the courts. The only other person who commanded respect like Onofrio or Uberto was Lorenzo. He could be charming, but also stern when he had to be. The bocce players turned to him to maintain the courts, since he lived close by and everyone thought that he had the time to do it. Besides, he was no longer an active wiseguy and was getting up in age (83 years). Lorenzo accepted the role assuming the help of his son, Alex. However, Alex was the opposite of Lorenzo. Whereas Lorenzo was engaging, Alex was aloof and unsociable. He had a foul mouth and lacked the scholarly training of his father. Besides, he didn't have the time to hang around the Bocce courts. He rarely played the game. He was helping only to please his father. Whatever little time he spent at the courts, Lorenzo just liked to quote poetry to anyone visiting. He had a captive audience, since he made the bocce balls from the shed available. In the end, Lorenzo was too sick with a heart condition to spend time at the courts. In summary, the old guards were withering away with no young blood willing to take over. Once Lorenzo was out of the picture, Alex was happy to quit. Besides, Alex was too busy organizing the annual banquet promoting the Abruzzo societies in which he was the main sponsor in addition to running nightclubs, restaurants, real estate, pizzerias, etc.

SEVENTEEN

To and From Bunker Hill

Just as birds migrate with the change of seasons, so do people. Some Canadians and New Englanders migrate south, mostly to Florida and Arizona, for the winter months. Floridians refer to these winter visitors as "snowbirds". The weather can be rather clammy and cold in New England States and Canada any time of the year, especially in the winter. There is an expression in Boston which typifies the weather there, "Don't worry about the weather today; it will change tomorrow". Sonny and Vito were brought up in warm weather. Southern Italy is often referred to as the "paesi del sole", "sunny towns". In fact, they never made peace with the climate in Boston, although they adapted to everything else there.

In the early 1990s, Vito and his wife took extended weekend trips to Miami, FL, with the intention of someday living there permanently upon retirement. As such, Vito and Fairmont University negotiated a special amendment to the employment contract whereby he would teach in the summer and take academic leave in the winter semester while maintaining his status as a tenured professor. This was a way for them to take a bite out of the winter months in Boston. Also, it was a win-win deal for both the university and Vito. The University had a difficult time staffing senior professors for the summer semesters, as most of them left the university for summer vacations or to visit other universities.

That warm, velvety and gentle trade wind caressing Vito and Anna on arrival in Miami convinced them once and for all that this was the place for retirement in the future. He was pleasantly surprised to see small lizards in

Miami. The last time he had seen them was in Avella more than fifty years earlier. Like a lizard, he also loved to bask in the sun. Every winter, they were hell bent to return to Miami. There were a lot of problems in Miami in the 1980s and 1990s as most business establishments in Miami Beach were boarded up. Local newspapers were full of scary stories about European tourists being mugged and/or killed near the airport. Nevertheless, that was the place for Anna and Vito to be in the winter. The Chairman of the Physics Department at the University of Miami invited Vito to give seminars in magnetism to faculties and students in the winter of 1991. Vito was assigned an office and offered a small stipend which he had to refuse in order to avoid conflict of interest. A professor cannot draw two salaries at the same time from two universities. The hospitality allowed him to continue his research in the winter and be in contact with his students in Boston. At that time, he headed the largest research group at Fairmont University.

Thus, it was paramount for Vito to be in constant contact with his students in Boston via e-mail, faxes, telephone and visits from his students to the University of Miami. The chairman provided secretarial support in order to facilitate those communications. Most importantly, he was able to distance himself from the constant demands of academia, panel reviews for funding agencies, and teaching. It allowed him to produce some of the best research of his career. He started collaborations with faculties at Miami University and established a student exchange program between the two Universities as well as with the University of Rome, where he spent his sabbaticals.

Sonny was itching to get back to Miami. There were many reasons to do so: the weather, looking up personal friends, and nostalgia. He came and assisted his live-in girl-friend, who managed Suffolk University women's softball team in exhibition games in Miami in early spring. Sonny welcomed those spring breaks, but, mentally, he was still in Boston. He wanted to keep his grandson on a short leash. It was about this time that grandson Anthony graduated from high school and began to flex his muscles as a free-wheeling teen-ager, much like his uncle Sal had. His whereabouts were a mystery to the family. In daytime he slept and at night he was nowhere to be found. He had no interest in pursuing further schooling, a job, or a desire to enroll in military service. How he was able to sustain himself financially was also a mystery. His mother had suspicions, but no hard evidence. To say that the family was in turmoil again, was an understatement.

As a little boy, grandson Anthony was an altar boy, and Sonny, the usher, collected church donations. Sonny was like a mother hen monitoring Anthony's whereabouts. As an altar boy, Anthony looked like a Raphael's Angel with rosy cheeks and curly black hair and was so well behaved. He was the pride and joy of Sonny. Being a con artist, Sonny tried to implant in Anthony's mind that he was going to be a medical doctor in the future by introducing him to people as the first doctor in the family. He urged his daughter, Carmela, to put her boys, Ken and Anthony, in private Catholic school in the North End. He wanted to keep his grandsons away from the young riff-raffs of the North End. He knew enough about them that they spelled "t-r-o-u-b-l-e".

The first sign of trouble was when Anthony reached the age of puberty. He was constantly out in the streets with friends, when his mother Carmela was holding down a job at City Hall and his father, Ryan, at the police station. The kids vandalized the school yard and engaged in brawls with kids from Charlestown. These two groups never got along. At festival time, all hell broke loose between them. Some kids were seriously wounded, but nothing was ever reported in the newspapers about the fights and injuries. The feeling among the adults was, "It is just kid stuff." What they didn't realize was that all the fighting was a prelude for things to come, usually not good. Sonny had seen that behavior before with his son and he wanted no part of it. He became furious with Carmela. He was of the old school where a mother stayed home to take care of her children. However, he didn't practice what he preached. Carmela was feminist and just as stubborn as her father. It was that goat spirit in both of them. Carmela turned to Ryan, her husband and police officer, to do something about Anthony. He explained that Anthony was going through a stage of his life that all teenagers go through. Hence, nothing to worry about. That lackadaisical attitude irritated the living shit out of Sonny.

As always, Sonny waited for his pal from Avella at the bocce courts in the afternoons, just like a faithful dog. He needed to unburden himself, mostly about his grandson Anthony and what to do about his drug problem. Vito surmised as much, as Anthony sometimes showed up at the bocce courts totally stoned. On one particular day, he showed up while Vito and Sonny were playing bocce. Vito could see out of the corner of his eye that Sonny was sad and somber. He wanted to say something to him, but Anthony was unreachable. Anthony talked gibberish about nothing. He was totally incoherent and hallucinating. Sonny tried to cover up for the embarrassing situation. Vito went over to Sonny to lend support by telling him that there was no need to explain anything. Sonny talked and talked to unburden himself about the episode. He reminisced about the good times, when Anthony was a bright and cheerful boy excelling in school and was the running back on the football team. He loved to say that Anthony was as popular with the cheerleaders as he was. Suddenly, he turned toward Vito and shouted at the top of his lungs: "What the f..k happened?" It was sad to see Sonny in such a miserable state of mind.

Sonny was to the bocce courts what a ringmaster is to the circus. The difference being that Sonny was also the clown. He could no longer pretend to be the clown at the park. While coaching his softball team, Sonny sometimes called time out and approached the umpire at the plate. The umpire came over to Sonny and asked him what the problem was. Sonny replied that he had changed his mind. The umpire and the spectators had no clue as to why Sonny called time out. Then all of sudden, Sonny started again shouting at the umpire and kicking dirt on the plate about an earlier call by the umpire. After twenty minutes of this charade, he would wink at the umpire, plant a kiss on his cheek, and walk away as if nothing happened. The players knew all along what was coming and they got a big chuckle out of it. The spectators were befuddled but entertained and soon accepted it as being the time for Sonny to be Sonny. It has long been suspected that Sonny and the umpires planned this whole charade, because he was never thrown out of a game for all the shenanigans. It was not as if the umpires were unaware of what was coming from Sonny. They needed a break too! This was his way of re-assuring his friends that he was still the ringmaster and the clown of the courts. After the game, Sonny came over to Vito and said: "Billy has nothing over me." Sonny, being a Red Sox fan, hated Billy, but was willing to copy Billy's style of managing or bullshitting around the umpire. With all that bravura, Sonny didn't fool Vito. He was hurting and Vito knew when Sonny was not being himself.

Sonny was careful about sharing his concerns about Anthony and never mentioned anything about the new wave of drug dealers. Doing so could only get Vito in trouble and that was the last thing in the world that he wanted to do, a map of the drug trade. Besides, there was no need to go there. Vito was well aware of the lay of the land in the North End. There were more undercover agents in the streets in the morning than tourists at times. Also, one saw at the bocce courts all of the comings and goings of new faces. They were either dealing in drugs or drugged out of their minds. Some of them looked wasted, lying on benches in a stupor. By and large, the new faces were young and an intimidating bunch from South Boston, Charlestown and the North End.

The situation at the private school in the North End became intolerable. Anthony was in his environment with kids around him of the same mind set, raising hell. They dared each other to do the unthinkable, like having a drinking party on the grounds of the pre-revolution Cobb's Hill Burying Ground. Even the locals were offended by the drinking parties and the noise late at night. The family solution was to ship Anthony away from the bad influence of kids in the North End. Little did they realize that it was Anthony who was the bad influence. They enrolled Anthony into another private school run by the Catholic church in Newton, Nonantum area of town. Most of the kids went there for disciplinary reasons and/or to motivate them to learn basic verbal and math skills for college preparation.

About this time, his best friend Vinny, from kindergarten days, died of a drug overdose. Apparently, the rumor in town was that Vinny had experimented with a new and powerful drug called "Angel Dust". At the funeral, attended by the immediate family and friends of Vinny, Anthony was crying, sobbing and murmuring Vinny's name over and over. They had had a lot in common in terms of pursuing their own identities. They were rebels at a very young age, determined to chart their own courses. It put a damper on Anthony's drug use. At least it sobered him up enough to curtail a lot of the shenanigans that he was involved with before the death of Vinny. That peaceful interlude did not last long. Sonny was determined to find the source of drugs pouring into the North End. He discovered that most of it was coming from Roxbury and South Boston through Haymarket during the market days. Not much Sonny could do about the trafficking of the drugs and the new killer, "Angel Dust".

Anthony was becoming acclimated to the new neighborhood in Newton, so much so that he was doing things with his new friends like in the old days at the North End, mostly smoking pot and drinking parties on weekends. During one recess period, a nun teacher caught him with a plastic container of marijuana and he was immediately expelled from school. Sonny prevailed upon a local politician to vouch for Anthony but to no avail. Thus, drugs were reaching towns like Newton, Needham, and many like them, which was unthinkable before. Sonny and his family could no longer insulate Anthony from drugs anyplace in the USA!

This was no longer kid stuff gone bad. This was bad adult behavior which was not condoned in the family, especially by Sonny. The family was upset. The mother and father could not acquiesce to that type of behavior, especially when the mother worked in the mayor's office and the father in the police department's drug enforcement. Sonny knew the danger in that behavior as he had seen it before with his son's health deteriorating to a vegetative state. Anthony transferred to Columbus High School for his senior year in the North End where he was back to his old stomping ground. Carmela was at her wits end as to what to do with him, but Sonny never gave up on him. He would keep tabs on Anthony almost on a daily basis, though it didn't do much good.

As soon as Anthony graduated from High School and turned eighteen, Carmela threw him out of the house. Anthony, coming home after his graduation ceremony, discovered that his favorite Levy pants was tucked under the tire of a car parked on Quarter Street. He walked up and down the street to discover more of his clothes. The wind had blown his clothes all over the neighborhood. This was a desperation act from his mother's part to convey to him that she meant business. She refused to see him even after he pleaded to let him back in the house. The neighbors were enjoying this spectacle, since Anthony had been a pain in the ass with all those night parties at the cemetery. The only recourse for him was to turn to his grandfather. Of course, Sonny took him into his studio apartment, although Anthony refused to clean up his mess from throwing clothes all over the room. Initially, the two made peace with the mess until Anthony stole and sold Sonny's heart and soul, the Vespa motor scooter. It was Sonny's only mode of transportation.

Happy-go-lucky Sonny on his Vespa,
courtesy of mastro Fernando Masi.

Sonny really loved his Vespa which was powered by battery. He would drive from his apartment to work and most often around the North End. It gave him the option of getting around and socializing with more people. At Puopolo Park he would drive his Vespa and get to know and meet people from one end of the park to the other. Before, he only socialized at the bocce courts. One day he showed up at the bocce courts without his beloved Vespa and was swearing, kicking dirt and just raising hell with everybody there. He shouted at the top of his lungs, "Who in the f..k stole my Vespa." To Sonny, this was no joke; he needed transportation as if his life depended on it. His whole being was challenged. He searched all over the North End to no avail.

There was a lull in the search. Surely, if it was not to be found in the North End, then where? In one lazy Sunday afternoon, a tourist came by to say hello to an old acquaintance at the bocce courts. This was part of the ritual for tourists returning to the area. One woman tourist remarked that she saw a "cute" motor scooter that she had once seen in Rome. It was buzzing around the Bunker Hill Monument in Charlestown and she was annoyed by the noise and the distraction caused by a teenager driving it around the monuments. As she described the "cute" motor scooter and the obnoxious teenager riding it, ears began to perk up, like radar antennae, and attention focused on the tourist. "Was the scooter blue?", inquired Sonny. "No, it was green", replied the tourist. "Too bad", murmured Sonny. Nevertheless, he decided to take a look at the scooter one day, just in case. Besides, that was the only lead he had so far. Sonny rarely ventured outside the North End. To him, going to Charlestown was like going to the wild-west, even though it was only a mile away to Bunker Hill.

Sonny dreaded going, but finally made the trek to Bunker Hill Monument one afternoon. He didn't have much hope of finding his Vespa. Indeed, he was right. There were only obnoxious kids running around on bicycles trying to be a nuisance to the tourists. What to do? He decided to return home, but, half-way down the hill, he stopped and turned around, looking back to the top of the hill. He was in a quandary as to what to do, go back to Bunker Hill or not. After all, that was the only lead and he finally decided that he should follow through to the end and determine what's what. He sat down on a bench and waited and waited, for time was irrelevant. He was on a mission. In the mean-time, he was staring at the monument wondering what really happened there in the Revolutionary War [17-1]. He had time to read the inscriptions about the statues and was so wrapped up in the monuments that he forgot why he was there. He started heading home, when at the corner of his eye he could see a scooter coming up from a side street heading for the hill.

He quickly went back up the hill to take a good look at the scooter. A teenager was riding a green Vespa, bypassing Sonny sitting on a metal bench. The Vespa looked just like the one he had, except it was green. No, it can't be, Sonny thought. However, on a quick glance at the front tire, he noticed that the front bumper was slightly bent and the hubcaps were blue, everything else green. The bend in the bumper was due to a bad habit of Sonny driving his Vespa right into a post or a tree anytime he parked it. His eyesight was not that focused to allow him to park without bumping into

Statue of William Prescott at Bunker Hill, Charlestown.

obstacles. There was no need to examine the scooter further. It was clear to him that it was his Vespa.

How did it get here? Sonny did not want to confront the teenager as he had a pretty good idea what happened. One advantage that he had over the teenagers was patience. He knew that sooner or later teenagers there would goggle over the Vespa and ask the driver about the toy, much like when he brought his Vespa to the bocce courts. Teenagers all gathered by the Colonel Prescott statue and peppered the driver with questions about the scooter. Sitting on a bench nearby, Sonny could hear the name Tony pop up a number of times. He surmised that Anthony sold the Vespa to the teenager. It didn't matter to Sonny why Anthony had sold it. The kid was a mess mentally and physically. Confronting Anthony would only make things worse for the whole family. Forever the optimist, it was time to put a lid on the whole affair. However, it put a whole different "light" on his grandson. Henceforth, the relationship would become more guarded, as Anthony was no longer that sweet little boy that he once knew. It was difficult for Sonny, or for any grandfather, to erase those sweet memories, but he had to be realistic about the situation. He bought another Vespa and locked it up in the shed at the softball field together with the softball equipment and had the only key.

That was not the only thing that disturbed Sonny. He confided to Vito a number of times about his difficulties with Anthony at the apartment.

Exasperation was oozing out of Sonny. In short, he was at his wits end as to what to do with Anthony as he was turning Sonny's life and the apartment upside down. Material things can be replaced, but his mental state was affected to the extent that he was talking to close friends about his dilemma. Before, Sonny was a happy-go-lucky type of guy, always with a sunny disposition. After Anthony moved into Sonny's apartment, Sonny became brooding, morose, and simply a nasty SOB to anyone close to him. Anthony would come to Sonny's apartment at any hour of the day, drunk or drugged out. He started wearing his grandfather's clothes, since he refused to do his own laundry, but these were minor infractions. Sonny never divulged the major ones as they were too embarrassing. The two friends arrived at the same conclusion without the need to state it and that was that this kid was living way beyond his means. Sonny had a plan to separate Anthony from the source of money and drugs. He concocted a plan to drag Anthony's ass to Florida during the softball spring season that Suffolk College scheduled each year. Anthony had no choice but to come along. He told Anthony, in no uncertain terms, that he didn't trust his being alone in the apartment and, therefore, he would lock him out in spring.

Sonny concluded that there was more than one source of drugs that Anthony had access to and there was no way to limit his access to them. The only way to do that was to get back into the drug business, and he was not about to get involved with that again. Besides, there were too many independent drug dealers since the departure of Whitey from Boston. Finally, Sonny admitted defeat and wanted to proceed with his intention of taking Anthony to Miami and to the in-laws, at least temporarily. Also, Sonny desperately wanted to put some distance between Anthony and his friends in the North End, i.e. throw a monkey wrench into whatever plans Anthony had with those friends.

Anthony had places to go and things to do in Boston that required his presence. Of course, he was not about to divulge details of his active life. Sonny was just as determined to not let Anthony use his apartment as his headquarters for nefarious activities. It was a stalemate that Sonny easily won. Steady income was needed to pay rent and Anthony didn't have a steady legitimate job to rent a place of his own. Besides, no one would hire him given his past behavior. He was well known in the North End as the brat that he was. It was and is a small town. Sonny had a hunch that he was up to no fucking good and that was good enough for him to assume a hard-nosed attitude toward his grandson. Finally, Anthony reluctantly acquiesced to the trip to Miami. Together with the Suffolk University women's softball team, they traveled by bus to Miami. Anthony had no choice. It was either the streets or Miami. Besides, he was becoming more of a pain in the ass to the family and to the neighborhood. Sonny's apprehension was that his grandson was going to end up like his son.

The bus ride from Boston to Miami, took about twenty-five hours. Miami Dade University hosted Suffolk University each year. The University is centrally located near the beaches, the softball fields, restaurants, entertainment, etc. For young people it was a plus to be able to have some fun on the beaches and at the same time put in the work to get in baseball shape. The trip south included an overnight stopover in Washington, DC and Atlanta, Georgia, where Sonny and Anthony shared a hotel room. During the trip, Sonny spent a lot of time with Anthony trying to find out what happened to Vinny, in particular who supplied his drugs. Sonny knew most of the networks operating in the area, although he was no longer active. However, Anthony didn't bite, claiming that he was not aware that Vinny was doing drugs. That was a lie and both knew it. Sonny postponed the confrontation for another day. There was not much socializing for Anthony on the bus trip as Sonny had warned Anthony that he might look but don't touch "the merchandise", meaning the girls in the bus. After all, Anthony was a strapping and good-looking young man. The girls flirted and teased him, but Sonny had him on a short leash. He wanted no more headaches with Anthony spoiling the trip.

Transportation to the fields and beaches was facilitated by the same bus as from Boston. Sonny was in the old stomping grounds of his youth with Jesse, especially when the group was driving to the beaches along Ocean Drive past the art-deco buildings. Sonny was taking Anthony on his nostalgic trip reminiscing about the days of his youth. As they drove past 20th St. and the spot where the restaurant Wolfie's, was once located in Miami beach, Sonny recalled to Anthony the time he met Meyer Lansky there, Mafia legend of the 1920s. It seemed that every mafioso in the North End must have met Lansky in Miami at one time or another. Anthony didn't have a clue as to what Sonny was talking about. "Just as well", Sonny thought. Further north on Ocean Drive toward Hollywood, FL, Sonny pointed out the spot where his brother and he opened a pizzeria, no longer in existence.

Although Anthony was upset about being dragged to Florida, the up side to it was that he was going to visit his grandmother, Jesse, in Miami for the first time. Jesse lived in a district of Miami called "Little Havana", where most Cuban refugees resided. She managed a family restaurant featuring mostly Cuban dishes. Anthony managed to escape Sonny's watchful eyes by staying at his grandmother's house for a couple of days. He took a taxi together with four women softball players to the Carina restaurant on Coral Way, where his grandma was working. Sonny didn't want to go for the simple reason of avoiding any potential embarrassment for Claire, his new companion. However, Jesse was looking for him, inquired about him and was upset, to say the least. Anthony invented a cock and bull story about nothing, explaining why Sonny couldn't be there. Obviously, Jesse missed Sonny and that was made known to him by Anthony.

Anthony's job at the softball games, playing on "home" field, was to do all the menial routine work, like carrying equipment, lining up the bases with white chalk powder, carrying water and drinks, etc. After the game, he was responsible for securing the equipment in a shed provided by the host college. "Home field' meant the field where the host college played their games. At games away from home field, Anthony had the responsibility of loading all the equipment of his team onto the bus. Sometimes, a girl's undergarment was suggestively slipped into the uniforms that were to be packed by Anthony for an away game. When the ruse came to Sonny's attention, he made sure to fib to the girls on the team that Anthony was on probation from the law and he was to do civic duties as part of the probation, such as janitorial work for a school. Sonny didn't want to encourage any shenanigans between Anthony and the girls. Sonny's obfuscation worked like a charm. The girls avoided Anthony like a plague. Surprisingly, Anthony actually liked the area after a couple of weeks and began to cultivate friends there. Sonny always liked the area for nostalgic reasons. It was the first safe place (away from Genovese) that his family settled in to call home, when they emigrated to USA and, also, it was the city where he got married and started a family.

As soon as there was a break in the schedule of games, Anthony and Sonny rented a car and drove to Miami to visit Jesse. Sonny didn't want to return to Boston without doing that. Anthony could see from Sonny and Jesse's body language that there was still that special spark between the two. They were still in love with each other. Anthony surmised that sooner or later the two would re-unite, since the strain between the two, due to raising the family, had lessened to some extent. Also, the deep hurt over the death of their son Sal was beginning to heal. The old man still had it. His Flamenco dancing at the nightclub that night, that they had often frequented in their younger days, was nothing less than exquisite and full of passion. Anthony blushed as he had never seen his grandfather like this before. He had only seen that stern and admonishing look.

In fact, Anthony looked forward to the trip for the following year, although he had worked his ass off on the fields in this visit. That was music to Sonny's ear. Hopefully, he thought, whatever spell his friends in the North End had over Anthony was broken. As it turned out, it was only the beginning of more heartaches. Anthony was scheming just like Sonny did at the same age. In a way, it was reminiscent of old times—something was frozen in time. Nothing changed from the times when Sonny was doing trafficking in contrabands. Anthony saw an opportunity to smuggle cocaine to Boston, which was readily available in Miami, via the bus used to transport the equipment for the softball team. The plan was rather simple. Switch a regular softball base to one filled with cocaine and transport it to Boston with the rest of the softball gear north. As much as two kilograms of cocaine could be packed in a softball base. The street value was then about $80,000. A net profit of $70,000 to $75,000 could be realized. Everything was in place: people, place, transport, etc., to carry out the scheme. He spent the whole stay in Miami setting it up. He was organizing a network of contacts, just like old times, as Sonny once did.

The return trip to Boston was uneventful except for the mess that Anthony had to unscramble in the shed at Miami Dade University. The shed contained equipment belonging to both Miami Dade and Suffolk University. He had to separate equipment, uniforms, cleats and helmets before the team and coaches showed up at the bus terminal. All softball bases looked the same. It was impossible to ascertain the identity of the softball bases. Suffolk brought their own bases which were identical to the ones belonging to the host college. The same problem arose when dropping the equipment into the shed near the softball fields in Puopolo Park. The teams, women's and men's, stored their equipment there, including that of Suffolk University's team, Sonny's team and that of other colleges. It was more as though they threw the equipment in the shed. What Anthony had in mind, was the perfect mess to the sheds to carry out his plan for switching bases to transport cocaine to Boston.

Sonny and Anthony arrived at a truce in maintaining the apartment in a decent, livable condition. They did laundry together every two weeks. However, this time Sonny kept the new Vespa in the apartment rather than tying it up in the shed or outside the apartment. Sonny never revealed to Anthony what he discovered about the disappearance of the previous Vespa. He could not antagonize Anthony, especially when he had to live with him. In Sonny's lexicon, frigetz (forget about it) about the other Vespa was his best option, especially when things improved between the two. However, appearance was deceiving.

Anthony claimed to be attending a local community college, taking night classes to train in the new computer technology to become a computer technician. That was just a ruse for Anthony to run out at night. It was clear to Sonny that Anthony was living beyond his means and, yet, he was not holding down a job. Sonny's sources from past contacts and personal networks were not volunteering any information about Anthony's whereabouts. That was exactly what worried Sonny the most. His friends were shutting him out of their inner sanctum of gossip. He was no longer privy to all the gossip in town. There was no way for him to get back in good grace with them. Anthony was an up-and-coming star in their eyes, perhaps an earner like Sonny had been at one time. It was a riddle that Sonny just could not solve about Anthony's hidden life, but he knew something did not add up. Anthony was flashing money left and right, but had no steady job. That thought was haunting Sonny.

Sonny was busy with work at the restaurant and part time jobs, from morning to night, and didn't have the time to wonder about what Anthony was up to every hour. His days of raising a child were over a long time ago. The whole family was resigned to the fact that Anthony was hell bent on charting his own course. Anthony showed up at the softball field whenever the Suffolk women's softball team had a game scheduled at the park. He would help in lining up the fields and putting away equipment in the shed after the game. He was just scheming to go back for the ride to Miami with the Suffolk team. The kid was sly as a fox.

By helping out, it helped his cause to come along for the ride to Miami. By that time, he was getting comfortable doing the janitorial work around the softball field. The following year, Anthony was again invited by Suffolk to help out in field maintenance in Miami. As for Sonny, he would sneak out sometimes to watch the Red Sox at Fort Myers. He didn't mind the two-hour drive along Alligator Alley on the way to the Red Sox spring training camp, but he hated the thought that, one of these days, an alligator might pop up from the canal and surprise him on the highway. That was one of the payoffs in his coming to help—to see Red Sox players in training. The other payoff was the time he spent in Miami with Jesse. They decided to re-unite and go back to Boston together later in the spring. This meant that Anthony would have to go back to Boston on the bus alone with the Suffolk team, surrounded by all those women. What a price to pay! For Anthony, women were the last thing on his mind at that time. It suited him just fine to get rid of Sonny on the ride home as he didn't want to involve Sonny in his scheme of transporting cocaine north. Since Anthony was mainly responsible for the upkeep of the softball bases, he could easily switch a base loaded with cocaine for a regular one.

Miami has been known as the capital city of cocaine trafficking in the USA as far back as the 1930s. The contact between drug dealers in the North End and the cocaine network in Miami had been established long before Anthony appeared on the scene. The financial arrangement, of course, organized by the wannabes of the North End could only have been done with established means of communications, more or less established by Davide and Sonny, when they were in Miami. Anthony was just the conduit between these two groups of people, the Miami network and the wannabes of the North End. The plan was for Anthony to leave the shed open at the softball field in Miami Dade the evening before departure for Boston. Someone would come by the shed and exchange a regular base bag with one loaded with cocaine. With this plan, Anthony could always claim innocence, if it failed. The plan was carried out by Anthony as smoothly as possible. In the morning of departure from Miami, the softball equipment together with the cocaine loaded base, was placed onto the bus by Anthony along with other regular softball bases.

As always, things never work out as planned and this was no exception—Murphy's law. On the way back, the bus driver was cited for speeding in North Carolina. South and North Carolina are known as the speed trap states of America. Surprisingly, the driver was not aware of this well-known speed trap. The thought did cross Anthony's mind that, perhaps, the state police were on a lookout for drugs, when he heard the sirens. However, when the police approached the bus, there were no dogs sniffing for drugs. Anthony breathed a sigh of relief. Back in Boston, the softball bases, including the "loaded" one and the rest of the equipment were stored in the shed near the bocce court. As planned, the shed was left open with the lock hanging loose. The loaded softball base was later picked up by a friend of Anthony, who had been waiting for the bus to arrive. The friend mingled among spectators watching bocce games prior to the arrival of the bus. The softball base loaded with cocaine was replaced with a regular one and the shed, in turn, was locked up. That was Anthony's first drug delivery to wannabes in the North End and he handled it very smoothly. Indeed, time stood still. Fifty years earlier or more similar types of activities took place from Florida to Boston via pizzerias.

Sonny remained in Miami until the end of April waiting for the weather to improve in Boston. By March in Cervinara there are flowers all over the hills and the sun is smiling and inviting people to come out of hibernation. Early spring may be windy, but it rarely snowed in the town itself. In contrast, March snow blizzards are not uncommon occurrences in Boston. Sonny kept threatening Vito that one day he might move into his apartment in Miami, just a joke between the two. However, he and Jesse did visit Vito in Miami to enter a bocce tournament in Griffith Park. He confided to Vito that he felt at home in Miami. In a way, He was torn between returning to Boston or staying in Miami, with Jesse opening a pizzeria even though he was blind as a bat. He had no intention of dealing with cocaine again.

Claire was well aware of Sonny's special connection to the area and his recent dalliances with his former wife. She, in fact, welcomed the reconciliation between Jesse and Sonny. She was moving on to bigger Title IX programs at other big-time schools in the mid-west and west coast. She was appointed volley ball coach at Washington State University, knowing full well that Sonny had no desire to move to the West coast. All of his friends lived on the East coast. Sonny and Claire had had a beautiful relationship, but it was time to move on. Time has a way of healing all wounds and past memories.

To Sonny's surprise, Jesse wanted to return to Boston. She missed her children and grandchildren and was anxious to get back. After much deliberations, they decided that Jesse would move in with Sonny. This meant that Anthony had to move back with his mother, assuming it was acceptable to Carmela. Sonny was happy with the new arrangement for Anthony was one big pain in the ass. Besides, Sonny wanted his studio apartment back. It was out of the question for Jesse to move in with Sonny and Anthony in such a small apartment. They would have been at each other's throats within a matter of minutes. Carmela was ecstatic to learn that her mother was coming back to Boston to live with Sonny. They rented a U-Haul truck to load all of Jesse's personal possessions and drove north on Highway 95, which was so familiar to Sonny from his past life. On the way back, they stopped at a pizzeria where many years ago Sonny made stops to deliver cocaine powder.

EIGHTEEN

Return of the Prodigal Grandson

In the post era of Whitey's empire, whether it be Irish or Italian gangs, they were very disorganized. The gangs fragmented into many independent illicit operations. The Winter Hill and the South Boston Irish gangs broke up into many drug dealing groups, since drugs were so accessible. Many of the Mafia underbosses were still in jail due to the eavesdropping work by the FBI, thanks to Whitey. This was a great time for young wannabes who were not in jail and had not yet made the FBI files. For Anthony, it was easy to be associated with local wannabes. This meant that each small subgroup operated independently. Davide's operation in Medford was totally legitimate. His pizza business alone was well established and popular in town and was thriving financially. Hence, there was no need to delve into cocaine trafficking. Uberto's operation in East Boston was involved with laundering money derived from drug dealings. Sonny worked at Davide's pizzeria only when he was in need of money.

Thus, a whole new generation of wannabes appeared on the scene and they were striving to be recognized. Soon after Anthony's return from Miami, he and his friends were involved in a violent fracas with the boys of Charlestown just before one of the summer festivals in the North End. Usually, a few get hurt in these yearly confrontations, but this time it was different. The commotion heard by the bocce crowd and by tourists from the brawl was loud, and gunshots could be heard coming from behind the skating rink. Uberto rushed from the bocce courts and Sonny, hearing the shots from the softball field, rushed there. A crowd of bocce players and tourists gathered at the skating rink building facing the ocean side. By this time, all the combatants involved in the brawl had disappeared except for one teenager and a young man sprawled on the ground. The teenager was shot once in the arm, and was bleeding profusely, and the other victim was stabbed in the stomach, his intestines clearly visible. Blood was gushing from both the victims. It was none other than Anthony who was bleeding from the stomach. It was a drug deal that had gone bad, details of which are still murky to this day. Most likely, it had something to do with cocaine secured by Anthony in Miami.

View of the skating rink from Charlestown. The indoor bocce courts are located in the smaller building attached to the skating rink. The brawl occurred to the right of the bocce courts building, next to the pier. Cobb's Hill Burying Ground is besides the tallest tree in the background. The Old North Church is a block from the Cemetery.

Sonny went berserk, when he arrived on the scene. For the first time in his life, he got on his knees, clutching Anthony, tearing his tee shirt from his back, wrapping it around Anthony's stomach and gently caressing and reassuring him. Uberto rushed back to his van and drove over the sidewalk to the back of the skating rink; he loaded both the teenager and Anthony into the back of the van. He and Sonny, in the passenger seat, drove them to the MGH Emergency room. By this time, the emergency staff welcomed both Uberto and Sonny as the good Samaritans, since lately Sonny had been taking sick and injured people quite regularly to the emergency room. Within a few minutes, the two young men received medical attention and were assigned a hospital room. Sonny waited patiently for the doctor's prognosis. It did not look good. Anthony had lost a lot of blood. There was a real danger that other organs may have been infected. Sonny's tee shirt was soaking wet with blood, and his upper torso, covered in the team uniform, were soaked in blood.

Minutes after Uberto left the crime scene, the Boston Police showed up at the scene of the shooting. Officer O'Toole, Anthony's father, led the investigation. He secured the area and collected evidence in a plastic bag containing cocaine powder, an empty bullet cartridge and a bloody knife. The gun was never found. Most likely, it was thrown into the ocean. Officer Ryan became aware of who the victims were, since a big crowd of people began to circle around the crime scene. One of them shouted to officer O'Toole that Uberto drove Anthony to MGH. He had a suspicion that Anthony had been involved with a bad drug deal and decided to pocket the plastic bag containing the powdered cocaine. Immediately, Ryan left the scene to head toward MGH and his colleague took over the investigation. As an officer of the law, he was responsible for writing a report of the crime scene and turning in all evidence. However, as the cruiser stopped by the Boston Garden, he emptied the plastic bag containing cocaine powder into the street sewer and the knife into a garbage container. Although the relationships among Sonny, Ryan and Anthony were, at best, strained, Ryan was not about to incriminate Anthony for any potential crime involving cocaine.

Sonny and Ryan maintained vigilance the entire night waiting and praying for a prognosis from any of the medical staff. His grandmother, mother, father and brother, took turns waiting for reports at the hospital. Sonny stayed there for three straight days. When he received word that the infection was localized and the wound stabilized, he went home to rest for he was sleepy and exhausted. Besides, he was getting tired of hospital cafeteria food. He even volunteered to cook for them. An intern lent a nurse's blue uniform to cover Sonny's torso during his stay in the hospital. How ironical that, on one hand, Anthony was dealing in drugs, and, on the other hand, Sonny organized a bocce tournament under the banner, "North End Against Drugs".

Anthony remained in the hospital for a month. Doctors removed the stitches and the threat of infection spreading through vital organs seemed to have vanished. However, he could not physically exert himself much. Even lifting a bottle of water was an effort for him. During the convalescence period, he moved back to his parents' home under the watchful eye of Jesse. Even Ken pitched in, helping Jesse do chores such as picking up medicines and brought soup instead of pizza for Anthony. In his mind, Ken was already practicing to be a doctor. Ken and Anthony began to re-acquaint after many years of fighting each other, making up for lost time. Anthony was the prodigal grandson who came back home, except here the prodigal grandson was the elder brother.

For the first time in his life, Anthony was no longer restless and on the go. He had no choice in the matter. His wound was very serious and it required long rehabilitation. He was at peace with himself and was resigned to do better toward the family. Ken had Anthony all for himself and was happy to tell Anthony about performing Sinatra's song at the festival. Ken was a self-made entertainer emulating Sinatra. The North End was and is Sinatra country. Sinatra had been invited to sing at the festivals for many years, but, as always, prior engagements prevented him from coming. His commitments extended for more than two years ahead of scheduled events. Societies who collected money for the festivals could make commitments for only one year in advance, since the cycle of banquets, donations and special events were renewed yearly. At the end of the calendar year, the money was committed for the upcoming festival only. Most likely, it was a money issue. Sinatra was not going to come on a bag of peanuts or IOUs! Ken was invited to the festivals as a substitute and only on Friday night stage events. That night, local talent was invited to perform at no cost to the organizers. The North End crowds loved to have performers who sang any song made popular by Sinatra, especially when Ken was on stage.

Anthony was proud of Ken for the first time in his life. For once in his young life, he appreciated Ken for what he represented to the family and he wanted to be part of that. Something magical happened. Anthony cried and apologized to Ken for the way he had treated him in the past. According to Anthony, not even a dog should be treated that way and he wanted to amend for his past behavior. Anthony must have done a lot of soul searching during that month in bed.

Ken enrolled at the University of Massachusetts, majoring in biology. His dream was to eventually study to be a medical doctor. He worked in the summer at MGH. His career as a singer took a slight detour thereafter. He was able to get singing engagements at weddings, festivals and at private parties. However, his primary goal was to become a medical doctor. Of course, he was goaded by Sonny. Sonny went out of his way to organize singing contests among young people at his bocce tournaments. He absolutely reserved the right to introduce Ken on stage as the only doctor from the North End. In fact, there were more than twenty doctors who had been born in the North End. It didn't bother him to lie about that, as long as the intended target was Ken.

Sonny didn't want anyone in the immediate family getting hurt by snooping around in the drug business, as Ryan did. It was, then and now, an extremely dangerous endeavor. According to Sonny, they were all a bunch of double-crossers in that business, both the police and drug dealers. Drug dealing was getting to be very complex and combustible. There were too many dealers who were fiercely independent. Then again, in the courtyard, where he once lived, police officers and mafiosi lived side-by-side for years without many incidents. Although, Sonny gave his blessing for the marriage many years ago, the relationship between Sonny and Ryan was somewhat strained. It was peaceful co-existence for many years. In public, they acknowledged each other's presence, but that was the extent of it. There were no pleasant exchanges between the two. Formality prevailed.

The drug scene in South Boston was hot and heavy even though Whitey left. Ryan was also very familiar with the people there and the drug scene. His family once settled in South Boston and lived there for 10–15 years. Also, being in the drug and enforcement division allowed him to investigate known drug hangouts. When Ryan first appeared in South Boston, Whitey was a legend there as well as in neighboring districts like Dorchester. People looked upon him as a "Robin Hood" of South Boston. The difference being that this modern-day Robin Hood took it from the poor and destitute and gave crumbs back to the ones drugged out who, in turn, returned the money by purchasing more drugs. Thus, money made a full cycle back to Whitey.

Initially, Ryan thought of Whitey as a modern day Robin Hood, until he discovered the misery that Whitey brought to South Boston and vicinity with drug imports, despite denials from Whitey. Some of the victims from drug overdoses were among his best friends. He rose through the ranks to be the lead investigator in that precinct. South Boston was not the only place where drugs could be found. There was an epidemic of drugs throughout the Boston area. Laws were passed to deter the use of drugs. First time offenders of possession of drugs were automatically jailed. Still, the new laws had no impact on their use and distribution of drugs. Bribes to police officers were common, especially if confiscated drugs by police disappeared from holding cells and returned to dealers. The monetary payoffs in returning drugs were enormous compared to their salaries.

When Whitey went on the lam from the law, more independent drug dealers or gangs sprang up in South Boston and elsewhere. There was no one to be accountable to, since Whitey was not going to be around to shake them down for protection money. The big-time drug dealers, like the cartels didn't care with whom they did business, since their network dealt directly with street dealers, no middlemen or people like Whitey. The source of drugs was finite, but the number of dealers increased substantially with Whitey gone. This created a lucrative market for policemen to be corrupt, since competition for drugs raised the price of drugs and bribes. It enticed people like Anthony to get involved in this lucrative business.

One incident stood out at Haymarket. Most established vendors were aware that there was an undercurrent of illicit trade not visible to most shoppers. Tourists tended to romanticize the outdoor farmer's market similar to the ones in Europe, especially Italy, but locals knew better. Like the rest of the North Enders, Friday and/or Saturday was reserved for shopping at Haymarket. A habit instilled by their forebears. During the 1950s, the farmer's market extended from Salem to Merrimac Streets and it was a must thing to do for immigrants from all over the area. It allowed them to purchase food at lower prices. Sonny warned Vito, "Get your shopping done early and quickly and get the f..k out of there." He never explained to Vito why. However, Sonny was in constant contact with vendors and they sensed that something was brewing with these recently employed part-time helpers. One didn't question Sonny about it, one just did as told. New helpers showed up every week with no knowledge of their products, fruits and vegetables. They appeared totally stoned, drugged out, and obviously waiting for something to arrive and it wasn't fruit and vegetable cartons. By late Saturday afternoon, there was a frenzy to clean up the mess created by the previous two days of shopping.

Like condors, people scavengers descended on the scene out of nowhere looking for unsold products of fruits and vegetables. Most of it was unfit to eat, but it didn't stop them from looking all over. People searched among discarded garbage boxes containing mostly rotten products. This was the "perfect storm" or "perfect chaos" to conduct illicit business. Part of the crowd scavenged all over while others were heading home from shopping. Vendors scurried around to pack their canvases, tables, and baskets into their cars, trucks and vans and go home. Drug dealers, who were the hired helpers there, utilizing the commotion of people scurrying about, waited for drug shipments to be loaded into their vehicles. In a mad rush, these so-called helpers rushed to an oncoming van picking up boxes of assortment of drugs. The so-called helpers disappeared within a few seconds. It was a bold and brazen plan, since it took place in the late afternoon on Saturday among so many people whose focus was on something else. Drug dealers used the timing of people's commotion all around to their advantage, the perfect man-made chaos.

However, the old-time vendors were not fooled as they were highly suspicious of those new hired helpers. They were hired to do menial work in carrying heavy equipment to vehicles belonging to vendors, not to accommodate themselves and leave soon after the customers left Haymarket. Besides, where did those boxes laden with drugs come from? Certainly, it was not part of the vendors' inventory. They smelled a rat, although the area was infested with real ones. The old-timers were confused as to their identity, but not Sonny. He figured out that these boys were not from the North End, but most likely from South Boston and vicinity. The dots were connected between the points in question, when Ryan and Carmela were brought into the picture. Ryan instantly recognized those young men. They were part of a drug ring from South Boston and Dorchester. His investigative unit had been surveying the drug activities in South Boston for a number of years. Also, he saw them grow up from kids and knew their parents from the time he resided in South Boston. Unbelievable as it may have seemed, there was a collaboration between Ryan and an old time mafioso, Sonny. As in the movie "To Catch a Thief", sometimes it takes a thief to catch one.

Thus, Ryan concluded that the source of drugs was via Haymarket, away from the everyday drug dealing in South Boston and Dorchester. Haymarket was put under surveillance by the Boston police drug enforcement division. Ryan organized a dragnet to trap the dealers in the van. Police officers dressed in regular everyday clothes were observing the comings and goings of all the vendors and helpers there including the new faces pretending to be vendors. Out of nowhere, underground policemen jumped into action and raided the van being unloaded with boxes full of drugs. The drug dealers were apprehended with the boxes in their possession as well as the helpers. The boxes were full of a variety of drugs: cocaine, heroin, marijuana, etc.

As in any drug raid, the confiscated drugs were stored at the police station or precinct. In Ryan's report, he listed fifteen boxes. The drug dealers caught in the raid were out in the street long before the story appeared in the local newspapers and evening TV news. The next day, inventory of all confiscated drugs stored in the police station revealed that there were fourteen boxes rather than fifteen. Naturally, all eyes turned to Ryan. He protested over the attention being focused on him. He actually never counted the boxes; someone else did the counting. He was accused of stealing one box and was suspended from the police force without pay. Fortunately for Ryan, a police officer at the precinct, came forward to inform the supervisors that indeed he counted fifteen boxes, when first received. This meant that another police officer confiscated one of the boxes. This episode, however brief, together with Anthony being at MGH put tremendous pressure on the family. Nothing was going right for Carmela's family.

Although the relationship between Sonny and Ryan had been strained over the years, Sonny not only supported but helped Ryan during this trial period. To Ryan, a mafioso was always a mafioso and Sonny was one of "them". Omerta is a lifetime oath that one cannot dismiss readily. Doing so can be consequential. However, Sonny was the glue and the cheerleader that bound the family together. Finally, Ryan saw the human side of Sonny, a pussycat wanting to be patted. Ryan thanked him for believing in him during that trial period. After all those years of looking at each other suspiciously, Ryan and Sonny came to the realization that family was more important than anything else. Ryan realized that Sonny had "retired" from the Mafia and it was all in the past. Sonny had turned the page and he realized that he should too. However, Sonny did not become harmless after his "retirement" from the Mafia. He was always harmless even when associated with them. It was remarkable that Sonny had survived from such a harsh environment in his younger days. Somebody upstairs must have looked over his shoulders so that he didn't have to do that anymore in old age.

NINETEEN

The Lone Ranger and Tonto

In 2013, Sonny qualified for disability retirement from Social Security. He was happy as a clam. He savored this moment that he had been waiting for a long time. Rumor circulated around town that someone in the Social Security Office "cooked the books" for Sonny which was totally false. Yes, there was a person who helped him in the application process. Dealing with that office can be exasperating and time consuming. The person helping Sonny just pointed which door to knock or who to call to get the correct information. However, once disability was confirmed, the process moved rapidly. He could finally get some proper medical attention for his eyes from experts at MGH, rather than from the friendly pharmacist at the drug store in town. He scheduled two appointments to see eye specialists. Both medics concurred that Sonny needed eye surgery in both eyes. He had procrastinated forever about having surgery. In the meantime, he drove his Vespa all over town even though he couldn't distinguish the color of traffic lights.

When he played bocce, he could not distinguish the difference between burgundy and green colored bocce balls. On every toss of the bocce ball, he approached the pallino just to see where his ball stopped relative to others. A player had to tell him which colored ball to toss. Too bad Iaccarino had left town; he would have had a field day with Sonny. Vito warned Sonny about driving at night especially in dark streets where his visibility was somewhat limited. In order to encourage Sonny to ask for someone else to drive at night, Vito would say to him: "You know, Sonny, the Lone Ranger was half blind too, like you. He asked Tonto to help him ride even in open valleys in broad daylight. Imagine that!" The implication was that the Lone Ranger didn't ride at night and neither should he. Of course, Vito lied. The trails in the valleys were as wide as the length of a football field and there were no Vespa scooters there where the Lone Ranger chased the "bad" guys. Besides, the Lone Ranger didn't need any help from Tonto. Everybody there at the bocce courts got a big chuckle from the snipe from Vito, but Sonny would not let anyone else smirk or chuckle at his expense, except for Vito, Luca, Lorenzo and Alex. Others simply could not. They were told in no uncertain terms to "fuck off". Sonny turned to Vito smiling, and winked, "I know". He just wanted to forget about his medical condition and surgery in particular.

Ryan showed up more and more at the bocce courts to help Sonny in running the bocce tournament and the talent show for young kids. In addition, Ryan assisted Sonny in managing the softball team. The two of them seemed to be inseparable and got along nicely in those days even though their backgrounds were as different as night and day. He admired Sonny for reaching out to kids, especially handicapped children, and older people around the bocce courts given Sonny's condition. At other times, Carmela was there to help run the tournament together with Ryan. Ryan was demoted to a beginner level as a bocce player. Sonny was preparing those two for the time when he was not going to be around anymore. Being a highly superstitious man, he must have felt some sort of premonition that that day was coming soon.

At each tournament organized by Sonny, Luca was in charge of grilling hotdogs and hamburgers as well as providing soft drinks, salad, potato chips, watermelon, etc. at no cost to Sonny. He owned the Luca restaurant, and clowned around with Sonny each day while serving him breakfast. Sonny and Luca went back a long time, all the way back to the town of Cervinara. Luca's family owned farmland on the mountains where Sonny's sheep grazed the land. Vito discovered by accident that Luca was his distant uncle. Luca was a distant cousin of Vito's aunt. In the heydays of Sonny, when he was an earner, the two of them owned two thoroughbred horses that ran in races all over the USA. These cozy relationships between the two did not help either of them at tournaments. Both wanted to annihilate each other on the bocce courts. Some tourists thought that they were about to shoot each other. It was just a show for the benefit of the locals and that deep desire to win at all costs. The regular players were totally indifferent to that, as they had seen it a number of times.

Often, Sonny had breakfast at Luca's restaurant. Luca absolutely wanted to be the one to serve food at Sonny's table, although two waiters worked for him. He relished serving breakfast only for Sonny. He never charged Sonny for breakfast or lunch and the restaurant was closed for dinner. In the late afternoon, Sonny moseyed two blocks over to the restaurant where he worked as a waiter. From time to time, Vito went to that restaurant for dinner with the family, just to see how he was doing. The occasion, in reality, was to socialize like old times, reminisce about past friends, and think about entering the next tournament. At the restaurant, Sonny would not allow Vito to place an order, since he knew best what to cook for Vito's family. So, he was left alone to cook the usual authentic Italian farm food that Vito adored. As a former "goat", he knew Vito's taste in food. Sonny's specialty dish was the tripe dish (goat intestine). He refused any tip and was offended at even the thought of a tip from Vito. Not tipping was sacrilegious to any other waiter, but not to Sonny. Usually, after working at the restaurant, Sonny drove his Vespa to take his usual ride around the bocce courts, just to be a pain in the ass to the people assembled there, but the locals knew what was coming their way. Of course, there was no harm intended unless taken.

Much sadness caught up with a lot of people who Sonny cared for very much during this period of time. Unexpectedly, Alex died of a heart attack. At the funeral Mass in church, Lorenzo and his family sat in the first row with his two illegitimate grandchildren. Alex's wife, Maria, and her two sons, Marco and Domenico (Dino), did not attend the Mass. Half of the North End residents attended the funeral at Sacred Heart church, and also some well-dressed out-of-towners from the New York City-New Jersey area, who gave the locals the creeps. No doubt, they were wiseguys from different Mafia factions. It was a shock to the locals. But what was more shocking to them was the appearance of the two-year old illegitimate son of Alex in the arms of nonno, grandfather Lorenzo. A baby girl was in the arms of nonna, grandmother Felicia. That was the start of much gossip in the North End. One rumor placed Alex in the arms of his mistress, when he died. Sonny was one of the pallbearers at the Church and gave a beautiful eulogy. He praised Alex so much that heaven had to be the next destination.

After the Mass, the priest reminded Sonny that there were no other special ritual induction ceremonies in Heaven. Saint Peter will be there, screening people at the front gate.

Alex was survived by two sisters, his wife and two children, his mistress and their two children, and parents. He was tall as he was wide and weighed 350 pounds. His stomach had been "stapled" or reduced in size, but he was still overweight. The heart attack was the result of his weight. He was a protégé of Sonny, who taught him to make pizza, and to traffic in cocaine. Besides the pizzeria, he owned a real estate company, a steak house in downtown Boston, a restaurant in the North End, a nightclub in Medford, properties in Florida and another restaurant in Nashua, NH. He was a major earner. Everybody in the Mafia respected him and, most likely, he was on his way to being the next capo of the Mafia in the North End.

The dalliance between Alex and his mistress started about ten years before his death. Her name was Sarah and she was born in Long Island near West Hampton Beach. She was an aspiring actress whose main ambition was to appear in a Broadway show. She worked at odd jobs here and there as a model, waitress, bartender and nightclub singer in order to support herself in New York City, although her family was affluent. Sarah left home after graduating from Barnard College, where she majored in sociology and theater. She was a strikingly beautiful blonde who was very sociable. She first appeared at the bocce courts in the company of Alex and Lorenzo.

Apparently, Alex met her at a nightclub in New York City, where she worked as a bartender. He offered her the same job at his nightclub/restaurant in downtown Boston at twice the salary she was making. It was not the money that attracted her to Boston. It was her restlessness as a young woman on the move. Besides, she needed a break from her pursuit of Broadway. She accepted his offer on the spot. The old timers at the bocce courts went gaga over her good looks. The fact that she was in the company of Alex, made them take the liberty of approaching her and they started to entertain her with their nonsensical gibberish. She enjoyed all of that and more so much that every Sunday afternoon she came back to the courts like clockwork to partake in the kibitzing and bullshitting. For some reason, she needed to forget about New York City, and this was the best therapy for her.

However, there were long periods of time when she was out of sight in the North End and the nightclub in downtown Boston. No one had a clue as to why she disappeared. When she re-appeared, her first visit was to the courts. She was very much liked by the players who constantly chatted her up. However, they all sensed that she was special to Alex and, therefore, any romantic moves toward her were forbidden. In the latter years, her routine changed in order to spend more time in NYC to again chase her dream. After Alex died, she never appeared again at the bocce courts or at the nightclub. No one was aware that she was Alex's mistress and had two children with him. Apparently, she must have had her babies whenever she was away for an extended period of time. Alex's parents took care of them.

Alex's family was split with regard to the illegitimate children. After Maria discovered that Alex fathered two more children besides their own two, she fired Alex's two sisters from the realty company that she then owned. Also, she took possession of the pizzeria, steakhouse, houses in suburbia, Boston and Naples, Florida. Alex had put up the cash originally for the purchase of the properties, but the deeds were put in her name to avoid scrutiny from the government. She had the legal right to claim the properties. She was rightly upset that no one of Lorenzo's family and friends had informed her about Alex's indiscretions, especially when Sarah's children were raised by Alex's parents. It is somewhat of a mystery how Alex' parents were able to hide from Maria that these two were Alex's children. From Lorenzo's perspective, he loved all of his grandchildren, illegitimate or not.

After Alex's death, there was no more bounce in Lorenzo's steps and no more poetry recitals at the bocce courts. His health soon deteriorated to the point where he couldn't even walk to the bocce courts, only two blocks away. That comradeship with the players was what had kept him alert and alive. He had that distant look of a broken man. He would sit on the bench and stare at the ocean below, as if he were in a trance ready to jump into the ocean. Friends quoted poetry just to get him started, as if they were revving up a dead motor. The rest of the players were anxiously looking for any sign of life or reaction from the poet. Nothing. The players at the bocce courts were somber and quiet. His bocce playing told it all, no enthusiasm whatsoever, deader that a door knob in terms of creativity on the courts. Sonny came up to Lorenzo and shouted at him in the most vile manner with an atrocious dialect just to get a spark out of him. No response. He aged very fast. About a year after Alex's death, he simply withered-away. He wanted to join Alex in the other world and give him advice once again.

People believed that it was not a matter of his health deteriorating that killed him, but his melancholy about his son. He died without ever again seeing his legitimate grandsons.

At the funeral home where Lorenzo's body was laid out in a casket, all the Bocce players and North End residents paid their respects to the family and relatives sitting in a semi-circular circle around the casket. All the poems that he composed were displayed on the wall along with pictures of friends and family. It was clear from pictures of him and notorious Mafia people that Lorenzo was connected. Photos of Lorenzo, Alex and Sonny were displayed, exhibiting Lorenzo's life from the day he was born to his death. In one photo, Sonny was pictured with well known Mafia bosses in Florida and New York City. Those pictures unsettled Vito as he had always had a suspicion that Sonny was connected, but the suspicion grew to a certainty on seeing those pictures. Chills ran up and down his spine. He made peace with that knowledge by rationalizing that as long as Sonny didn't declare who he was in the past, then he didn't know. There was no harm in not knowing.

Not even the Governor of Massachusetts received such an honorable send off from the funeral home to the church as Lorenzo. The whole town showed up for the procession. The local Roma band leading the procession played somber music. This time there was no hanky-panky music out of respect for Lorenzo. City Hall people showed up in force. At the church, who's who in the Mafia world showed up. The first ten rows were occupied by family and relatives. All of the immigrants from Abruzzo residing in suburbia showed up. Again, Maria and her two sons did not show up. However, the two illegitimate grandchildren were seated in the front row with nonna. Sarah was there dressed in a black dress next to her children. Behind the family, relatives occupied the remaining ten rows of seats. Locals and politicians were seated in the center section of the church, behind the relatives. Most of the seats on one side of the church were occupied by people who wore expensive suits and whose pictures appeared in newspapers regularly for being involved in various nefarious activities.

Before Mass, Sonny and Vito were having an espresso in a cafe across the street from the Church. Of all the people walking into the cafe, was none other than Carmine from New Jersey, with two bodyguards. Sonny and Carmine embraced each other like lost brothers. Vito excused himself to go to the bathroom. He didn't want to hear anything that they had to say. Most of it was bullshit talk anyway about nothing of interest to Vito. He wanted no part of Carmine; he left them and walked over to the Church. Vito sensed that Carmine was a very different mafioso than Sonny. Sonny retired from the Mafia and "jumped over the fence" to join a society of human beings and leave that dreadful cult society. Clearly, Carmine was not able to do the same, since he was still active. In Church, Sonny kept his distance from past notorious guests, since his role in organized crime was over. He had no desire to go back in time and resume his role as in the past. In fact, all the people who surrounded him in the photos as exhibited in the funeral home were dead from natural death or otherwise. He sat with Felicia, Lorenzo's two daughters, and Sarah with her two children. Vito and friends from the suburbs sat on the opposite side from where the notorious guests sat. The relationship between Sonny and Lorenzo must have been very strong in view of the fact that he delivered the eulogy.

In the eulogy, Sonny thanked Lorenzo for helping him with his move to Boston. Also, he traced Lorenzo's life from the time he lived in Sulmona. Lorenzo was the top student in his class at the Lyceum School and excelled especially in comparative classic literature. In order to avoid serving in the Italian Army, he enrolled in the Police Academy to qualify as a finance policeman (similar to custom police). His two brothers had no inclination for schooling and opted to help their parents in farming. He emigrated to America under the Refugee Act passed in Congress in the late 1940s. Lorenzo got involved in overseeing religious festivals so that they adhered to traditional ways. When he first arrived in the North End, he assisted the band leader in the music program of the Roma band which performed in festival processions in the streets. Being a religious man, he and Sonny formed a special committee to stop the Archbishop of Boston from closing Sacred Heart Church and other churches in the North End. Due to his diligence and perseverance the churches today are still open. In summary, Sonny saw Lorenzo as a visionary and a religious man, but also believed in traditions that made the community strong. In his final words, Sonny stated that Lorenzo will have a receptive audience for his poetry, since Iaccarino and Onofrio have now been taught Latin and Florentine Italian by Saint Peter. Although it pained him, he read one of Lorenzo's beautiful poems. As a final tribute to Lorenzo, Sonny invited the Roma band to play Ave

Maria, while one of the band members sang the song in Latin. Tears were flowing from people's eyes uncontrollably, including those of Sonny. This time the priest did not reprimand Sonny.

This period of time was probably the worst of times for Sonny in view of what happened to his two friends, Alex and Lorenzo. He thought things couldn't get any worse, but they did. Luca was a total wreck physically. He was on 36 pills a day regiment for his heart condition. Lucky for him, his son, a pharmacist from Medford, controlled the pill taking. However, those two feuded over the intake of foods forbidden by the medical doctors, like Italian pastries. Luca and Sonny were very different, but they got along like a hand in glove. Whereas Luca was soft spoken and unassuming, Sonny was loud and boisterous. One thing that they had in common was that they loved to tease the living shit out of each other. In fact, the only reason Luca fed Sonny breakfast and lunch every day was so that he could tease him to death and vice-versa. Nothing was out of bounds for the two of them. Was it love? Nah. They just liked each other's company and they were not homosexuals.

Unfortunately for Luca, his wife was in the beginning stage of dementia and, sometimes, she got lost when she went out on her own. Often, both Luca and Sonny would get on the Vespa to look for her all over town. That was outright crazy. They were nuts about getting on that Vespa, although Luca drove a Mercedes Benz. With Sonny's sight being what it was and Luca too preoccupied mentally to alert Sonny, it was like the blind leading the blind. Somebody in heaven must have looked over them to guide that Vespa. Although both enjoyed a good laugh, they could also be very stern. During an interlude at the bocce courts, a young wannabe pulled a gun to impress Luca that he owned one. Without hesitation or fear, Luca turned toward him and said: "Gimme that fucking gun or I will shove it up your ass and have you shot right here on this spot." He yanked the gun out of his hand and put it in his pocket and then went back to joking around with others. That wannabe never showed up again at the bocce courts.

It was bound to happen. For a man in his condition, sooner or later Saint Peter comes calling. The soft and gentle man, Luca, died of a heart attack. Sonny was not surprised. He knew it was coming, but still he wished other-wise. This time at the church funeral, the priest impressed upon Sonny, just before his eulogy, that Sainthood is approved at the Curia in Rome, not by him. Nevertheless, Sonny did make note of Luca's Sainthood in his eulogy.

Sonny was not the same man thereafter. He was no longer the court jester. He simply kept to himself and was in seclusion and mourning.

In the span of one year three of Sonny's closest friends had died and there was no letting up. Corvo and Sonny often chit-chatted about private matters that concerned only them. They started a contest between the two as to who would harvest the most tomatoes from plants that they placed in front of the buildings where they lived. They replaced flower beds planted by the city with their tomato plants in late springtime. The flower beds measured 2x2 square feet. They watered their plants and weeded anything else that grew there. They protected their plants from tourists and kids poking through a metal screen surrounding the plants. Corvo would sit in a chair in front of his apartment smoking Sicilian stogies just to drive kids away with that awful smoke. Once a week, Sonny and Corvo would get together to compare progress made by the other's growth of the plants. That was serious business, more so than any other former business that they engaged in. Corvo's plants were full of yellow flowers implying more tomatoes than Sonny's plants. By early September, the yellow flowers were still blooming, but no tomatoes. However, Sonny's plants did indeed produce tomatoes. There was keen interest from the bocce players about the tomato contest. All of them made suggestions or jokes about Corvo's plants. Sonny suggested to Corvo that next time he should use local seeds rather than Sicilian seeds. Most people then believed that Sonny sprayed something in the middle of the night on the flower buds to thwart the natural growth of the plants. They were forever toying with each other's mind, but they enjoyed their pranks.

Although Corvo, the Sicilian, and Sonny appeared to be confrontational at times to people who didn't know the two, in truth, they were bosom buddies who understood life in the Mafia better than anyone else. They had one thing in common; they both survived the Mafia and were still able to talk about it. In late summer, the apple tree near the courts was full of ripening apples. Everybody at the courts kept an eye on the tree to see when Corvo would show up to pick the apples. They loved to see the special contraption attached to a long wooden stick that Corvo built for picking the apples. He was too old to climb the tree. In a way it was entertaining to see the passion and determination that Corvo put into this task. People waited and waited but no Corvo. Finally, the bad news came. He died falling down the steps to the basement in his apartment complex. His body was discovered by his wife, who was an invalid, a day after his fall. He must have lain there in agony for awhile.

Thankfully, good news was just around the corner after a long period of bad news. Anthony was doing so much better and was out of danger. The infection cleared up and the doctor assigned him to a re-habilitation center nearby. The family was relieved and they all pitched in with the recovery process. His grandmother fed him and helped him dress. Sonny drove Anthony, on his Vespa, to the re-habilitation center. He had to learn to walk again, move left to right slowly and build up leg and stomach muscles. Like a faithful dog, Sonny watched his every move at the rehab center and had him repeat the steps, when they returned home. The recovery period lasted almost a year. Anthony was a changed man. In that year, Anthony seemed to mature ten years and he became more at ease with himself and the family. He was no longer restless and took the time to listen to family members. Sonny had believed all along that he was a good man capable of doing good things. He was no longer a young punk. The family bonded like never before.

As tournaments rolled around, Carmela and Anthony worked together in running Sonny's tournament and Sonny enjoyed being the ring master, giving orders and joking again with people. Carmela was a carbon copy of her father in running the tournament. She would have everybody pick a name from the lottery to be paired with a beginner. If a pair suited her, she would draw them from her pocket secretly. When players complained about her sleight of hand, she would tell them what they could do with themselves. Sonny was finally coming out of the funk that he was in after his friends had died. It restored his faith in accepting the good with the bad, as on the mountains. Ryan and Anthony worked together in managing the softball team. Again, Sonny did what he liked to do best, bullshit around with people and party after the game. Finally, the family was together as a unit. Anthony enrolled at a local university, making Sonny a very happy man.

TWENTY

Back Door to Heaven

In the past, Sonny had spent his afternoons at the bocce courts, but no more. Since the death of his friends, he was living a secluded life spending most of his time at the restaurant where he worked or sitting on the bench in front of the cafe staring at nothing in particular. That behavior was not in his character. Too much thinking. The only time that Sonny showed up at Puopolo Park was for the softball games that he managed, usually after work. If he stopped at the bocce courts and played a game, there was no life or spark to his game and he was no more the ringmaster and the clown of the courts.

As for Vito, the gig was up at the University. When students organized a game of bocce on campus, Vito could no longer walk around campus incognito of the game. His graduate students were well aware of Vito's other life, playing regularly at the courts in the North End. It didn't fool the students, when Vito naïvely asked, "How do you play the game?". They had seen him play many times at the bocce courts. They insisted that they wanted to try and play a "real" game of bocce in the North End, taught by the masters. Vito decided to introduce his graduate students to the other half of his world. This was going to be a seminar about the world of hard knocks rather than the comfortable world of academia. He organized a guided tour of the North End that included visits to the bocce courts, Sonny's restaurant, and pastries at a café. The students were ecstatic. He contacted Sonny and Uberto who had ample experience teaching the game to hand-icapped children. Sonny volunteered to prepare a light inexpensive lunch and pastries at Café Graffiti. Sonny chose this café so that students could leave their imprints on the wall along with their signatures. It was a hit! As usual the lunch was delectable and the wine was on the house, thanks to the owner. The pastries were "out of this world", according to the students.

The students were grateful to Sonny and Uberto for having so much patience in teaching them about bocce. One student remarked on how courteous and polite everyone was. Vito sighed, "If they only knew". He was sitting on the bench watching the spectacle and was amused by the con job. Sonny and Uberto got a whiff of academia and asked the students if they were interested in having a course in the game of bocce at Fairmont University. They rationalized that if athletes at the university could take courses in comic books, why not bocce? Sonny and Uberto were salivating at the prospect of making some money out of this. In the students, they had a receptive audience. Vito chuckled at the notion. "Once a hustler always a hustler." That was what he thought of those two con artists. They never had an audience as attentive as this one. Vito felt somewhat jealous that those students never concentrated as much in class as he saw them do on that bocce court. Sonny and Uberto gave it all they had to teach them about the game. It was satisfying for both parties. Vito stayed away from the "class" all the while. The outing seemed to rejuvenate both Sonny and Uberto.

There were odd questions from students. One asked: "Where is the headquarters for the Mafia?" Uberto replied with a straight face that there was one headquarter at Prince Street and the other one at Nashua Street. He conveniently omitted the fact that the one on Nashua Street was the jail house where Turiddu was incarcerated. He added: "The top position is vacant now, since the CEO went on semi-retirement about 30 years ago. A national search is underway for one." Vito and Sonny looked at each other and wondered, "Where in the f..k did that come from?" All three of them just smiled and looked toward the sky to anyone up there pleading, "Please no more of this bullshit." Another naïve question from a student was: "Are you Mafia?" Sonny took that question and said that he and Uberto didn't fit the profile for employment in the Mafia, since both of them were employed as waiters in restaurants and they were old. That was the last time Vito took students on a tour of the North End. It was too close for comfort. He could only take so much. As for Sonny and Uberto, they loved the energy and enthusiasm displayed by the students and they missed that from old times at the courts. Sonny needed that extra boost of energy from the young ones to be himself again. That was one reason Vito took the time to organize the get-together. It was a nostalgic moment that they both cherished.

At the next tournament organized by Sonny, there was a large banner displaying Sonny Alvaro Tournament. It used to read, North End Against Drugs Tournament, NEAD. Sonny was smiling from ear to ear. He was proud to inform Vito that the North End Community Center, with the approval of City Hall, re-named the tournament. What an honor. "Not bad for an old goat, eh", beamed Sonny. He was proud as a peacock. He deserved the honor. Sonny had provided free service to the park, for more than 30 years, as an instructor to handicapped children, was a softball team manager, liaison to college athletic departments, and assistant to old people on election days. His mantra was to cajole, push and do anything to get the youth into sports and arts. Probably, that was his purpose in life, to alleviate the misery of life through his wisdom and levity. A sentimentalist at heart. Vito was very proud of him. At least, someone from the mountains of Cervinara made a big difference in people's lives.

Sonny's tournament was managed by Carmela and Anthony. Although there were many teenagers (beginners) showing up, there were not enough old timers (team captains) to stage a full tournament. Onofrio and others like him had passed away, others lost interest and most of them stayed home. The spark plugs, Onofrio and Iaccarino, that had energized past tournaments were no longer there. No one else had stepped forward to take their places. The old gang was slowly but surely disappearing from the scene. Yuppies and students who resided in the North End were constant visitors at the courts, but they were transients who were just killing time for a year or so. They were more interested in having a party or a picnic with their friends than the game itself. For the few old-timers still around, it was boring to watch them play the game that they loved. That spark that once existed was gone. It was rare to see two-old timers at the courts play at any given time. Somewhat depressing. Often, Sonny came to the courts in the late afternoon, sitting on the bench contemplating where everyone had gone and how to relight the flame of the past.

Sonny's routine was pretty much the same from day to day. He would check-in at the restaurant, help-out with the cooking, and set up the tables. Then, he would take a break on his Vespa and drive to the courts with the hope of finding someone to play bocce with. Sometimes, Vito would show up and it was like old times in the mountains of Avella—taking no prisoner in the match. But at the end of the matches, the two went separate ways. No hard feelings, even if they tried to bust each other's balls during the matches. In the evenings or after work, he would get on his Vespa and drive past the courts on Commercial Street just to see who was around. Commercial Street was a four-lane road, not a highway and usually traffic was heavy due to the influx of busses with tourists coming into the North End and workers going home to suburbia.

Every Thursday evening, a tour bus, called "Ghost Ride", full of tourists parked on the inside lane across from the bocce courts. Copp's Hill Burying Ground was located 50 steps straight up from the bus stop. A tourist guide would step out of the bus onto the sidewalk with a lantern, in a special dress uniform reflecting the times of the Revolutionary War, and guide the tourists like sheep up the steps to the Cemetery starting at 10:00 pm. Traffic was diverted to the passing lane around the bus, as the bus blocked the inside lane next to parked cars by the sidewalk. On a sultry summer evening, Sonny was heading home from work, taking his usual drive-by the bocce courts, checking for any friends along Commercial Street heading toward the back of the bus. Sonny drove the Vespa around the bus onto the passing lane only to bump into the back of a tricycle. The tricycle had just pulled out of the inside lane to the passing lane in front of the Vespa. Tourists rented tricycles and/or horse drawn wagons to take in the historic sites of Boston. The collision flipped Sonny into a cartwheel motion over the tricycle onto the asphalt road.

His skull was fractured and within 5–10 minutes he was in a hospital bed. The initial prognosis did not look good. His head swelled to about twice its normal size. The first members of the family to arrive at the hospital were Anthony and Ken. Jesse, Ryan and Carmella followed soon after. The last time Anthony cried so hard was when he was in Sonny's arms as a baby and Sonny had cuddled him to stop him from crying. Again, Sonny smiling, extended his arm and patted Anthony's arm to comfort him. That was the last smile; he was forever the optimist. Thereafter, Sonny lapsed into a coma for two weeks. It was a foregone conclusion that he was brain dead and he never did recover.

At the funeral home, pictures of Sonny in the early days as a pizza chef, his wedding ceremony, his children and grandchildren were displayed. In addition, pictures of friends from Florida were prominently displayed. Seeing those pictures, confirmed once again what Vito had suspected all along. The final exhibition of pictures was that of his friends from the bocce courts and the tournaments that Vito and he had competed as a team. Vito was moved to tears. Sonny came from the mountains, and his heart was just as big as the mountains. With all that had happened in his lifetime, nothing changed

View from Copp's Hill Burying Ground toward the men's softball field. The bocce courts are to the left of the field. The tour bus stopped besides the light pole.

The goat in him never left. He found what others pursued all their lives, peace of mind and that special spirit. That was the message that Sonny wanted to convey to Vito, not that rough and tough character of a mafioso as in movies. He was just a human being who got off on the wrong track. Vito always had faith in Sonny to do the right thing and he did. He fulfilled his purpose in life, just like anything else in this universe.

At the funeral Mass, Sonny's friend, Father Cucu, celebrated the Mass and gave the eulogy. He made the trip from Rome, as soon he heard the bad news. Father Cucu was promoted to Monsignore by the Vatican and was allowed to give Masses at Sacred Heart Church for a couple of days during his visit, although he was a Silesian Order priest. The Franciscan Order was in charge of Sacred Heart. He enumerated all the good things that Sonny did for others as well as for the church without expecting anything in return. Most importantly, Sonny loved children and devoted much of his time to handicapped and autistic children, organizing picnics, tournaments and art festivals. His family meant everything to him and he was willing to go through a brick wall for the welfare of his family. He was indeed the good shepherd. Father Cucu made the point that Saint Peter will clear the street of traffic to heaven to welcome Sonny with his Vespa and all traffic lights will be green. As such, Sonny need not worry about the color of those lights. His friends Lorenzo, Onofrio, Luca, and Iaccarino will be waiting for him. Lorenzo, in particular, can't wait to teach him the classic languages and recite poetry to him. At the end of the eulogy, Father Cucu came to Vito and said: "Sonny recognized you the minute that you showed your face in the North End. He wanted to convey to you that he was extremely grateful for your accepting him for what he was as in the old times and not as a mafioso. You knew that he was no Angel." Vito responded deferentially, "Father Cucu, I am as sure as the sky is blue and the ocean is deep that Guido, Sonny, is going to put in a good word for you to Saint Peter so that the two of you, Lorenzo and Williams can play golf together again." Father Cucu smiled and walked away pleased at the thought of being with Guido Alvaro.

TWENTY-ONE

Twice Upon a Hill

After the death of Sonny, Uberto was the only one left of the old guards to maintain the courts on weekends. There was still a handful of old timers who got together usually then to play bocce. Tournaments were devoid of top-notch players like Sonny, Onofrio, etc. Players from suburbia now dominated the tournaments. There was really no interest in bocce by the younger generation in the North End. Anna and Vito had many friends in the North End, but it was not the same as being on the bocce courts that brought something different and interesting each day. What made it interesting was the old generation. They represented cultural views of where they came from. These ranged from classical poetry to riddles, proverbs and everything in between. It was this contrast from the American culture that made it so interesting, which is not to say that one was bad and the other good. The cultures complemented each other to embellish both. The neighborhood now had more yuppies and students from neighboring colleges. Most of the original immigrants from after WW II had left for the suburbs or passed away. Vito was spending more time on campus and in his research laboratory. He took more sabbatical leaves to universities in Rome and Copenhagen to interact with colleagues who were eager to have him around as a research collaborator.

Since Rome is only about 120 miles north of Avella/Cervinara, Vito took the occasion to visit those towns and drive to the top of Monte Avella, where Sonny (Alvaro) and he spent their youth in those small haystack houses. The winding road to the top was built only within the past ten years in order to

277

accommodate new housing halfway up the mountain. The shack were still there. A new generation of shepherds were surprised to see Vito and Anna atop the mountain. Nothing had changed. It was as if the mountains were saying to Vito: "Welcome back, we missed you." It was an eerie and sort of a surreal feeling of serenity with nature, as if the mountains sensed that something had been missing for a long time. Vito felt that the mountains were in mourning, as the water dripped from the melting snow like tears of sorrow for their beloved Guido.

In Vito's last year at Fairmont University, he taught juniors and seniors a course that he first introduced as part of the curriculum about thirty-five years earlier. In the first day of class, as usual, he reviewed the roster, taking the time to pronounce student's names correctly. Those with strange sounding names appreciated that a teacher took the time to properly pronounce his or her name. He came across one name that he was very familiar with, Anthony O'Toole, Sonny's grandson. Nah, that can't be! Indeed, it was. After class, Vito invited Anthony to have coffee at the University cafeteria. They talked about personal things related to Anthony's interest in academics. Basically, Vito was shocked and at the same time happy to see him in such an advanced undergraduate class. Anthony came a long way from the rat holes and gutters of the North End.

Vito asked what brought the change in his life. Anthony related that after Sonny's death his grandmother, Jesse, told him that Sonny knew all along that Anthony was the one who sold his beloved Vespa. Sonny forgave him. He forgave him, because he didn't want to put another roadblock in his future. Sonny desperately wanted Anthony to straighten out his life. Finally, she told Anthony straight that there was nothing to admire about Sonny's past life as a mafioso. It had only been a life of misery and uncertainty and he didn't want Anthony to pursue that. In short, one had to have eyes in front and in back of the head to survive in that world.

As usual, Vito arrived at his laboratory at 9:30 am sharp at the end of the regular semester to collect notes for the summer course coming up. One of the graduate students shouted from across the laboratory, "Vito, there is an undergraduate student waiting for you in your office". Vito was surprised to hear that, since students were heading home or to jobs for their summer recess. However, it was not unusual for students to be waiting for Vito in his laboratory during the academic semester. Office hours were available for students the whole day, every day. Therefore, he never posted office hours at the door, as required by the University. He would tell students in class, "If you need help in your school work or want to explore ideas, just come to my laboratory and wait for me until I show up in case I am on University errands".

When Vito opened his office door, Anthony was waiting for him smiling. Vito assumed that he received a good grade, but that was not the reason for his visit. Something was brewing. Vito recognized Anthony's mischievous smile, so emblematic of Sonny's. Anthony came to thank him profusely not so much for the grade, but for Vito's persistence in demanding more and more out of the students each day. However, as a parting remark, he said: "You have been massaging our minds, making us believe that we are geniuses. That is a bunch of bullshit. Sonny and you are one and the same, sly old con artists. Sonny tried to implant the idea in my head that I could be anything that I wanted to be. You made us believe, in this class, that we are in the forefront of a wave pushing the knowledge base. It must be that mountain air that you, Sonny and the goats were breathing". The kid is all right, Vito mused. He's got some marbles in his head. He was right. Anthony continued that he was going to breathe the same air next month. Uncle Davide was going to take him and Ken for a visit to those beautiful mountains of Cervinara and Avella.

The trip to Cervinara had been planned for a long time. Initially, Davide and Sonny and their wives were planning to go together. Besides nostalgic reasons, the brothers decided to sell the grassland on the mountains where they had spent their youth taking the sheep to the grazing grass fields. They and their children were never going to go back and re-settle in Cervinara, so, why not sell the land and just visit their beloved mountains and breathe that fine and clean air. In the planning stages, Sonny passed away and, therefore, changes in their plans were called for. Since Davide was footing all the expenses, he asked both Ken and Anthony to come along. The boys were ecstatic about going to the place where Sonny and Davide were born, to discover the rest of the family, and go back to their roots.

Their cousins in Cervinara were keepers of the land. Their uncle, Alfredo, who was a Camorra member and a former Mayor of the town after World War II, was still alive and active in politics. Alfredo's grandson was now Mayor of Cervinara. Time stood still in Cervinara. Alfredo still yielded power behind the scenes. He came up with the great scheme that the city should buy the grassland from Davide and convert it into a national park, called Sonny Alvaro National Park. What a scam. Davide would get top euro for the property, thanks to his uncle. How could Davide argue with that deal. Furthermore, it brought honor to the family to have the Alvaro name attached to the park. This meant that, as in the past, shepherds would take the sheep to the park, but this time there was no fee for grazing the fields.

The grassland where Guido and Vito spent time when shepherding on Monte Avella. Small pebbles from there were taken back to Boston by Davide.

At the site of the park, a plaque to Sonny was commemorated. There followed a small ceremony in which the Mayor, Uncle Alfredo, and other dignitaries made speeches recounting stories of Sonny (Guido) as a young shepherd. The audience was made up mostly of shepherds, who knew or had heard of Alvaro name, from the towns of Cervinara and Avella. After the ceremony, as people left the site, Davide gathered the two nephews, Ken and Anthony, and began to collect small pebbles round and about the haystack and near the bocce court. The boys were perplexed as to the purpose of collecting little stones to transport them back to the USA. Davide smiled and explained it as mementos to take back.

New house settlements had been driving away wolves and other wild life that had existed before in the high mountains. It is just a matter of time before new settlements will begin to appear on the high mountains as well as on the grass fields which shepherds called their home. Sooner or later they will be displaced just like the wolves and wildlife. Although Ken and Anthony were taken to popular touristic places like Sorrento, Amalfi, Pompei, etc., they preferred the mountain scenery, and, especially, the farm food of the locals in Cervinara. Anthony assumed the role of head of the family representing Sonny's family interest. He was protective of Ken much as Davide once had been protecting Sonny.

They finally got to taste the unadulterated farm food of Cervinara. It didn't taste anything like the food that they had tasted in the North End.

Dishes of porcini mushrooms, rice, lamb, sausages, bacon and beans were cooked routinely. Up in the mountains, even a simple dish like pasta e fagioli (beans) soup tasted extraordinary. The taste of lamb cooked in Arabic style in a pit of hot charcoal for hours is delectable. The two brothers got a glimpse of what life was like at the time when Sonny and Davide were roaming the mountains. Also, they experienced the arduous work of being up in the mountains. Davide organized a party to hunt down wild boars with Ken and Anthony.

The outing on the hills was both exhilarating and scary. Wild boars are nothing like domesticated pigs. They are ferocious and courageous, a bad combination for hunters. The sight of wild boars brought them a high sense of both alertness and trepidation. One bad move on their part and the boars would have no hesitation charging directly at them. Hunting dogs provided some protection, but ultimately it came down to a moment of truth: shoot the boar or climb a tree. This was one experience that both Ken and Anthony would never forget and, most importantly, they could picture for themselves how both Davide and Sonny experienced life in the mountains.

Wild boars roaming the mountains.

Finally, the two brothers had an opportunity to tend sheep on the high mountains on an excursion with other shepherds and Davide. They started the trip at five in the morning and ended it three days later. The trip was instructive in that they appreciated the incredulous trek traveled by Sonny and what he represented. As for Davide, he was one happy man. Most importantly, he accomplished what he set out to do, collect pebbles on Monte Avella for when he returned home, he would make a special trip to the cemetery. As he meditated about the loss of Sonny, he planted small pebbles around Sonny's grave; it fulfilled his purpose for the trip, to bring that special spirit full circle, from the hills of Monte Avella back to Sonny.

As for the other shepherd, Vito moved to Coral Gables, Florida, upon retirement. He loved the idea of entering bocce tournaments in nearby Naples. On one such occasion, Vito teamed up with a former North Ender, Giorgio, who retired in Naples. At the tournament, Carmine, former arch-nemesis of Sonny in the last tournament, had entered came over to Vito to convey his condolences about Sonny and said that he was truly sorry to hear about the death of "vostro amico"/ "your friend". Vito thought, "For sure, he was never tuo amico/your friend!" Of course, Vito knew very well what he was talking about. That was Carmine's way of not mixing his world with "non-connected" people. It was much to-do with the omerta bullshit. Carmine went on to add that all those extra-curricular activities and charades at the last tournament were just a show between themselves. In truth, they were acquaintances from way back, when Sonny was in Sturmville. He claimed that Sonny was always an earner and nothing more than that. There was not an ounce of meanness in that man. He couldn't even do a knee job! Vito whispered to himself, Amen.

Yes, Sonny carved a living within the harsh world of a secret cult-society, but, in the end, he jumped over that magical fence to join a society of human beings. More importantly, he returned home. Home was not a place, but a special state of mind that very few people are graced with, peace of mind. He found a purpose in life. As a young shepherd, he saw the awesome power, splendor and serenity of nature and felt that special spirit once upon that hill. Often, at the bocce courts, he muttered, sometimes shouted to no one in particular, "These f...g blood suckers", at the bocce courts. Just like parasites sucking blood, organized crime syndicates (cults) do the same to society—literally and physically.

Epilogue

Both Guido and Vito were raised by peasant families who were fiercely independent. It fostered self-reliance in the boys and, therefore, they reached maturity at an early age in life. Vito channeled his aspiration in pursuing books and Sonny (Guido) into the lure of money. A life of contrabands was a way of life for Guido to rise above poverty as a young orphan after World War II in Italy. There were no other choices. The narrator of this story did much of the historical research to correlate the life of actual notorious and so called "honorable" mobsters with that of Guido.

As a boy shepherd, Guido went through traumatic experiences when threatened by violent storms up on the Apennine mountains, Italy. He was terrified and scared for his life. He was often left alone while adult shepherds searched for grass fields and food. He learned that it was easier to accept mother nature on her terms, good or bad. Besides, after the storm, he was rewarded in the tranquility, splendor and awesome beauty of nature all around him. As such, he arrived at a state of mind that can best be described as peace of mind at a young age. That was his mantra for the rest of his life.

Guido's dream in the land of plenty turned into a nightmare, when he emigrated to the USA. Constant internal and external turmoil followed him throughout his adult life. Contrabands, greed, corruption, money and fame only brought misery, constant fear for his life, stress and grief to him and his family. Clearly, Sonny's journey was spinning out of control much like during the violent storms up on the mountains. As Charles Chaplin once remarked, God must have been the travel Agent who set out the itineraries, bookings and destinations for Sonny. Going blind and desperate for a change, he turned to things that mattered most to himself, family, people in need and friends. As on the mountains of Avella, Italy, he re-discovered tranquility and peace of mind by helping others in greater need. Ultimately, it became his purpose in life which is the essence of all things in this universe. Sonny understood the difference between a cult society which worshipped money at all costs and one that believed in the frailty, goodness and beauty in people. He jumped over the "fence" to join a society of civilized human beings. Very few, if any, mafiosi have been able to make that transition.

Acknowledgement

Writing a book is like painting on a canvas or sculpting a statue. Only the editors can tell authors what they "see". It is their feedback that an author needs the most. As such, I want to thank the following for editing my book: Charlotte Frank, Bernard Nemtzow, Mildred Vittoria and Rie Vittoria. It is remarkable that after their editing, we are still the best of friends. I wish to thank mastro Fernando Masi for his beautiful paintings exhibited on the cover as well as in the text.

Bibliography[*]

[1-1] - E.T. Salmon, Samnium and the Samnites, Cambridge University Press, Cambridge (2010).

[1-2] - A. Everitt, Cicero, Random House, Inc., New York (2001).

[1-3] - P. Togliatti, Per La Liberta (For the Liberty), L'Unita, Rome (1944).

[1-4] - C.R.S. Harris, Allied Military Administration of Italy,, 1943–45 (HMSO, 1957).

[1-5] - C. Vittoria, Bitter Chicory To Sweet Espresso, Purpo, Inc., Key Biscayne (2017).

[1-6] - S. Legomsky, Immigration and Refugee Law and Policy, Foundation Press, New York (2015).

[1-7] - C. Levi, Christ Stopped at Eboli, Farrar, Strauss and Giroux, New York (1974).

[1-8] - R. Saviano, Gomorrah, Arnoldo Mondatori Editore, Milan (2008).

[1-9] - N. Lewis, Naples 44, Pantheon Books, New York (1978).

[1-10] - D. Frasca, Vito Genovese: King of Crime, Avon Books, New York (1963).

[1-11] - M.A. Gosch and R. Hammer, Lucky Luciano, Little Brown and Company, Boston (1975); S. Feder and J. Joesten, Luciano Story, Da Capo Press, New York (1994).

[2-1] - G. Reavill, Mafia Summit, Thomas Dunne Books, New York (2013).

[2-2] - P. Maas, The Valachi Papers, Bantam Books, New York (1968).

[2-3] - Laura Fermi, Atoms in the Family, My life with Enrico Fermi, University of Chicago Press, Chicago (1954).

[4-1] - S. Raab, Five Families, Saint Martin Press, New York (2005).

---

[*] The references are designated as [**x-y**]. The number **x** designates the chapter. The number **y** designates the specific reference.

[4-2] - D. Eisenberg, U. Dan and E. Landau, Meyer Lansky, Paddington Press, New York (1979).

[4-3] - W.B. Miller, Violence by Youth Gangs…, Monograph, U.S. Printing Office, Washington, DC (1975).

[4-4] - S.M. Deitche, The Silent Don, Barricade Books, Tampa Bay (2007).

[5-1] - S. Alexander, The Pizza Connection, Diane Publication Co.,New York (1988).

[5-2] C. Sifakis, The Mafia Encyclopedia, Publisher Facts on File, Inc., New York (2005).

[5-3] - R. Quirk, Fidel Castro, W.W. Norton & Company, New York and London (19913.

[5-4] - J. Rasenberger, The Brilliant Disaster, Charles Scribner and Sons, New York (2011).

[5-5] - W. Brashler, The Don: The Life and Death of Sam Giancana, Harper and Row, New York (1977).

[5-6] - S. Giancana, C. Giancana and B. Giancana, Double Cross, Skyhorse pub., New York (1992).

[5-7] - J.H. Davis, Mafia Kingfish: Carlos Marcello and the Assassination of John F. Kennedy, McGraw-Hill, New York (1989); W. Bonanno, Bound by Honor: A Mafioso Story, Publishers Weekly, New York (1999); C. Rappleye and E. Becker, All American Mafioso: The John Rosell Story, Barricade Books, Inc., New York (1995); "How the Outfit Killed JFK, Playboy (Nov. 2010); J. Anderson and L. Whitten, Mob May Have Been Behind Kennedy Assassination, The Free Lance-Star, Fredericksburg, VA (1976).

[5-8] - A. Sloane, Hoffa, MIT Press, Boston (1991); "Hoffa Lawyer: Jimmy Recruited Mob for JFK Hit", Associated Press, January 14, 1992; F. Ragano and S. Raab, Mob Lawyer, Carles Scribner's and Sons, New York (1994).

[5-9] - T. Reppetto, Bringing Down the Mob, MacMillan, Boston (2007).

[5-10] - K. Weeks, and P. Karas, Brutal, The Untold Storyof My Life Inside Whitey's Bulger Irish Mob, Harper Collins, New York (2007).

[6-1] - H. Carr, The Brothers Bulger, Grand Central Publishing, Boston (2006).

[6-2] - D.K Goodwin, The Fitzgeralds and the Kennedys, Simon & Schuster, New York (1987); T. Schwarz, Joseph P. Kennedy, Wiley, New York, (2003).

[6-3] - T.J. English, Paddy Whacked, Harper-Collins, New York (2005).

[6-4] - E. Sweeney, Boston Organized Crime, Arcadia Publishing, Boston (2012).

[6-5] - L. O'Neil and D. Gerard, Black Mass, Harper Collins, New York (2001); K. Cullen and S. Murphy, Whitey Bulger, W.W. Norton, New York (2013).

[6-6] - J. Burke, A profile in Political Power, JAMMAR Productions, Boston (2010).

[6-7] - H. Carr, Hitman: The Untold Story of Johnny Martorano, Tom Doherty Associates, New York (2011).

[6-8] - G. O'Neil and D. Lehr, The Underboss, Public Affairs, Boston (1989).

[7-1] - Lincoln Research Laboratory which is associated with M.I.T. is funded by the AF.

[8-1] - J. Beatty, The Rascal King, ISBN 9780201175998 (1992).

[8-2] - M.A. Ross, The Jewish Friendship Trail, Boston Walks Publisher, Boston (2003); S. Puleo, The Boston Italians, Beacon Press, Boston (2007); T.H. O'Connor, The Boston Irish, Northeastern University Press, Boston (1995).

[10-1] - D.H. Fischer, Paul Revere's ride, Oxford University Press, New York (1994); D. Federhen, From Artisan to Entrepreneur, Paul Revere Memorial Association, Boston (1988).
[10-2] - R. Wachtel, Old Ironsides, Children Press, New York (2003).

[11-1] - Transcript of William Bulger's Congressional testimony, The Boston Globe, June 19, 2003.

[11-2] - This Mafia hitman, Fotios 'Freddy', Geas hated 'rats'. South China Morning Post, Nov. 1, 2018.

[12-1] - R. Phillips, Rogue FBI agent sentenced to 40 years in mob hit, cnn.com, January 15, 2009; The Readers Digest, The Exonerated", March, 2008.

[13-1] - M. Pagnoni, Joy of Bocce, Publisher Author House, Springfield (2004).

[16-1] - M. Paulson, "A Church Seeks Healing", Boston Globe, Dec. 4, 2002, "Church Allowed Abuse by Priests for Years", Boston Globe, January 6, 2002.

[16-2] - G. Haven and T. Russell, Life of Father Taylor, the Sailor Preacher, Boston Port and Seamen's Society, Boston (1904).

[17-1] - R.E. Hubbard, Major General Israel Putnam, McFarland & Company, Inc., Jefferson, NC, (2017).

Index